PHILOSOPHY IN A NEW CENTURY

John R. Searle has made profoundly influential contributions to three areas of philosophy: philosophy of mind, philosophy of language, and philosophy of society. This volume gathers together in accessible form a selection of his essays in these areas. They range widely across social ontology, where Searle presents concise and informative statements of positions developed in more detail elsewhere; Artificial Intelligence and cognitive science, where Searle assesses the current state of the debate and develops his most recent thoughts; and philosophy of language, where Searle connects ideas from various strands of his work in order to develop original answers to fundamental questions. There are also explorations of the limitations of phenomenological inquiry, the mind-body problem, and the nature and future of philosophy. This rich collection from one of America's leading contemporary philosophers will be valuable for all who are interested in these central philosophical questions.

JOHN R. SEARLE is Slusser Professor of Philosophy at the University of California, Berkeley. His most recent publications include *Mind: A Brief Introduction* (2004), *Consciousness and Language* (2002), *Rationality in Action* (2001, 2003), and *Freedom and Neurobiology* (2007).

PHILOSOPHY IN A NEW CENTURY

Selected Essays

JOHN R. SEARLE

University of California, Berkeley

CAMBRIDGE
UNIVERSITY PRESS

CAMBRIDGE UNIVERSITY PRESS

Cambridge, New York, Melbourne, Madrid, Cape Town, Singapore, São Paulo, Delhi

Cambridge University Press
The Edinburgh Building, Cambridge, CB2 8RU, UK

Published in the United States of America by Cambridge University Press, New York

www.cambridge.org
Information on this title: www.cambridge.org/9780521731584

First published 2008

Printed in the United Kingdom at the University Press, Cambridge

A catalogue record for this publication is available from the British Library

Library of Congress Cataloguing in Publication data
Searle, John R.
Philosophy in a new century : selected essays / John R. Searle.
p.   cm.
Includes index.
ISBN 978-0-521-51591-7 (hardback) – ISBN 978-0-521-73158-4 (pbk.)
1. Philosophy.   I. Title.
B1649.S261   2008
191 – dc22   2008033464

ISBN 978-0-521-51591-7 hardback
ISBN 978-0-521-73158-4 paperback

For Dagmar

Contents

Original place of publication of the essays

1 "Philosophy in a new century," in *Philosophy in America at the Turn of the Century*, APA Centennial Supplement, *Journal of Philosophical Research* (2003).

2 "Social ontology: some basic principles," in "Searle on institutions," *Anthropological Theory*, vol. 6, no. 1 (2006).

3 "The Turing Test: fifty-five years later," in Robert Epstein, Gary Roberts, and Grace Beber (eds.), *Parsing the Turing Test: Philosophical and Methodological Issues in the Quest for the Thinking Computer* (Springer, 2008).

4 "Twenty-one years in the Chinese room," in John Preston and Mark Bishop (eds.), *Views into the Chinese Room, New Essays on Searle and Artificial Intelligence* (Oxford/New York: Oxford University Press, 2002).

5 "Is the brain a digital computer?", Presidential Address to the APA, *Proceedings of the American Philosophical Association*, 1990.

6 "The phenomenological illusion," in M. E. Reicher and J. C. Marek (eds.), *Experience and Analysis* (Vienna: öbvahpt, 2005).

7 "The self as a problem in philosophy and neurobiology," in Todd E. Feinberg and Julian Paul Keenan (eds.), *The Lost Self: Pathologies of the Brain and Identity* (New York: Oxford University Press, 2005).

8 "Why I am not a property dualist," *Journal of Consciousness Studies* (2002).

9 "Fact and value, 'is' and 'ought,' and reasons for action," in G. O. Mazur (ed.), *Twenty-Five Year Commemoration to the Life of Hans Kelsen (1898–1973)* (New York: Semenenko Foundation, 1999).

10 "The unity of the proposition," previously unpublished.

Introduction

The writing of these essays was scattered over nearly two decades, and they were addressed to many different sorts of audiences. They exemplify my general preoccupations with three areas of philosophy: philosophy of mind, philosophy of language, and what I call the philosophy of society. The first essay, which gives the title to the volume, was written for the American Philosophical Association as part of the centennial issue of the Association's proceedings. It is a revision of an article originally written for the Royal Society[1] in a volume which discussed the future of various scientific and academic subjects in the twenty-first century. In a sense, the real introduction to this volume is Chapter 1, because in it I state my general conception of philosophy and its future and the articles which follow exemplify that general conception.

The second essay, "Social ontology: some basic principles," originally appeared in the journal *Anthropological Theory*, in a special issue dedicated to my account of social ontology. Following this lead-off article, there were a series of other articles together with replies by me. My aim in this article, as in earlier and later work, is to give an account of the fundamental structure of social reality. I argue that the basic social mechanism, the glue that holds human society together, is what I call "status functions," functions that can be performed only in virtue of collective acceptance by the community that the object or person that performs the function has a certain status, and with that status a function that can be performed in virtue of that collective acceptance and not in virtue of the physical structure of the object or person alone. The next question then becomes, How are status functions created and maintained? I now believe that there is a simpler account than the one I gave in this chapter, though it is a continuation

---

[1] John R. Searle, "The future of philosophy," *Philosophical Transactions of the Royal Society*, Millennium Issue (29 December, 1999).

of the one I gave, and for that reason I have added an addendum to the second chapter.

The third, fourth and fifth chapters are part of my continuing, ongoing investigation of, and indeed controversy with, the computational theory of the mind. Chapter 3, "The Turing Test: fifty-five years later," was originally prepared for a volume dedicated to problems concerning "the thinking computer." The fourth chapter, "Twenty-one years in the Chinese Room," was written for a volume assessing the whole history of the Chinese Room Argument. Chapter 5, "Is the brain a digital computer?", was my presidential address to the American Philosophical Association in 1990 and it criticizes the computational conception of the mind from a different angle from that of the Chinese Room, but one I think is just as important, and perhaps more important, even though it has not received anything like the attention that the Chinese Room Argument received. The Chinese Room demonstrates that the syntax of the implemented program is not sufficient to guarantee the semantics of actual mental contents. Implemented programs are defined syntactically and semantics is not intrinsic to syntax. But this article goes to the next stage and asks the question, What fact about a physical system makes it computational? And I discover what now seems to me obvious: that computation is not intrinsic to the physics of the system, but is a matter of our interpretation. Computation, in short, is not discovered in nature, but is imposed on nature and exists relative to our interpretation. This does not mean that computational interpretations are arbitrary. But it does mean that computation does not name an observer-independent phenomenon like digestion, photosynthesis or oxidization. Just as the Chinese Room argument showed that semantics is not intrinsic to syntax, this argument shows that syntax is not intrinsic to physics.

Chapter 6, "The phenomenological illusion," was originally presented at the annual Kirchberg Wittgenstein conference in 2004. In it I discuss what is for me an unusual area of publication, namely an appraisal of the inadequacies of certain phenomenological authors. The general problem I find with them is that they have a kind of perspectivalism that makes all of reality seem to exist only from a certain perspective. This prevents them from giving an adequate account of the real world and the relationship of our experience to the real world. The result of my assessment is that from my point of view, at least, several of the standard phenomenological authors seem to me not too phenomenological, but rather not nearly phenomenological enough.

Chapter 7, "The self as a problem in philosophy and neurobiology," originally appeared in a neurobiological volume dedicated to problems of neurobiology and the self. In it I try to show how my general approach to the philosophy of mind deals with the special problems having to do with the self.

The philosophy of mind as a theme continues in Chapter 8, "Why I am not a property dualist." This article originally appeared in the *Journal of Consciousness Studies*. Because I insist on the *ontological* irreducibility of consciousness while insisting at the same time that consciousness is *causally* reducible to its neuronal base, I am frequently accused of property dualism. In this article I try to answer that charge. The ambiguity of the title is deliberate. It can mean either or both: what grounds have I for rejecting property dualism, and what grounds are there for denying that I am already a property dualist?

Chapter 9, "Fact and value, 'is' and 'ought,' and reasons for action" was originally published in the twenty-fifth anniversary commemoration volume of the great legal theorist Hans Kelsen. I resume in this article a discussion that I first began in 1964 with an article in the *Philosophical Review*: "How to derive 'ought' from 'is'". But in this article, as well as in my book *Rationality*, I situate this whole discussion within the theory of speech acts, the theory of rationality, and the theory of reasons for action. I think that if you are clear about the basic philosophical issues, then the answer to the question, Can you derive 'ought' from 'is'? will seem fairly obvious, indeed, almost trivial.

The last chapter, Chapter 10, "The unity of the proposition," is previously unpublished. I wrote it some years ago and have never previously prepared it for publication. One of the many marks of a philosophical sensibility is an obsession with problems which most sane people regard as not worth bothering about. Here is a typical philosopher's question: How do the words in a sentence hang together to make a sentence and not just a word jumble? How do the elements of a proposition hang together to make a proposition and not just a soup of concepts? In this article I offer answers to these questions.

In addition to the gratitude expressed in the individual essays, I would like to thank Jennifer Hudin for preparing the index, Asya Passinsky for assistance in the preparation of the volume, and especially my wife, Dagmar Searle, for her constant help and inspiration. This book is dedicated to her.

CHAPTER I

Philosophy in a new century

General ruminations on the state and future of philosophy often produce superficiality and intellectual self-indulgence. Furthermore, an arbitrary blip on the calendar, the beginning of a new century, would not seem sufficient, by itself, to override a general presumption against engaging in such ruminations. However, I am going to take the risk of saying some things about the current and future state of philosophy, even though I think it is a serious risk. A number of important overall changes in the subject have occurred in my lifetime and I want to discuss their significance and the possibilities they raise for the future of the subject.

I. PHILOSOPHY AND KNOWLEDGE

The central intellectual fact of the present era is that knowledge grows. It grows daily and cumulatively. We know more than our grandparents did; our children will know more than we do.

We now have a huge accumulation of knowledge which is *certain, objective, and universal,* in a sense of these words that I will shortly explain. This growth of knowledge is quietly producing a transformation of philosophy.

The modern era in philosophy, begun by Descartes, Bacon, and others in the seventeenth century, was based on a premise which has now become obsolete. The premise was that the very existence of knowledge was in question and that therefore the main task of the philosopher was to cope with the problem of skepticism. Descartes saw his task as providing a secure foundation for knowledge, and Locke, in a similar vein, thought of his *Essay* as an investigation into the nature and extent of human knowledge. It seems reasonable that in the seventeenth century those philosophers took epistemology as the central element of the entire philosophical enterprise, because while they were in the midst of a scientific revolution, at the same time the possibility of certain, objective, universal knowledge seemed problematic. It was not at all clear how their various beliefs could be established with certainty, and it was not even clear how they could be made consistent. In particular there was a nagging and pervasive conflict between religious faith and the new scientific discoveries. The result was that we had three and a half centuries in which epistemology was at the center of philosophy.

During much of this period the skeptical paradoxes seemed to lie at the heart of the philosophical enterprise. Unless we can answer the skeptic, it seemed we cannot proceed further in philosophy or, for that matter, in science. For this reason epistemology became the base of any number of philosophical disciplines where it would seem that the epistemological questions are really peripheral. So, for example, in ethics the central question became, "Can there be an objective foundation for our ethical beliefs?" And even in the philosophy of language, many philosophers thought, and some still do, that epistemic questions were central. They take the central question in the philosophy of language to be, "How do we know what another person means when he says something?"

I believe the era of skeptical epistemology is now over. Because of the sheer growth of certain, objective, and universal knowledge, the possibility of knowledge is no longer a central question in philosophy. At present it is psychologically impossible for us to take Descartes's project seriously in the way that he took it: We know too much. This is not to say that there is no room for the traditional epistemic paradoxes, it simply means they no longer lie at the heart of the subject. The question, "How do I know that I am not a brain in a vat, not deceived by an evil demon, not dreaming, hallucinating," etc.? – or, in a more specifically Humean vein, "How do I know I am the same person today that I was yesterday?" "How do I know that the sun will rise in the East tomorrow?" "How do I know that there really are such things as causal relations in the world?" – I regard as like Zeno's paradoxes about the reality of space and time. It is an interesting paradox how I can cross the room if first I have to cross half of the room, but before that, half of the half, and yet before that, half of that half, etc. It seems I would have to traverse an infinite number of spaces before I can even get started and thus it looks like movement is impossible. That is an interesting paradox, and it is a nice exercise for philosophers to resolve the paradox, but no one seriously doubts the existence of space or the possibility of crossing the room because of Zeno's paradoxes. Analogously, I should like to say, no one should doubt the existence of knowledge because of the skeptical paradoxes. These are nice exercises for philosophers, but they do not challenge the existence of objective, universal, and certain knowledge.

I realize that there is still a thriving industry of work on traditional skepticism. I am suggesting, however, that the traditional forms of skepticism cannot have the meaning for us that they had for Descartes and his successors. Whether we like it or not, the sheer weight of accumulated knowledge is now so great that we cannot take seriously arguments that attempt to prove that it doesn't exist at all.

One clarification I need to make immediately. When I say that philosophy is no longer about epistemology I mean that the professional paradoxes of epistemology, the skeptical paradoxes, are no longer central to the philosophical enterprise. But in addition to epistemology in this specialized professional sense, there is, so to speak, "real-life" epistemology. How do you know that the claims you make are really true? What sorts of evidence, support, argument, and verification can you offer for the various claims you make? Real-life epistemology continues as before, indeed, it is as important as ever, because, for example, in the face of competing real-life claims about the cause and cure of AIDS, or the rival claims of monetary policy and fiscal policy in managing the economy, it is as important as ever that we insist on adequate tests and verification. So when I say that we are in a post-epistemic era, I mean we are in a post-skeptical era. Traditional philosophical skepticism I regard as now obsolete. But that does not mean we should abandon rational standards for assessing truth claims. On the contrary.

I just said that we have a large and growing body of knowledge which is *certain, objective, and universal.* I emphasize these three traits because they are precisely what is challenged by a certain contemporary form of extreme skepticism sometimes called "post-modernism," with such subsidiary branches as "deconstruction," "post-structuralism," and even some versions of pragmatism. According to this skeptical challenge, it is at best a mistake, and at worst a kind of totalitarian impulse, that leads us to say that we can have certainty, objectivity, and universality. According to this view, we never attain certain, objective, and universal knowledge at all. This is supposedly shown by certain investigations of science, such as those conducted by Thomas Kuhn and Paul Feyerabend that emphasize the irrational elements in the development of scientific theories. On this view, scientists do not attain truth; rather, they rush irrationally from one paradigm to another. Furthermore, the story goes, it is impossible to have objectivity, because all claims to knowledge are always perspectival; they are always made from a certain subjective point of view. And finally, it is impossible to have universality, because all science is produced in local, historical circumstances and is subject to all of the constraints imposed by those circumstances. I believe that these challenges are without merit, and I want to briefly say why. The main point I want to make is that what is true in the skeptical challenges is in no way inconsistent with certainty, objectivity, and universality.

One of the problems that we have, in coming to terms with the huge growth of knowledge, is to see how all of these features can exist simultaneously. How can knowledge be at the one and the same time *certain* and yet *tentative* and *corrigible*, how can it be totally *objective* and yet always from one *subjective* perspective or another, how can it be absolutely *universal*, and yet the product of *local* circumstances and conditions? Let us go through these in order. The certainty in question derives from the fact that the evidence for the claims in question is so overwhelming, and the claims themselves are so well embedded in a systematic set of interrelated claims, that are all equally well supported by overwhelming evidence, that it is simply irrational to doubt these truths. At present it is irrational to doubt that the heart pumps blood, that the earth is a satellite of the sun, or that water is made of hydrogen and oxygen. Furthermore, all of these items of knowledge are embedded in very powerful theories, the theories of human and animal physiology, the heliocentric theory of our planetary system and the atomic theory of matter. But at the same time it is always possible that there could be a scientific revolution that will overthrow these whole ways of thinking about things, that we might have a revolution comparable to the way in which the Einsteinian Revolution assimilated Newtonian mechanics as a special case. Nothing in any state of knowledge, however certain, can preclude the possibility of future scientific revolutions. This tentativeness and corrigibility is not a challenge to certainty. On the contrary, at one and the same time, we have to recognize certainty, and yet acknowledge the possibility of future major changes in our theories.

I want to emphasize this point: There is a very large body of knowledge that is known with certainty. You will find it in the university bookstore, in, for example, textbooks on engineering or biology. The sense in which we know with certainty that the heart pumps blood, for example, or that the earth is a satellite of the sun is that, given the overwhelming weight of reasons that support these claims, it is irrational to doubt them. *But certainty does not imply incorrigibility.* It does not imply that we could not conceive of circumstances in which we would be led to abandon these claims. It is a traditional mistake, one I am now trying to overcome, to suppose that certainty implies incorrigibility by any future discovery. We are all brought up to believe that certainty is impossible because claims to knowledge are always tentative and subject to further correction. But this is a mistake. Certainty is not inconsistent with tentativeness and corrigibility. There is no question that we know a great many things with certainty, and yet those things are revisable by future discoveries.

That leads to the second combination of features: how can knowledge at one and the same time be completely objective and yet perspectival, always stated and assessed from one perspective or another? To say that a knowledge claim is epistemically objective is to say that its truth or falsity can be established independently of the feelings, attitudes, prejudices, preferences, and commitments, of investigators. Thus, when I say that "Water is composed of H_2O molecules," that claim is completely objective. If I say, "Water tastes better that wine" – well, that claim is subjective. It is a matter of opinion. It is characteristic of knowledge claims, of the sort that I have been discussing, that when I say that such knowledge grows cumulatively, the knowledge in question is, in this sense, epistemically objective. But such objectivity does not preclude perspectivality. Knowledge claims are perspectival in the obvious and trivial sense that all claims are perspectival. All representations are from a perspective, from a point of view. So when I say, "Water consists of H_2O molecules," that is a description at the level of atomic structure. At some other level of description, at the level of subatomic physics, for example, we might wish to say that water consists of quarks, muons, and other sundry sub-atomic particles. The point for our present discussion is that the fact that all knowledge claims are perspectival does not preclude epistemic objectivity.

I want to state this point emphatically: All representation of reality, human or otherwise, and a fortiori all knowledge of reality, is from a point of view, from a certain perspective. But the perspectival character of representation and knowledge does not imply that the knowledge claims in question are dependent on the preferences, attitudes, prejudices, predilections, of observers. The existence of objectivity is in no way threatened by the perspectival character of knowledge and representation.

Finally, knowledge claims of the sort that I am talking about, where we make claims about how the world works, are universal. What is true in Vladivostok is also true in Pretoria, Paris, and Berkeley. But the fact that we are able to formulate, test, verify, and conclusively establish such claims as certain, universal, and objective, requires a very specific socio-cultural apparatus. It requires an apparatus of trained investigators, and the social cultural conditions necessary for the existence of such training and such investigation. These have developed most strongly in Western Europe and its cultural offshoots in other parts of the world, especially North America, during the past four centuries. There is a trivial and harmless sense in which all knowledge is socially constructed. In this trivial and harmless sense knowledge is expressed in statements, in claims; and these claims have to be formulated, formalized, tested, verified, checked and rechecked. That we are able to do this requires a very specific sort of socio-cultural structure, and in that sense, our knowledge claims are socially constructed. But social construction in this sense is not in any way in conflict with the fact that knowledge so arrived at is universal, objective, and certain.

I want to emphasize this third point just as I did the first two: Knowledge claims are made, tested, and verified by historically situated individuals working against the background of specific cultural practices. In this sense all knowledge claims are socially constructed. But the truth of such claims is not socially constructed. Truth is a matter of objective facts in the world that correspond to our knowledge claims.

So far I have considered three objections to the commonsense view that we have a large body of knowledge that is certain, objective, and universal. First, knowledge is always tentative and corrigible; second, it is always stated from a point of view; and third, it has to be arrived at by cooperative human efforts working in particular historically situated social contexts. The chief point I am making is that there is nothing inconsistent between these theses and the claim that knowledge so arrived at is often *certain, objective, and universal.*

If by "modernism" is meant the period of systematic rationality and intelligence that began in the Renaissance and reached a high point of self-conscious articulation in the European Enlightenment, then we are not in a post-modern era. On the contrary, modernism has just begun. We are, however, I believe, in a post-skeptical or post-epistemic era. You will not understand what is happening in our intellectual life if you do not see the exponential growth of knowledge as the central intellectual fact. There is something absurd about the post-modern thinker who buys an airplane ticket on the internet, gets on an airplane, works on his laptop computer in the course of the airplane flight, gets off of the airplane at his destination, takes a taxicab to a lecture hall, and then gives a lecture claiming that somehow or other there is no certain knowledge, that objectivity is in question, and that all claims to truth and knowledge are really only disguised power grabs.

II. THE POST-SKEPTICAL ERA

Assuming that I am right about these features of knowledge and about the fact that knowledge continues to grow, what are the implications for philosophy? What does philosophy look like in a post-epistemic, post-skeptical era? It seems to me that it is now possible to do systematic theoretical philosophy in a way that was generally regarded as out of the question a half a century ago. Paradoxically, one of Wittgenstein's great contributions to philosophy is one that he himself would reject. Namely, by taking skepticism seriously and attempting to cope with it, Wittgenstein has helped to pave the way for a type of theoretical and systematic philosophizing that he himself, in his later work, abominated and thought impossible. Precisely because we are no longer worried about the traditional skeptical paradoxes and about their implications for the very existence of language, meaning, truth, knowledge, objectivity, certainty, and universality, we can now get on with the task of general theorizing.

The situation is somewhat analogous to the situation in Greece after the transition from the philosophy of Socrates and Plato to the philosophy of Aristotle. Socrates and Plato took skepticism seriously; Aristotle was a systematic theoretician.

With the possibility of developing general philosophical theories, and the decline of the obsession with skeptical worries, philosophy has eliminated much of its isolation from other disciplines. So, for example, the best philosophers of science are as familiar with the latest research as are specialists in those sciences.

There are a number of topics I could discuss concerning the future of philosophy, but for the sake of brevity, I will confine myself to six subjects.

1. The traditional mind-body problem

I begin with the traditional mind-body problem, because I believe it is the contemporary philosophical problem most amenable to cooperation between scientists and philosophers. There are different versions of the mind-body problem but the one most intensely discussed today is: What exactly are the relations between consciousness and the brain? It seems to me the neurosciences have now progressed to the point that we can address this as a straight neurobiological problem, and indeed several neurobiologists are doing precisely that. In its simplest form, the question is how exactly do neurobiological processes in the brain *cause* conscious states and processes, and how exactly are those conscious states and processes *realized in* the brain? So stated, this looks like an empirical scientific problem. It looks similar to such problems as, "How exactly do biochemical processes at the level of cells cause cancer?" and, "How exactly does the genetic structure of a zygote produce the phenotypical traits of a mature organism?"

However, there are a number of purely philosophical obstacles to getting a satisfactory neurobiological solution to the problem of consciousness, and I have to devote some space at least to trying to remove some of the worst of these obstacles.

The single most important obstacle to getting a solution to the traditional mind-brain problem is the persistence of a set of traditional but obsolete categories of mind and body, matter and spirit, mental and physical. As long as we continue to talk and think as if the mental and the physical were separate metaphysical realms, the relation of the brain to consciousness will forever seem mysterious, and we will not have a satisfactory explanation of the relation of neuron firings to consciousness. The first step on the road to philosophical and scientific progress in these areas is to forget about the tradition of Cartesian dualism and just remind ourselves that mental phenomena are ordinary biological phenomena in the same sense as photosynthesis or digestion. We must stop worrying about how the brain *could* cause consciousness and begin with the plain fact that it *does*. The notions of both mental and physical as they are traditionally defined need to be abandoned as we reconcile ourselves to the fact that we live in one world, and that all the features of the world from quarks and electrons to nation states and balance of payments problems are, in their different ways, parts of that one world. I find it truly amazing that the obsolete categories of mind and matter continue to impede progress. Many scientists feel that they can only investigate the "physical" realm and are reluctant to face consciousness on its own terms because it seems not to be "physical" but "mental," and several prominent philosophers think it is impossible for us to understand the relations of mind to brain. Just as Einstein made a conceptual change to break the old conception of space and time, so we need a similar conceptual change to break the bifurcation of mental and physical.

Related to the difficulty brought about by accepting the traditional categories is a straight logical fallacy which I need to expose. Consciousness is, by definition, subjective, in the sense that for a conscious state to exist it has to be experienced by some conscious subject. Consciousness in this sense has a first-person ontology in that it only exists from the point of view of a human or animal subject, an "I," who has the conscious experience. Science is not used to dealing with phenomena that have a first-person ontology. By tradition, science deals with phenomena that are "objective," and avoids anything that is "subjective." Indeed, many philosophers and scientists feel that because science is by definition objective, there can be no such thing as a science of consciousness, because consciousness is subjective. This whole

argument rests on a massive confusion, which is one of the most persistent confusions in our intellectual civilization. There are two quite distinct
senses of the distinction between objective and subjective. In one sense,
which I will call the epistemic sense of the objective/subjective distinction,
there is a distinction between objective knowledge and subjective matters
of opinion. If I say, for example, "Rembrandt was born in 1606," that statement is epistemically objective in the sense that it can be established as true
or false independently of the attitudes, feelings, opinions, or prejudices of
the agents investigating the question. If I say, "Rembrandt was a better
painter than Rubens," that claim is not a matter of objective knowledge,
but is a matter of subjective opinion. In addition to the distinction between
epistemically objective and subjective claims, there is a distinction between
entities in the world that have an objective existence, such as mountains
and molecules, and entities that have a subjective existence, such as pains
and tickles. I call this distinction in modes of existence, the ontological
sense of the objective/subjective distinction.

Science is indeed epistemically objective in the sense that scientists
attempt to establish truths which can be verified independently of the attitudes and prejudices of the scientists. But epistemic objectivity of method
does not preclude ontological subjectivity of subject matter. Thus there is
no objection in principle to having an epistemically objective science of an
ontologically subjective domain, such as human consciousness.

Another difficulty encountered by a science of subjectivity is the difficulty in verifying claims about human and animal consciousness. In the
case of humans, unless we perform experiments on ourselves individually,
our only conclusive evidence for the presence and nature of consciousness
is what the subject says and does, and subjects are notoriously unreliable.
In the case of animals, we are in an even worse situation, because we have
to rely on the animal's behavior in response to stimuli. We cannot get any
statements from the animal about its conscious states. I think this is a real
difficulty, but I would point out that it is no more an obstacle in principle
than the difficulties encountered in other forms of scientific investigation
where we have to rely on indirect means of verifying our claims. We have
no way of observing black holes, and indeed, strictly speaking, we have no
way of directly observing atomic and subatomic particles. Nonetheless, we
have quite well-established scientific accounts of these domains, and the
methods we use to verify hypotheses in these areas should give us a model
for verifying hypotheses in the area of the study of human and animal
subjectivity. The "privacy" of human and animal consciousness does not
make a science of consciousness impossible. As far as "methodology" is

concerned, in real sciences methodological questions always have the same answer: In order to find out how the world works, you have to use any weapon that you can lay your hands on, and stick with any weapon that seems to work.

Assuming, then, that we are not worried about the problem of objectivity and subjectivity, and that we are prepared to seek indirect methods of verification of hypotheses concerning consciousness, how should we proceed? Most scientific research today into the problem of consciousness seems to me to be based on a mistake. The scientists in question characteristically adopt what I will call the building block theory of consciousness, and they conduct their investigation accordingly. On the building block theory, we should think of our conscious field as made up of various building blocks, such as visual experience, auditory experience, tactile experience, the stream of thought, etc. The task of a scientific theory of consciousness would be to find the neurobiological correlate of consciousness (nowadays called the "NCC"), and, on the building block theory, if we could find the NCC for even one building block, such as the NCC for seeing the color red, that would in all likelihood give us a clue to the building blocks for the other sensory modalities, and for the stream of thought. This research program may turn out to be right in the end. Nonetheless, it seems to me doubtful as a way to proceed in the present situation for the following reason. I said above that the essence of consciousness was subjectivity. There is a certain subjective qualitative feel to every conscious state. One aspect of this subjectivity, and it is a necessary aspect, is that conscious states always come to us in a unified form. We do not perceive just the color or the shape, or the sound, of an object, we perceive all of these at once simultaneously in a unified conscious experience. The subjectivity of consciousness implies unity. They are not two separate features, but two aspects of the same feature.

Now, that being the case, it seems to me the NCC we are looking for is not the NCC for the various building blocks of color, taste, sound, etc., but rather what I will call the basal, or background, conscious field, which is the presupposition of having any conscious experience in the first place. The crucial problem is not, for example, "How does the brain produce the conscious experience of red?" but rather, "How does the brain produce the unified, subjective conscious field?" We should think of perception not as *creating* consciousness, but as *modifying* a preexisting conscious field. We should think of my present conscious field not as made up of various building blocks, but rather as a unified field, which is modified in specific ways by the various sorts of stimuli that I and other human beings receive. Because we have pretty good evidence from lesion studies that consciousness is not distributed over the entire brain, and because we also have good evidence that consciousness exists in both hemispheres, I think what we should look for now is the kind of neurobiological processes that will produce a unified field of consciousness. These, as far as I can tell, are likely to be for the most part in the thalamocortical system. My hypothesis, then, is that looking for the NCCs of building blocks is barking up the wrong tree, and that we should instead look for the correlate of the unified field of consciousness in more global features of the brain, such as massive synchronized patterns of neuron firing in the thalamocortical system.[1]

2. The philosophy of mind and cognitive science

The mind-body problem is one part of a much broader set of issues, known collectively as the philosophy of mind. This includes not only the traditional mind-body problem, but the whole conglomeration of problems dealing with the nature of mind and consciousness, of perception and intentionality, of intentional action and thought. A very curious thing has happened in the past two or three decades – the philosophy of mind has moved to the center of philosophy. Several other important branches of philosophy, such as epistemology, metaphysics, the philosophy of action, and even the philosophy of language, are now treated as dependent on, and in some cases even as branches of, the philosophy of mind. Whereas fifty years ago the philosophy of language was considered, "first philosophy," now it is the philosophy of mind. There are a number of reasons for this change, but two stand out. First it has become more and more obvious to a lot of philosophers that our understanding of the issues in a lot of subjects – the nature of meaning, rationality and language in general – presupposes an understanding of the most fundamental mental processes. For example, the way language represents reality is dependent on the more biologically fundamental ways in which the mind represents reality and, indeed, linguistic representation is a vastly more powerful extension of the more basic mental representations such as perception, intentions, beliefs, and desires. Second, the rise of the new discipline of cognitive science has opened to philosophy whole areas of research into human cognition in all its forms. Cognitive science was invented by an interdisciplinary group,

---

[1] I have discussed these issues in much greater detail in my, "Consciousness," *The Annual Review of Neuroscience* 23 (2000): 557–578.

consisting of philosophers who objected to the persistence of behaviorism in psychology, together with like-minded cognitive psychologists, linguists, anthropologists, and computer scientists. I believe the most active and fruitful general area of research today in philosophy is in the general cognitive science domain. The basic subject matter of cognitive science is intentionality in all of its forms.

Paradoxically, cognitive science was founded on a mistake. There is nothing necessarily fatal about founding an academic subject on a mistake; indeed many disciplines were founded on mistakes. Chemistry, for example, was founded on alchemy. However, a persistent adherence to the mistake is at best inefficient and an obstacle to progress. In the case of cognitive science the mistake was to suppose that the brain is a digital computer and the mind is a computer program.

There are a number of ways to demonstrate that this is a mistake but the simplest is to point out that the implemented computer program is defined entirely in terms of symbolic or syntactical processes, independent of the physics of the hardware. The notion "same implemented program" defines an equivalence class that is specified entirely in terms of formal or syntactical processes and is independent of the specific physics of this or that hardware implementation. This principle underlies the famous "multiple realizeability" feature of computer programs. The same program can be realized in an indefinite range of hardwares. The mind cannot consist in a program or programs, because the syntactical operations of the program are not by themselves sufficient to constitute or to guarantee the presence of semantic contents of actual mental processes. Minds, on the other hand, contain more than symbolic or syntactical components, they contain actual mental states with semantic content in the form of thoughts, feelings, etc., and these are caused by quite specific neurobiological processes in the brain. The mind could not consist in a program because the syntactical processes of the implemented program do not by themselves have any semantic contents. I demonstrated this years ago with the so-called Chinese Room Argument.[2]

A debate continues about this and other versions of the computational theory of the mind. Some people think that the introduction of computers that use parallel distributed processing ("PDP," sometimes also called "connectionism"), would answer the objections I just stated. But I do not see how the introduction of the connectionist arguments makes any

---

[2] John R. Searle, "Minds, Brains and Programs," *Behavioral and Brains Sciences* 3 (1980): 417.

difference. The problem is that any computation that can be carried out on a connectionist program can also be carried out on a traditional von Neumann system. We know from mathematical results that any function that is computable at all is computable on a universal Turing machine. In that sense no new computational capacity is added by the connectionist architecture, though the connectionist systems can be made to work faster, because they have several different computational processes acting in parallel and interacting with each other. Because the computational powers of the connectionist system are no greater than the traditional von Neumann system, if we claim superiority for the connectionist system, there must be some other feature of the system that is being appealed to. But the only other feature of the connectionist system would have to be in the hardware implementation, which operates in parallel rather then in series. But if we claim that the connectionist architecture rather than connectionist computations are responsible for mental processes, we are no longer advancing the computational theory of the mind, but are engaging in neurobiological speculation. With this hypothesis we have abandoned the computational theory of the mind in favor of speculative neurobiology.

What is actually happening in cognitive science is a paradigm shift away from the computational model of the mind and toward a much more neurobiologically based conception of the mind. For reasons that should be clear by now, I welcome this development. As we come to understand more about the operations of the brain it seems to me that we will succeed in gradually replacing computational cognitive science with cognitive neuroscience. Indeed I believe this transformation is already taking place. Advances in cognitive neuroscience are likely to create more philosophical problems than they solve. For example, to what extent will an increased understanding of brain operations force us to make conceptual revisions in our commonsense vocabulary for describing mental processes as they occur in thought and action? In the simplest and easiest cases we can simply assimilate the cognitive neuroscience discoveries to our existing conceptual apparatus. Thus, we do not make a major shift in our concept of memory when we introduce the sorts of distinctions that neurobiological investigations have made apparent to us. Even in popular speech we now distinguish between short-term and long-term memory, and no doubt as our investigation proceeds, we will have further distinctions. The concept of iconic memory is already passing into the general speech of educated people. But in some cases it seems we are forced to make conceptual revisions. I have thought for a long time that the commonsense conception of memory as a storehouse of previous experience and knowledge is both psychologically and biologically inadequate. My impression is that contemporary research bears me out on this. We have to have a conception of memory as a creative process rather than simply a retrieval process. Some philosophers think even more radical revisions than this will be forced upon us by the neurobiological discoveries of the future.

I give the example of memory as one instance where an ongoing research project raises philosophical questions and has philosophical implications. I could have given other examples about linguistics, rationality, perception, and evolution. I see the development of a more sophisticated cognitive science as a continuing source of collaboration between what was traditionally thought of as the two separate realms of "philosophy" and "science."

3. The philosophy of language

I said that the philosophy of language was the center of philosophy for most of the twentieth century. Indeed, as I remarked, during the first three-quarters of the twentieth century, the philosophy of language was taken to be "first philosophy." But by the end of the century that had changed. Less is happening in the philosophy of language now than in the philosophy of mind, and I believe that the currently most influential research programs have reached a kind of dead end. Why? There are many reasons of which I will mention only two.

First, one of the main research programs in the philosophy of language suffers from the epistemic obsession that I have been castigating. A commitment to a certain form of empiricism and in some cases even behaviorism led some prominent philosophers to try to give an analysis of meaning according to which the hearer is engaged in the epistemic task of trying to figure out what the speaker means either by looking at his behavior in response to a stimulus, or by looking at the conditions under which he would hold a sentence to be true. The idea is that if we could describe how the hearer solves the epistemic problem we would thereby analyze meaning. This preoccupation with the epistemic aspect of language use leads to the same confusion between epistemology and ontology that has bedeviled the Western philosophical tradition for over three centuries.

This work, I believe, is going nowhere, because its obsession with how we know what a speaker means obscures the distinction between *how* the hearer knows what the speaker means and *what* it is that the hearer knows. I think that epistemology plays the same role in the philosophy of language as it does, for example, in geology. The geologist is interested in such things as tectonic plates, sedimentation, and rock layers, and will use any method that comes to hand to try to find out how these phenomena work. The philosopher of language is interested in meaning, truth, reference, and necessity, and analogously should use any epistemic method that comes to hand to try to figure out how these phenomena work in the minds of actual speakers and hearers. What we are interested in is what are the facts which are known; and to a much lesser extent are we interested in the question, how we come to know these facts.

Finally, I think the greatest source of weakness in the philosophy of language is that its currently most influential research project is based on a mistake. Frege was anxious to insist that meanings were not psychological entities, but he did think that they could be grasped by speakers and hearers of a language. Frege thought that communication in a public language was possible only because there is an ontologically objective realm of meanings, and that the same meaning can be grasped equally by both speaker and hearer. A number of authors have attacked this "internalist" conception. They believe that meaning is a matter of causal relations between the utterances of words and objects in the world. So the word "water," for example, means what it does to me not because I have some mental content associated with that word, but rather because there is a causal chain connecting me to various actual examples of water in the world. This view is called "externalism," and it is usually opposed to the traditional view, called "internalism." Externalism has led to an extensive research project of trying to describe the nature of the causal relations that give rise to meaning. The problem with this research project is that nobody has ever been able to explain, with any plausibility whatever, the nature of these causal chains. The idea that meanings are something external to the mind is widely accepted, but no one has ever been able to give a coherent account of meaning in these terms.

My prediction is that no one will ever be able to give a satisfactory account of meanings as something external to the head, because such external phenomena could not function to relate language to the world in the way that meanings do relate words and reality. What we require in order to resolve the dispute between internalists and externalists is a more sophisticated notion of how the mental contents in speakers' heads serve to relate language in particular, and human agents in general, to the real world of objects and states of affairs.

Frege's real mistake, and it is one that I repeated, is to suppose that the way in which language relates to reality – the "mode of presentation" – also fixes propositional content. Frege assumed both that sense determines reference and that propositional content consists in sense. But if by the notion of "proposition" we are interested in that which we assess as true or false, then it is not the case that sense is identical with propositional content, because often we are interested in the actual objects that are referred to rather than the mode in which they are referred to. This is especially true of indexicals. We need to separate the question, "How do words relate to the world?" from the question, "How is propositional content determined?" However, the correct observation by the externalists, that the content of a proposition cannot always be specified by what is internal to the mind, does not show that the contents of the mind are insufficient to fix reference. I have discussed these issues in some detail elsewhere and will not repeat the discussion here.[3]

4. The philosophy of society

It is characteristic of the history of philosophy that new branches of the subject are created in response to intellectual developments both inside and outside of philosophy. Thus, for example, in the early part of the twentieth century, the philosophy of language in the sense in which we now use that expression was created largely in response to developments in mathematical logic and work on the foundations of mathematics. A similar evolution has occurred in the philosophy of mind. I would like to propose that in the twenty-first century we will feel a pressing need for, and should certainly try to develop, what I will call a philosophy of society. At present we tend to construe social philosophy as either a branch of political philosophy (thus the expression "social and political philosophy"), or we tend to construe social philosophy as a study of the philosophy of the social sciences. A student today taking a course called "Social Philosophy" is likely either to be studying Rawls on justice (political philosophy) or Hempel on covering law explanations in the social sciences (philosophy of social science). I am proposing that we should have a freestanding philosophy of society, which stands to social sciences in the same way that the philosophy of mind stands to psychology and cognitive science, or the philosophy of language stands to linguistics. It would deal with more general framework questions. In particular, I think we need much more work on questions of the ontology of social reality. How is it possible that human beings, through their social interactions, can create an objective social reality of money, property, marriage, government, games, etc. when such entities, in

---

[3] John R. Searle, *Intentionality: An essay on the philosophy of mind* (Cambridge: Cambridge University Press, 1983), chaps. 8–9.

some sense, exist only in virtue of a collective agreement or a belief that they exist? How is it possible that there can be an objective social reality that exists only because we think it exists?

When questions of social ontology have been properly sorted out it seems to me that the questions of social philosophy, namely the nature of explanation in the social sciences and the relation of social philosophy to political philosophy, will naturally fall into place. I attempted to begin this research project in my book *The Construction of Social Reality*.[4]

Specifically, I believe that in our study of political and social reality we need a set of concepts which will enable us to describe political and social reality, so to speak from the "middle distance." Our problem in attempting to cope with social reality is that our concepts are either immensely abstract, as in traditional political philosophy, for example the concepts of the social contract or the class struggle, or they tend to be essentially journalistic, dealing with day-to-day questions of policy and power relations. Thus we are quite sophisticated in abstract theories of justice, and with the developing criteria for assessing the justice or injustice of institutions. Much of the progress in this area is owed to John Rawls, who revolutionized the study of political philosophy with his classic work *A Theory of Justice*.[5] But when it comes to political science, the categories traditionally do not rise much above the level of journalism. Therefore, if, for example, you read a work in political science as recent as twenty years old, you will find that much of the discussion is out of date.

What we need, I believe, is to develop a set of categories which would enable us to appraise social reality in a way which would be more abstract than that of day-to-day political journalism, but at the same time, would enable us to ask and answer specific questions about specific political realities and institutions in a way that traditional political philosophy was unable to do. Thus, for example, I think the leading political event of the twentieth century was the failure of ideologies such as those of fascism and communism, and in particular the failure of socialism in its different and various forms. The interesting thing from the point of view of the present analysis is that we lack the categories in which to pose and answer questions dealing with the failure of socialism. There are different definitions of "socialism," but they all have one thing in common: a system can only be socialist if it has public ownership and control of the basic means of production. The failure of socialism so defined is the single most

---

[4] John R. Searle, *The Construction of Social Reality* (New York: Free Press, 1995).
[5] John Rawls, *A Theory of Justice* (Cambridge, Mass.: Harvard University Press, 1971).

important social development of the twentieth century. It is an amazing fact that that development remains unanalyzed and is seldom discussed by the political and social philosophers of our time.

When I talk of the failure of socialism, I am referring not only to the failure of Marxist socialism, but also to the failure of democratic socialism as it existed in the countries of Western Europe. The socialist parties of those countries continue to use some of the vocabulary of socialism, but the belief in the basic mechanism of socialist change, namely the public ownership and control of the means of production, has been quietly abandoned. What is the correct philosophical analysis of this entire phenomenon?

A similar sort of question would involve the appraisal of national institutions. So, for example, for most political scientists, it would be very difficult to attempt to analyze the backwardness, corruption, and general dreadfulness of the political institutions of several contemporary nation states. Most political scientists, given their commitment to "scientific objectivity," and the limited categories at their disposal, cannot even attempt to describe how dreadful many countries are. Many countries have apparently desirable political institutions such as a written constitution, political parties, free elections, etc., and yet the way they operate is inherently corrupt. We can discuss these institutions at a very abstract level, and Rawls and others have provided us with the tools to do so. But I would like an expanded social philosophy which would give us the tools for analyzing social institutions as they exist in real societies in a way that would enable us to make comparative judgments between different countries and larger societies, without rising to such a level of abstraction that we cannot make specific value judgments about specific institutional structures. The work of the economist-philosopher Amartya Sen is a step in this direction.

5. Ethics and practical reason

For much of the twentieth century the subject of ethics was dominated by a version of the same skepticism that has affected other branches of philosophy for several centuries. Just as the philosophy of language was damaged by the urge to treat the users of language as essentially researchers engaged in an epistemic task of trying to figure out what a speaker of a language means, so ethics was obsessed by the question of epistemic objectivity. The principal issue in ethics was about whether or not there could be objectivity in ethics. The traditional view in analytic philosophy was that ethical objectivity was impossible, that you could not, in Hume's phrase, derive an "ought" from an "is," and consequently that ethical statements could not literally be either true or false, but functioned only to express feelings or to influence behavior, etc. The way out of the sterility of these debates is not, I think, to try to show that ethical statements are true or false in a way that, for example, scientific statements are true or false, because there are clearly important differences between the two. The way out of the impasse, I believe, is to see that ethics is really a branch of a much more interesting subject of practical reason and rationality. What is the nature of rationality in general and what is it to act rationally on a reason for action? This, I believe, is a more fruitful approach than the traditional approach of worrying about the objectivity of ethical statements.

Something like the study of rationality, as a successor to ethics as it was traditionally construed, seems to be already happening. Currently there are, for example, a number of attempts to revive Kant's doctrine of the categorical imperative. Kant thought that the nature of rationality itself set certain formal constraints on what could count as an ethically acceptable reason for an action. I do not believe these efforts will succeed, but much more interesting than their success or failure is the fact that ethics as a substantive branch of philosophy – freed from its epistemic obsession to find a form of objectivity, and the inevitable skepticism when the quest for objectivity fails – seems now to have become possible again. I am not sure what the reasons for the change are, but my impression is that, more than any other single factor, Rawls's work not only revived political philosophy but made substantive ethics seem possible as well.

6. The philosophy of science

In the twentieth century, not surprisingly, the philosophy of science shared the epistemic obsession with the rest of philosophy. The chief questions in the philosophy of science, at least for the first half of the century, had to do with the nature of scientific verification, and much effort was devoted to overcoming various skeptical paradoxes, such as the traditional problem of induction. Throughout most of the twentieth century the philosophy of science was conditioned by the belief in the distinction between analytic and synthetic propositions. The standard conception of the philosophy of science was that scientists aimed to get synthetic contingent truths in the form of universal scientific laws. These laws stated very general truths about the nature of reality, and the chief issue in the philosophy of science had to do with the nature of their testing and verification. The prevailing orthodoxy, as it developed in the middle decades of the century, was that science proceeded by something called the "hypothetico-deductive method." Scientists formed a hypothesis, deduced logical consequences from it, and then tested those consequences in experiments. This conception was articulated, I think more or less independently, by Karl Popper and Carl Gustav Hempel. Those practicing scientists who took an interest in the philosophy of science at all tended to admire Popper's views, but much of their admiration was based on a misunderstanding. What I think they admired in Popper was the idea that science proceeds by acts of originality and imagination. The scientist has to form a hypothesis on the basis of his own imagination and guesswork. There is no "scientific method" for arriving at hypotheses. The procedure of the scientist is then to test the hypothesis by performing experiments and reject those hypotheses that have been refuted.

Most scientists do not, I think, realize how anti-scientific Popper's views actually are. On Popper's conception of science and of the activity of scientists, science is not an accumulation of truths about nature, and the scientist does not arrive at truths about nature, rather all that we have in the sciences are a series of so far unrefuted hypotheses. But the idea that the scientist aims at truth, and that in various sciences we actually have an accumulation of truths, which I think is the presupposition of most actual scientific research, is not something that is consistent with Popper's conception.[6]

The comfortable orthodoxy of science as an accumulation of truths, or even as a gradual progression through the accumulation of so far unrefuted hypotheses, was challenged by the publication of Thomas Kuhn's *The Structure of Scientific Revolutions* in 1962.[7] It is puzzling that Kuhn's book had the dramatic effect that it did because it is not strictly speaking about the philosophy of science, but about the history of science. Kuhn argues that if you look at the actual history of science, you discover that it is not a gradual progressive accumulation of knowledge about the world, but that science is subject to periodic massive revolutions, where entire world-views are overthrown when an existing scientific paradigm is overthrown by a new paradigm. It is characteristic of Kuhn's book that he implies, though as far as I know he does not state explicitly, that the scientist does not give us truths about the world, but only a series of ways of solving puzzles, a series of ways of dealing with puzzling problems within a paradigm. And when the paradigm reaches puzzles that it cannot solve, it is overthrown

[6] For an interesting criticism of Popper's views see David Stove, *Against the Idols of the Age* (Somerset, N.J.: Transaction, 1999).
[7] Thomas Kuhn, *The Structure of Scientific Revolutions* (Chicago: University of Chicago Press, 1962).

and a new paradigm is erected in its place, which again sets off a new round of puzzle-solving activity. From the point of view of this discussion, the interesting thing about Kuhn's book is that he seems to imply that we are not getting progressively closer to the truth about nature in the natural sciences, we are just getting a series of puzzle-solving mechanisms. The scientist essentially moves from one paradigm to another, for reasons that have nothing to do with giving an accurate description of an independently existing natural reality, but rather for reasons that are in greater or lesser degree irrational. Kuhn's book was not much welcomed by practicing scientists, but it had an enormous effect in several humanities disciplines, especially those connected with the study of literature. Kuhn seemed to have refuted the claim that science gives us truths about the world; rather science gives us no more truth about the real world than do works of literary fiction or works of literary criticism. Science is essentially a set of irrational processes whereby groups of scientists form theories which are more or less arbitrary social constructs, and then abandon these in favor of other theories, which are equally arbitrary social constructs.

Whatever Kuhn's intentions, I believe that his effect on general culture, though not on the practices of real scientists, has been unfortunate, because it has served to "demythologize" science, to "debunk" it, to prove that it is not what ordinary people have supposed it to be. Kuhn paved the way for the even more radical skeptical view of Paul Feyerabend, who argued that as far as giving us truths about the world, science is no better than witchcraft.

My own view is that these issues are entirely peripheral to what we ought to be worried about in the philosophy of science, and what I hope we will dedicate our efforts to in the twenty-first century. I think the essential problem is this: Twentieth-century science has radically challenged a set of very pervasive, powerful philosophical and commonsense assumptions about nature, and we simply have not digested the results of these scientific advances. I am thinking especially of quantum mechanics. I think that we can absorb relativity theory more or less comfortably, because it can be construed as an extension of our traditional Newtonian conception of the world. We simply have to revise our ideas of space and time, and their relation to such fundamental physical constants as the speed of light. But quantum mechanics really does provide a basic challenge to our world-view, and we simply have not yet digested it. I regard it as a scandal that philosophers of science, including physicists with an interest in the philosophy of science, have not so far given us a coherent account of how quantum mechanics fits into our overall conception of the universe, not only as regards causation and determinacy but also as regards the ontology of the physical world.

Most philosophers, like most educated people today, have a conception of causation which is a mixture of common sense and Newtonian mechanics. Philosophers tend to suppose that causal relations are always instances of strict deterministic causal laws, and that cause and effect relations stand to each other in simple mechanical relations like gear wheels moving gear wheels, and other such Newtonian phenomena. We know at some abstract level that this picture is not right, but we still have not replaced our commonsense conception with a more sophisticated scientific conception. I think that working through these issues is one of the most exciting tasks of the twenty-first century philosophy of science. We need to give an account of physical theory, especially quantum theory, that will enable us to assimilate physical results to a coherent overall world-view. I think that in the course of this project we are going to have to revise certain crucial notions, such as the notion of causation; and this revision is going to have very important effects on other questions, such as the questions concerning determinism and free will. This work has already begun.

III. CONCLUSION

The main message I have tried to convey is that it is now possible to do a new kind of philosophy. With the abandonment of the epistemic bias in the subject, such a philosophy can go far beyond anything imagined by the philosophy of a half century ago. It begins, not with skepticism, but with what we all know about the real world. It begins with such facts as those stated by the atomic theory of matter and the evolutionary theory of biology, as well as such "commonsense" facts as that we are all conscious, that we all really do have intentional mental states, that we form social groups and create institutional facts. Such a philosophy is theoretical, comprehensive, systematic, and universal in subject matter.[8]

---

[8] This article is a revision of "The Future of Philosophy," which was written for a scientific rather than a philosophical audience and published in a special millennium issue of the *Philosophical Transactions of the Royal Society*, series B, London, 354 (1999): 2,069–2,080. I am indebted to Dagmar Searle for discussion of all these issues.

CHAPTER 2

Social ontology: some basic principles

I. THE PROBLEM OF SOCIAL ONTOLOGY

The aim of this chapter is to explore the problem of social ontology. The form that the exploration will take is a development of the argument that I presented in *The Construction of Social Reality* (Searle, 1995). I will summarize some of the results of that book and then develop the ideas further.

First of all, why is there a problem about social ontology at all? We are talking about the mode of existence of social objects such as the United States of America, the San Francisco Forty Niners football team, the University of California and the Squaw Valley Property Owners Association, as well as such large-scale institutions as money or private property. We are also talking about social facts, such as the fact that I am a citizen of the United States, that the piece of paper that I hold in my hand is a $20 bill, and that France is a member of the European Union. We are also talking about social processes and events, such as the presidential election campaign, the collapse of communism and the last World Series. We are talking, in short, about social facts, social objects, and social processes and events. To repeat the question, why is there a problem about these phenomena?

The problem arises in various forms, but one is this: we know independently that the world consists entirely of physical particles in fields of force (or whatever the ultimately correct physics tells us are the final building blocks of matter) and that these physical particles are organized into systems and that some of the carbon-based systems have evolved over a period of about 5 billion years into a very large number of animal and plant species, among which we humans are one of the species capable of consciousness and intentionality. Our question, in its most broad and naive form, is: How can such animals as ourselves create a 'social' reality? How can they create a reality of money, property, government, marriage and,

26

perhaps most important of all, language? A peculiarly puzzling feature of social reality is that it exists only because we think it exists. It is an objective fact that the piece of paper in my hand is a $20 bill, or that I am a citizen of the United States, or that the Giants beat the Athletics 3–2 in yesterday's baseball game. These are all objective facts in the sense that they are not matters of my opinion. If I believe the contrary, I am simply mistaken. But these objective facts only exist in virtue of collective acceptance or recognition or acknowledgment. What does that mean? What does 'collective acceptance or recognition or acknowledgment' amount to?

An absolutely fundamental distinction we need to make before we can even begin to discuss these issues is that between those features of reality that exist independently of us, features I will call *observer-independent*, and those features that depend on us for their existence, which I will call *observer-relative*. Examples of observer-independent phenomena are force, mass, gravitational attraction, the chemical bond, photosynthesis, the solar system, and tectonic plates. Examples of observer-dependent facts are the sort of examples I mentioned earlier, such as that I am a citizen of the United States, that baseball is a game played with nine men on a side, and that the United States of America contains fifty states. Roughly speaking, we can say that the social sciences are about observer-relative facts; the natural sciences are about observer-independent facts. A simple rough-and-ready test for whether or not a fact is observer-independent is this: Could it have existed if there had been no conscious agents at all? If the fact could have existed even if there had never been any human beings or other conscious agents, for example, the fact that there is gravitational attraction between the earth and the moon, then the fact is observer-independent. If, however, the fact requires conscious agents for its very existence in the way that facts about money, property, government, and marriage require conscious agents, then the fact is at least a candidate for being observer relative. I said this was only a rough-and-ready test. The reason it is not sufficient as it stands is that the existence of consciousness and intentionality, on which observer-dependent facts rest for their very existence, are themselves observer-independent phenomena. The fact that the piece of paper in front of me is a $20 bill is observer-relative; that fact exists only relative to the attitudes of the participants in the activities of buying, selling and so on. But the attitudes that those people have are not themselves observer-relative. They are observer-independent.

I think it is worth going through this matter carefully. The piece of paper in my hand is a $20 bill. What fact about it makes it a $20 bill? Its physics and chemistry are not enough. If we wanted to go into detail, a complex legal story would have to be told about the US government, the Department of the Treasury and the Bureau of Engraving and Printing. But a crucial element of the story is the attitudes of the people involved. To put the matter crudely, a necessary condition of its being money is that people have to intend it to be, and think it is, money. So its existence as money is observer-relative. But what about the attitudes? Suppose I now think, "This is a $20 bill." That attitude and countless others like it are constitutive of the observer-relative fact that things of this sort are money. But the attitudes of the observers are not themselves observer-relative. I can think that it is money regardless of whether others think that I think that it is money. So the observer-relative existence of social phenomena is created by a set of observer-independent mental phenomena, and our task is to explain the nature of that creation.

You might think that these issues would long ago have been resolved because we have, after all, a rather long tradition of discussion of foundational issues in the social sciences, and we are, of course, much indebted to the great founders of the social sciences such as Max Weber, Georg Simmel, Emile Durkheim, and Alfred Schutz. Before them we had such great philosophers as David Hume, Jean Jacques Rousseau, and Adam Smith – one could continue the list back to Aristotle's *Politics*. What can we add to this great tradition? There is a serious weakness in all the classical discussions of the existence of social reality: all the thinkers I have mentioned took language for granted. Weber, Shutz, Simmel, and Durkheim all presuppose the existence of language and then, given language, ask about the nature of society. And they are in very good company because the tendency to presuppose language when discussing the foundations of society goes back to Aristotle. It is, for example, an amazing fact about the social contract theorists that they presupposed a community of humans who had a language and who then got together to make an original contract which founded society. I would want to say, if you share a common language and are already involved in conversations in that common language, you already have a social contract. The standard account that presupposes language and then tries to explain society has things back to front. You cannot begin to understand what is special about human society, how it differs from primate societies and other animal societies, unless you first understand some special features of human language. Language is the presupposition of the existence of other social institutions in a way that they are not the presupposition of language. This point can be stated precisely. Institutions such as money, property, government, and marriage cannot exist without language, but language can exist without them. Now one might feel that

we have overcome this lacuna in the twenty-first century as various sociological theorists have been sensitive to the problem of language. In addition
to a rich tradition of linguistic anthropology, we have the recent writings
of sociological theorists, especially Bourdieu and Habermas, and perhaps
Foucault as well. But I am afraid even they take language for granted.
Bourdieu, following Foucault, states correctly that people who are capable
of controlling the linguistic categorizations that are common in a society have a great deal of power in that society, and Habermas emphasizes
the importance of speech acts and human communication in producing
social cohesion. But, again, all three fail to see the essentially *constitutive*
role of language. Language does not function just to categorize and thus
give us power, à la Bourdieu, and it does not function just, or even pri-
marily, to enable us to reach rational agreement, à la Habermas. It has
much more basic and fundamental functions, which I will get to in a few
moments.

One last distinction before we go to work. Our culture makes a great
deal of the distinction between objectivity and subjectivity, but this distinction is systematically ambiguous between an epistemic sense and an
ontological sense. If I say, "Rembrandt was born in 1606," that statement
is epistemically objective. It can be ascertained as true or false independent
of the attitudes of observers. But if I say, "Rembrandt was a better painter
than Rubens," that statement is, as they say, "a matter of opinion." It is
"subjective." But in addition to the distinction between epistemic objectivity and subjectivity – and in a way the foundation of the distinction
of epistemic subjectivity and objectivity – is an ontological distinction
between ontological subjectivity and ontological objectivity. Mountains,
molecules, and tectonic plates have an existence that is independent of
the attitudes and feelings of observers. But pains, tickles, itches, emotions,
and thoughts have a mode of existence that is ontologically subjective in
the sense that they only exist insofar as they are experienced by human
or animal subjects. Now, the importance of this distinction for our discussion is this: the fact, for example, that George W. Bush is president
of the United States; and the fact that, for example, the piece of paper
I have in my hand is a $20 bill are epistemically objective facts. But the
important thing to emphasize is that such social institutional facts can be
epistemically objective even though human attitudes are part of their mode
of existence. That is, *observer-relativity implies ontological subjectivity but
ontological subjectivity does not preclude epistemic objectivity*. We can have
epistemically objective knowledge about money and elections even though
the kind of facts about which one has epistemically objective knowledge

are themselves all ontologically subjective, at least to a degree which we need to specify.

So let us just summarize where we are right now. We need the distinction between observer-relative and observer-independent facts. We also need a distinction between epistemic objectivity and subjectivity on the one hand and ontological objectivity and subjectivity on the other hand. Most of the phenomena that we are discussing, such phenomena as money, governments, and football games, are observer-relative. But at the same time, they contain components of observer-independent but ontologically subjective human attitudes. Though the constitution of society thus contains ontologically subjective elements as absolutely essential to its existence, all the same the ontological subjectivity of the domain does not prevent us from getting an epistemically objective account of the domain. In a word, epistemic objectivity does not require ontological objectivity. If it did, the social sciences would be impossible. Now with all that by way of preliminaries, we can state the basic logical structure of human societies. Here goes.

II. THE LOGICAL STRUCTURE OF SOCIETY

Human societies have a *logical structure*, because human attitudes are constitutive of the social reality in question and those attitudes have propositional contents with logical relations. Our problem is to expose those relations. Now it might seem that this is too daunting a task. Human societies are immensely complex and immensely various. If there is one thing we know from the cultural anthropology of the past century, it is that there is an enormous variety of different modes of social existence. The assumption I will be making, and will try to justify, is that, even though there is an enormous variety, the principles that underlie the constitution of social reality are rather few in number. What you discover when you go behind the surface phenomena of social reality is a relatively simple underlying logical structure even though the manifestations in actual social reality in political parties, social events, and economic transactions are immensely complicated. The analogy with the natural sciences is obvious. There is an enormous difference in the physical appearance of a bonfire and a rusty shovel, but the underlying principle in each case is exactly the same: oxidization. Similarly, there are enormous differences between baseball games, $20 bills, and national elections, but the underlying logical structure is the same. All three consist of the imposition by collective intentionality of status functions, a point I will shortly explain in more detail.

To describe the basic structure of social-institutional reality, we need exactly three primitives: collective intentionality, the assignment of function, and constitutive rules and procedures. (Here I am going to be very brief because I am repeating things I have said elsewhere.)

First, human beings have a remarkable capacity, which many other species also have, and that is to engage in cooperative behavior and sharing of attitudes with con-specifics. Human beings can collaborate in a number of ways, and one has only to observe any typical human interaction to see this. Two people carrying on a conversation, an orchestra playing a symphony, and two teams playing football, are all examples of cooperative behavior. I want to introduce a technical term for this. I call this *collective intentionality*. I will explain this term. 'Intentionality' is the word philosophers use to describe that feature of minds by which mental states are *directed at* or *about* objects and states of affairs in the world. Thus, for example, if I have a belief it must be a belief that such and such is the case; if I have a desire it must be a desire that such and such should be the case. Intentionality, in this technical sense, includes not only intending in the ordinary sense, in which I might intend to go to the movies, but also beliefs, hopes, desires, emotions, perceptions, and lots of others. In addition to individual intentionality, which is described in the first-person singular forms such as "I desire," "I believe," "I intend," there is also collective intentionality, which is described in the form, "we believe," "we desire," "we intend."

Collective intentional action is especially important in any theory of society. In such cases, I am doing something only as part of *our* doing something. For example, I am playing the violin as part of our playing the symphony. I am pitching the ball as part of our playing a baseball game. Collective intentionality is the intentionality that is shared by different people, and just as there can be shared intentions to do things, so there can be shared beliefs and shared desires. The church congregation, for example, reciting the Nicene Creed, is expressing a shared belief, a common faith.

It is common in social philosophy, and perhaps in the social sciences as well, to use the notion of "intersubjectivity." I have never seen a clear explanation of the concept of intersubjectivity, and I will have no use for the notion. But I will use "collective intentionality" to try to describe the intentionalistic component of society; and I suspect that if intersubjectivity is a legitimate notion at all, it must amount to collective intentionality. I am confident that collective intentionality is a genuine biological phenomenon, and though it is complex, it is not mysterious or inexplicable. I have tried to describe some of the complexities elsewhere (Searle, 1990).

Collective intentionality is the psychological presupposition of all *social* reality and, indeed, I define a social fact as any fact involving collective intentionality of two or more human or animal agents. So, on this definition, both a wolf pack hunting together and a supreme court making a decision are cases of collective intentionality and thus cases of social facts. My main problem in this article is to explain how such institutional social phenomena as the Supreme Court making a decision go beyond the social ontology present in social animals. The interesting problem arises not with *social* facts but with such *institutional* facts as those involving money, governments, political parties and economic transactions. Institutional facts are a subclass of social facts.

The second primitive notion we need is that of the assignment of function. Humans, and some animals, have the capacity to assign functions to objects, where the object does not have the function intrinsically but only in virtue of the collective assignment. All functions are observer-relative. Something has a function only relative to the attitudes of humans or other animals. We are blinded to this by the fact that in biology we frequently discover functions in nature. But when we discover, for example, that the function of the heart is to pump blood, we can only make that discovery within a presupposed teleology. It is because we value life and survival that we say the function of the heart is to pump blood. If we thought the most important thing in the universe was to glorify God by making a thumping noise, then the function of the heart would be to make a thumping noise. If we thought death and extinction were valuable above all else, then hearts would be dysfunctional and cancer would perform an important function. Lots of people disagree with me that all functions are observer-relative, but the argument that seems to me conclusive is that the notion of *function* contains a normative component not contained in the notion of *cause*. Roughly speaking, functions are causes that serve a purpose. Where do the purposes come from? In any case it is not essential for the main argument of this article that functions are observer-relative, though I note it in passing.

So far, then, we have collective intentionality and the assignment of function. It is easy to see how these can be combined. If one person can use a stump as a chair, a group of people can use a log as a bench. The collective intentionality enables the collective assignment of a function.

But it is the next move which is the distinguishing mark that separates humans from other species. Sometimes the collective assignment of function is imposed on a person or an object where the function is not performed in virtue of the physical features of the person or the object, but rather, in virtue of the fact that the collective intentionality assigns a certain status to that person or object and that status enables the person or object to perform a function which could not be performed without the collective acceptance of that status. An obvious example is money. The piece of paper in my hand, unlike the knife in my pocket, does indeed perform a function, but it performs the function not in virtue of its *physical* structure but in virtue of *collective attitudes.* The knife has a physical structure that enables it to cut and perform other knife-like functions, but money has no such physical structure. The physical structure is more or less irrelevant, provided only that it meets certain general conditions (such as being easy to recognize as money, easy to transport, hard to counterfeit and so on). I like to illustrate the move from the assignment of functions to what I call status functions with a parable. Suppose a community builds a wall around its dwellings. The wall now has a collectively assigned function, which function it can perform in virtue of its structure. But suppose the wall gradually decays until the only thing that is left is a line of stones. But suppose that the people continue to *recognize* the line of stones as a *boundary*, they continue to *accept* that they are *not supposed to* cross. The line now performs the function that the wall once performed, but it performs the function not in virtue of its physical structure but in virtue of the collective acceptance that the line of stones now has a certain *status* and with that status a *function* which can only be performed in virtue of the collective acceptance of that status. I want this to sound rather harmless and innocuous, but I think that in fact it is the decisive move that distinguishes humans from other animals. It is this move whereby we create *status functions* that marks the difference between social reality in general and what I will call institutional reality. Human institutions are matters of status functions.

I have tried to state the logical form of the assignment of a status function when it becomes regular, and thus a matter of a rule, as that of the constitutive rule of the form, X counts as Y, or more commonly, *X counts as Y in context C.* Thus, such and such counts as a $20 bill in our society. George W. Bush counts as president of the United States. Such and such a move in chess counts as a legal knight move. Such and such a position counts as a check, and such and such a form of check counts as checkmate. All of these are of the form X counts as Y in context C. Now, you might think that if that is all there is to human institutional reality, if that is what distinguishes us from the lower beasts, then it does not seem like much to go on. But it has two formal properties that are truly remarkable. First, it can iterate upwards indefinitely. Thus, making such and such noises counts as uttering a sentence of English, and uttering such and such a sentence of English counts as making a promise, and uttering such and such a promise counts as undertaking a contract. Notice what is going on in these cases. At the bottom level, X_1 counts as Y_1, but at one level up, $Y_1 = X_2$ counts as Y_2. And $Y_2 = X_3$ counts as Y_3 and so on upward indefinitely. Furthermore, the structure not only iterates upward, but it expands laterally, also indefinitely. We never just have one institutional fact but we have a series of interlocking institutional facts. Thus, I do not just have money, but I have money in my bank account at a certain financial institution, it is placed there by my employer, the University of California, and I use it to pay my credit card debts and my state and federal income taxes. All of those are institutional notions, and the example illustrates the way institutions interlock with each other. To repeat, you do not just have one institutional fact, you have a series of interlocking institutional facts, and thus, you have a series of interlocking institutions.

But still, you might say, what is the importance of all this? Who cares if we assign all these status functions? The answer is that status functions are the vehicles of power in society. The remarkable thing is this: we accept the status functions and in so accepting, we accept a series of obligations, rights, responsibilities, duties, entitlements, authorizations, permissions, requirements, and so on. As a shorthand, I call these *deontic* powers. Thus, for example, if someone is my wife, if a piece of property is my property, if I have received a parking ticket, if I am a professor at the University of California, all of these are matters of deontic powers both positive and negative. Thus, if it is my property, I have a certain *authority* over it, and I am *required by* law to pay the taxes on it. If I have received a parking ticket, I have an *obligation* to pay the fine. There is nothing like this in the animal kingdom. What we have in society is a set of deontic power relations. But again, one might ask the question, why should we care about these deontic power relations? Who gives a damn about my rights, duties, and obligations? The answer is important: What we are discussing here are reasons for action, and to recognize something as a right, duty, obligation, requirement, and so on is to recognize a reason for action. Furthermore, it is a specific kind of reason for action that is absolutely essential to human society and which, as far as I can tell, does not exist in the animal kingdom. These deontic structures make possible desire-independent reasons for action.

If I have a piece of property, and other people recognize that it is my property, then they have desire-independent reasons for not violating my property rights, and so on with rights generally. Contrast the territoriality of animals with the property rights of human societies. There are lots of differences but, for the purpose of this discussion, the crucial point is that, as far as we can tell, animals lack a deontology.

So again, it is this combination – status functions, deontic powers, and desire-independent reasons for actions – that gives us the specific human forms of socialization that enable us to distinguish human beings from other social animals, even from other primates. Now, we ought to allow ourselves to be astounded by this. The other primates are genetically very close to us. All the same, there is an enormous difference, or, rather, there is a series of enormous differences, between the ontology of human social life and that of animals (Kummer, 1971).

The most fundamental difference between us and other animals, and this point has been made by a number of philosophers, perhaps most famously Descartes, is that we have a language and other animals do not. It is, however, seldom made clear exactly what is involved in having a language. If you read standard sociobiologists such as Wilson (1975) or Barash (1977) you get the impression that many species of animals have signaling systems, but that humans are special in that we have a more elaborate signaling system than other animals. I think this is an inadequate conception of language. This is not the place for me to develop my entire theory of speech acts, but let me say just this much. The essential thing about human beings is that language gives them the capacity to *represent*. Furthermore, they can represent not only what is the case but what was the case, what will be the case, and what they would like to be the case. Even more spectacularly, they can lie. They can represent something as being the case even though they believe that it is not the case.

We can now state with a little bit more precision exactly what is special about language in the constitution of institutional reality. Institutional reality can only exist insofar as it is represented as existing. Something can be money, a football game, a piece of private property, a marriage, or a government only insofar as it is represented as such. In order for something to be any of these phenomena, it has to be thought of in a certain way, and these thoughts will represent it in a certain way. But the representation of these institutional facts always requires a language. Now, why is that? Why could not one just think that such and such is a government or such and such is a football game? The answer is, there is no phenomenon there other than the brute facts and their representation as having an institutional status. There is nothing in the bare physical facts that would provide the semantic content which we would need to have to be able to think that such and such was a government or a football game. Let me illustrate this with an example. My dog can see a person carry a ball across a line; but what he cannot see is the person scoring a touchdown. Now, why not? Is his vision not good enough? Does he need glasses? Suppose we decided that we were going to train the dog to see touchdowns. How would we go about it? We might train him to bark when he sees a man crossing a line while carrying a ball, but in order to see a man scoring a touchdown, he has to be able to represent something more than these physical facts. The physical facts that the dog sees and the physical facts that I see are exactly the same. What I have, that the dog does not have, is the capacity to represent those facts in a certain way, to represent them as existing at the higher level, to represent them as the Y term, in the X counts as Y formula. Now, this is the secret by which human beings can create an institutional reality and other animals cannot. Human beings have the capacity for seeing and thinking at a double level. We can both see the piece of paper and the dollar bill. We can both see the man carry the ball across the line and see the man score a touchdown. At first sight, this looks like a familiar case of *seeing as*. We see the figure now as a duck, now as a rabbit. But what is special about human beings is that they have the capacity, which the dog does not have, to see and think an institutional reality, but that is impossible just on the basis of the sheer physical facts because there is nothing in the physical facts to give the semantic content either to the thought or to the perception. The light waves striking my eyes when the man crossed the goal line and the light waves striking the dog's eyes are the same, but I literally saw the man score a touchdown, and the dog did not literally see that. In such cases, institutional reality so infects our perceptual and other forms of cognitive apparatus that the immediate processing of perceptual inputs is already done at the institutional level. Just as I can literally see a man score a touchdown, so I can literally see a man pay for groceries in a supermarket, and I can literally see my neighbor voting in an election.

Let us explore these ideas by going through some of the steps in which language is involved in the constitution of institutional reality.

We have the capacity to count things as having a certain status, and in virtue of the collective acceptance of that status, they can perform functions that they could not perform without that collective acceptance. The form of the collective acceptance has to be in the broadest sense linguistic or symbolic because there is nothing else there to mark the level of status function. There is nothing to the line and the man and the ball that counts as a touchdown, except insofar as we are prepared to count the man with the ball crossing the line as the scoring of a touchdown. We might put these points in the most general form by saying that language performs at least the following four functions in the constitution of institutional facts.

First, the fact can only exist insofar as it is represented as existing and the form of those representations is in the broadest sense linguistic. I have to say "in the broadest sense" because I do not mean to imply that full-blown natural languages with relative clauses, iterated modal operators, and quantificational scope ambiguities are essential to the constitution of institutional reality. I do not believe they are. Rather, I believe that unless an animal can symbolize something as having a status, which it does not have in virtue of its physical structure, then the animal cannot have institutional facts; and those institutional facts require some form of symbolization – what I am calling language in the broad sense. The symbolization has to carry the deontic powers, because there is nothing in the sheer physical facts that carries the deontology by itself.

Second, and this is really a consequence of the first point, the forms of the status function in question are almost invariably matters of deontic powers. They are matters of rights, duties, obligations, responsibilities, and so on. Now, animals cannot recognize deontic powers because without having some linguistic means of representation they cannot represent them. Let me state this point with as much precision as I can. Animal groups can have an alpha male and an alpha female, and other members of the group can make the proper responses to the alpha male and the alpha female, but this hierarchy is not established by the undertaking or imposition of such things as rights and obligations. What the animals do not have is the deontology, the obligations, requirements, duties, and so on that go with the recognition of the higher status. For those obligations, requirements, and duties to exist, they have to be represented in some linguistic or symbolic form. Again, when a dog is trained to obey commands, he is just taught to respond automatically to certain specific words or other signals.

(By the way, I frequently make remarks about animal capacities. I do not think we know enough about animal capacities to be completely confident in the attributions we make especially to the primates. But, and this is the point, if it should turn out that some of the primates are on our side of the divide rather than on the side of the other animals, in the sense that they have deontic powers and deontic relationships, then so much the better for them. In this article, I am not making a plea for the superiority of our species, rather, I am trying to mark a conceptual distinction, and I assume, on the basis of what little I know, that where deontology is concerned we are on one side and other animals are on the other side of the dividing line. If it turns out that some of them are on our side, I have no problem with that.)

Third, the deontology has another peculiar feature. Namely, it can continue to exist after its initial creation and indeed even after all the participants involved have stopped thinking about the initial creation. I make a promise today to do something for you next week, and that obligation continues even when we are all sound asleep. Now, that can only be the case if that obligation is represented by some linguistic means. In general, one can say this: no language, no deontology. Human societies require a deontology, and the only way they can do this is by having language.

Fourth, a crucial function of language is in the recognition of the institution as such. It is not merely particular cases within the institution, that this is my property, that that was a football game, but rather, in order that this should be a case of property or that a case of a football game, one has to recognize an institution of property and football games. Where institutional reality is concerned, the particular instances typically exist as such because they are instances of a general institutional phenomenon. Thus, in order for me to own a particular item of property, or to have a particular dollar bill, there has to be a general institution of private property and money. Exceptions to this are cases where an institution is being created *de novo*. But these general institutions, in which the particular instances find their mode of existence, can only exist insofar as they are recognized and that recognition has to be symbolic, linguistic in the most general sense.

III. FURTHER DEVELOPMENTS IN THE THEORY OF SOCIAL ONTOLOGY

I want now to discuss some of the further developments in the theory of institutional reality since the publication of *The Construction of Social Reality* (Searle, 1995). I want to mention two such developments. First, in the original statement of the theory, I pointed out that in order for status functions to be recognized, there typically have to be some sort *of status indicators*, because there is nothing in the man or the object itself that will indicate its status, since the status is only there by collective acceptance or recognition. Thus, we have policemen's uniforms, wedding rings, marriage certificates, and passports, all of which are status indicators. Many societies find that they cannot exist without status indicators, as, for example, the proliferation of identity cards and drivers' licenses will attest. However, Hernando De Soto (2003) pointed out an interesting fact. Sometimes the status indicators acquire a kind of life of their own. How is this so? Well, he points out that in many underdeveloped countries, many people own land, but because there are no property deeds, because the owners of the property do not have title deeds to the property, they are, in effect, what we would call squatters, they do not have status indicators. This has two consequences of enormous social importance. First, they cannot be taxed by the governing authorities because they are not legally the holders of the property, but secondly and even more importantly, they cannot use the property as capital. Normally, in order for a society to develop, the owners of property have to be able to go to the bank and get loans against their property in order to use the money to make investments. But in countries like, for example, Egypt, it is impossible for the vast amount of private property to be used as collateral for investments because so much of this property is held without the benefit of a property deed. The owners of the property are in effect squatters, in the sense that they do not legally own the property, though they live in a society where their status function is acknowledged and generally recognized and hence, on my account, continues to exist and generate deontic powers. But the deontic powers stop at the point where the larger society requires some official proof of the status functions. Thus without official documentation they lack full deontic powers.

A second and equally important development was pointed out to me by Barry Smith (2003). Smith pointed out that there are some institutions that have what he calls "freestanding Y terms" where you can have a status function, but there is no physical object on which the status function is imposed. A fascinating case is corporations. The laws of incorporation in a state such as California enable a status function to be constructed so to speak out of thin air. Thus, by a kind of performative declaration, the corporation comes into existence, but there need be no physical object that is the corporation. The corporation has to have a mailing address and a list of officers and stockholders and so on, but it does not have to be a physical object. This is a case where the performative utterance "such and such counts as the creation of a corporation" does indeed create a corporation, but there is no physical object other than the relationship among certain people on which the status function is imposed. There is indeed a "counts as Y" but there is no X which counts as Y.

An even more spectacular example is money. The paradox of my account is that money was my favorite example of the "X counts as Y" formula, but I was operating on the assumption that currency was somehow or other essential to money. Further reflection makes it clear to me that it is not. You can easily imagine a society that has money without having any currency at all. And, indeed, we seem to be evolving in something like this direction with the use of debit cards. All you need in order to have money is a system of recorded numerical values whereby each person (or corporation, organization, and so on) has assigned to him or her a numerical figure which tells at any given point the amount of money they have. They can then use this money to buy things by altering their numerical value in favor of the seller, whereby they acquire a lower numerical value and the seller acquires a higher numerical value. Money is typically redeemable in cash, in the form of currency, but currency is not essential to the existence or functioning of money.

It is tempting in such cases to think that the representation of the money in the form of magnetic traces on computer disks or entries in ledgers has become money. After all, manipulation of the numerals in the ledgers or the magnetic traces on the computer disks can constitute buying and selling, paying and receiving, so why are they not money? Even in such cases, it is important to distinguish between the representation of the institutional phenomenon and the institutional phenomena represented. You can see this if you consider the case of chess. Just as currency is not essential to the functioning of money, so physical chess pieces are not essential to the playing of chess. In the case of blindfold chess, you play the game entirely using representations of the chess pieces in the forms of a symbolism that defines the pieces and their positions on the board. But neither the board nor the pieces as physical objects are essential. All that is essential is that there should be a set of formal relationships that are capable of being represented symbolically. The symbols that we use do not, then, become chess pieces, though they become functionally equivalent to chess pieces in that the manipulation of the symbols is functionally equivalent to the movement of the chess pieces. Exactly analogously, the existence of physical objects of currency, coins, and bills, is not essential to the functioning of money. All that is essential is that there should be a set of numerical values attaching to individuals and a set of formal relations between these whereby they can use their numerical assignment to buy things from other individuals, pay their debts and so on.

How can such things function if there is no physical object on which the status function is imposed? The answer is that status functions are, in general, matters of deontic power, and in these cases, the deontic power goes directly to the individuals in question. So my possession of a queen in the game of chess is not a matter of my having my grubby hands on a physical object, it is rather a matter of my having certain powers of movement within a formal system (and the formal system is "the board," though it need not be a physical board) relative to other pieces. Similarly, my having $1,000 is not a matter of my having a wad of bills in my hand but my having certain deontic powers. I now have the right, that is, the *power*, to buy things, which I would not have if I did not have the money. In such cases, the real bearer of the deontology is the participant in the economic transactions and the player in the game. The physical objects of chess pieces and dollar bills are just markers for the amount of deontic power that the players have.

In the early part of *The Construction of Social Reality*, I said that the basic form of the institutional fact was X counts as Y in C and that this was a form of the constitutive rule that enables us to create institutional facts. But a later formulation I gave in the book gives us a much more general account. I said that the basic power-creation operator in society is *We accept (S has power [S does A])* and that we could think of the various forms of power as essentially Boolean operations on this basic structure, so, for example, to have an obligation is to have a negative power. What then, exactly, is the relationship between the two formulae *X counts as Y in C* and *We accept (S has power [S does A])*? The answer is that, of course, we do not just accept that somebody has power, but we accept that they have power in virtue of their institutional status. For example, satisfying certain conditions makes someone president of the United States. This is an example of the *X counts as Y in* C formula. But once we accept that someone is president of the United States, then we accept that he has the power to do certain things. He has the positive power to command the armed forces, and he has the negative power, that is, the obligation, to deliver a State of the Union Address. He has the *right* to command the armed forces, and he has the *duty* to deliver the address. In this case we accept that S has power (S does A) because S = X, and we have already accepted that X counts as Y, and the Y status function carries with it the acknowledged deontic powers.

Continuing with the example of the corporation, we can say that so and so counts as the president of the corporation and such and such people count as the stockholders. This is an example of the *X counts as Y in C* formulation, but, of course, the whole point of doing that is to give them powers, duties, rights, responsibilities, and so on. They then instantiate the *We accept (S has power [S does A])* formula. But to repeat a point made earlier, the corporation itself is not identical with any physical object or any person or set of persons. The corporation is, so to speak, created out of nothing. The president is president *of* the corporation, but he is not identical with the corporation. The reasons for doing this are famous. By creating a so-called "fictitious person" we can create an entity that is capable of entering into contractual relationships and capable of buying and selling, making a profit and incurring debts, for which it is liable. But the officers and stockholders are not personally liable for the debts of the corporation. This is an important breakthrough in human thought. So what amounts to the corporation when we set it up? It is not that there is an X that counts as the corporation but, rather, that there is a group of people involved in legal relationships – thus, so and so counts as the president of the corporation, so and so counts as a stockholder in the corporation and so on – but there is nothing that need count as the corporation itself, because one of the points of setting up the corporation was to create a set of power relationships without having to have the accompanying liabilities that typically go with those power relationships when they are assigned to actual human individuals.

I regard the invention of the idea of the limited liability corporation, like the invention of double-entry bookkeeping, universities, museums, and money, as one of the truly great advances in human civilization. Such inventions are less famous than the invention of steam engines and airplanes, but they are of comparable importance. It is not at all necessary that there should be such things as corporations or universities, but it is clear that without them human civilization would be impoverished and limited.

It might seem paradoxical that I talk about institutional reasons for action as 'desire-independent reasons for action' because, of course, many of these are precisely foci of very powerful human desires. What is more a field for human desire than money? Or political power? I think this question raises a deep issue: by creating institutional reality, we increase human power enormously. By creating private property, governments, marriages, stock markets and universities, we increase the human capacity for action prodigiously. But the possibility of having and satisfying desires within these institutional structures – for example, the desire to get rich, to become president, to get a PhD, to get tenure – all presuppose that there is a recognition of the deontic relationships. Without the recognition, acknowledgment, and acceptance of the deontic relationships, your power is not worth a damn. It is only worthwhile to have money or a university degree or to be president of the United States if other people recognize your having this status, and they recognize that status as giving them desire-independent reasons for behaving in a certain way. The general point is very clear: the creation of the general field of desire-based reasons for action presupposed the acceptance of a system of desire-independent reasons for action. This is true both of the immediate beneficiaries of the power relationships, the person with the money or the person who has won the election, and of the other participants in the institution.

IV. HOW MANY KINDS OF INSTITUTIONAL FACTS ARE THERE?

I still do not have a taxonomy of status functions that I find satisfactory. I think it is rather easy and, indeed, rather uninteresting to do a taxonomy of different kinds of institutions because one would naturally classify institutions according to their purposes and subject matters, educational institutions, governmental institutions, financial institutions, social institutions, and so on. A much more interesting and profound question is: How many kinds of institutional *facts* are there? This is the question that gets at a taxonomy of status functions. I am inclined to think that a basic division occurs between those status functions that accrue to people where the physical properties are essential to the status function and those where they are not, between being a licensed driver or a surgeon or a certified public accountant on the one hand and being money or a corporation on the other. In the case where you are a licensed driver or you are authorized to perform surgery, you have to have certain abilities independent of the authorization. The authorization allows you to do something that you are able to do anyway, as far as your sheer abilities are concerned. But when it comes to money, that is not the case. The piece of paper or, for that matter, the magnetic trace on the computer disk in your bank, does not have any powers in virtue of its physical structure. It is, rather, the collective acceptance that creates the power in the first place.

If we were going to attempt a taxonomy of institutions, I think the right way to go about it would be to do a taxonomy of institutional powers, because the whole purpose of having institutions is to create and distribute human power, specifically deontic power. The first thing we would have to recognize are those powers that have to do with *certifying* or *authorizing* people to do things, after ascertaining that they are competent to do them. This applies to certified public accountants, lawyers, doctors, ski instructors, licensed drivers, credentialed teachers, and also, of course, to tests for roadworthiness of vehicles and seaworthiness of ships, and to safety inspections of buildings and bridges. Such authorization allows the functioning of a pre-existing fitness and capacity.

This distinction is already prefigured in the theory of speech acts. I distinguish between declarations that simply create a state of affairs by declaring it to exist, such as a declaration of war, and what I call assertive declarations, where there is first a finding of fact and then the assignment of a status. For example, if it is found that the defendant did the act alleged against him, then he is pronounced "guilty as charged," an assertive declaration. Analogously with some status functions. First there is an examination of the facts. Can the applicant actually drive a car? Then, on the basis of an affirmative answer, he is assigned the status function of "licensed driver."

We will also need to distinguish certifications from authorizations. Thus, for example, a driving test will certify me as a competent driver and the issuance of a driving license or driving permit will authorize me to drive, for example, in the state of California. Typically, authorizations require prior certifications, but not all certifications are authorizations. Thus, for example, if you receive a bachelor's degree from an American university, you are certified as having met the criteria for the degree, but what does the degree now authorize you to do? Well, it authorizes nothing specific in the way that being a certified public accountant or having your driver's license authorizes you to do something specific. Nonetheless, the certification is important because there is an indefinite range of authorizations now open. There are, for example, all sorts of employment for which a bachelor's degree is a prerequisite.

A second category would include what we might think of as institutional power as such. Thus, for example, the chairman of the department, the president of the United States, a congress person are given powers which they would not be able to exercise without the enabling status that gives them the power.

Where sheer institutional power is concerned, it seems to me we will need to make a distinction between positive and negative powers. The chief of police, the president of the corporation, and the commander of the army all have positive powers. The prisoner of war, the convicted criminal, and the driver in receipt of a traffic citation all have negative powers. Within the category of negative powers, we will also need to distinguish punishments from taxes. Owing $1,000 in taxes and being fined $1,000 are quite distinct status functions, even though the upshot is exactly the same in both cases: I have to pay $1,000 dollars to the authorities. The mirror image of this on the positive side would be the distinction between salaries and prizes. The opposite of the tax is the salary that I receive. The opposite of the punishment is the prize or the award. Thus, the person who makes a million dollars in the stock market and the person who receives the prize of a million dollars are both in receipt of a million dollars. But the status functions are quite different.

V. CONCEPTUAL ANALYSIS AND EMPIRICAL DATA

It seems to me quite likely that some people in cultural anthropology will feel that I am making generalizations on the basis of what seem to be very limited data. The data that I am familiar with are, for the most part, derived from cultures that I happen to inhabit or have inhabited, and some that I have read about. What makes me think that this provides us with a general theory of social ontology? To answer this question, I need to make a distinction between empirical generalization and conceptual analysis. There is no sharp dividing line between the two, but the nature of the investigation that I am conducting here is one of taking certain empirical facts and trying to uncover underlying logical structures. I do not discover status functions just by examining the data, but by uncovering the logical structure of the data I am familiar with.

The analogy with the theory of speech acts is illuminating. When I published a taxonomy of the five basic types of speech acts (Searle, 1979), one anthropologist (Rosaldo, 1982) objected that in the tribe that she studied, they did not make very many promises, and, anyway, how did I think I could get away with making such a general claim on the basis of such limited data?[1] But the answer, of course, is that I was not offering a general empirical hypothesis but a conceptual analysis. *These* are the possible types of speech acts given to us by the nature of human language. The fact that some tribe does not have the institution of promising is no more relevant than the fact that there are no tigers at the South Pole is relevant to a taxonomy of animal types. I am discussing the logical structure of language and getting the categorization of possible types of speech acts. In this investigation, I am examining the logical structure of human civilization and trying to get at the basic structure of status functions. But, again, that forces the question back one stage. Well, what makes me think that these status functions I discover in our civilization are likely to be pervasive? And the answer, of course, is that they are not. Not all communities have driver's licenses, for example. But, and this is the crucial point, the logical structure of the status function, I believe, is pervasive, and I now want to state why. All human societies have a language, and in that language there are certain limited possibilities for performing speech acts having to do with the very nature of meaning and the nature of speech acts (I have explored all this in some detail elsewhere; Searle, 1983, especially chap. 6). Now, that already gives you a set of deontic powers. That gives you the rights, duties and

---

[1] When this article first appeared I did not respond to it because I thought she had missed the point of my analysis. She thought I was making an empirical generalization to the effect that all cultures had certain types of speech acts, when I was in fact presenting a conceptual analysis of what it is possible to do with language. When tracking down the reference to her article on the web I discovered, to my amazement, that it is still used in anthropology courses, so the distinction is perhaps worth emphasizing here.

obligations that go with making a statement, making a promise or making a request, so the basic structure is already present in the theory of speech acts. Now, it is very hard for me to imagine a culture that does not have *any* rights, duties and obligations beyond those that derive from the performance of speech acts. But, even if there were such a culture, it is standing on the threshold of having institutional reality because once someone, in any language, is in a position to say "This is mine" or "He is the boss," you have already embarked on the creation of non-linguistic status functions even though the language itself, for reasons that I have tried to make clear, is constitutive of those status functions. The thesis advanced here, then, is not an anthropological empirical hypothesis. I am not hypothesizing that all societies have such and such logical structures. Rather, I am analyzing the logical structures, and any society that has what we would consider to be the deontology of even a minimal civilization will have to have something like these structures. Now, of course, even an a priori conceptual argument like that would be subject to empirical refutations if you could show me a society that had what were intuitively institutional structures but had nothing like the sorts of structures that I describe. But if an anthropologist tells me that in the tribe she studies they don't worry too much about obligations, and if she thinks that is an objection to the analysis, she will have missed the point.

VI. DIFFERENT KINDS OF "INSTITUTIONS"

I have not been attempting to analyze the ordinary use of the word "institution." I do not much care if my account of institutional reality and institutional facts matches that of ordinary usage. I am much more interested in getting at the underlying glue that holds human societies together. But let us consider some other sorts of things that might be thought of as institutions.

I have said that the fact that I am an American citizen is an institutional fact, but how about the fact that today is the 15th of July, 2004? Is that an institutional fact? What does the question ask? At least as much as this: Does identifying something as July 15, 2004 collectively assign a status function that carries with it a deontology? So construed, the answer is no. In my culture there is no deontology carried by the fact that today is July 15. In that respect, 'July 15, 2004' differs from Christmas Day, Thanksgiving, or, in France, July 14. Each of these carries a deontology. If it is Christmas Day, for example, I am *entitled* to a day off, and collective intentionality in my community supports me in this entitlement. We could easily imagine a subgroup for which being July 15 was an institutional fact, but I am currently not in such a subgroup.

I think there is a sense of the word "institution" in which the Christian calendar is a kind of institution, but it is not the kind of institution that I am attempting to analyze. Similarly with other verbal systems. Different societies have different color vocabularies, but that does not make the fact that the cloth in front of me is magenta into an institutional fact. Similar remarks could be made about systems of weights and measurements. The fact that I weigh 160 pounds is the same fact as the fact that I weigh 72 kilos even though this same fact can be stated using different systems of measuring weights.

More interesting to me are those cases where the facts in question are on the margin of being institutional. I think that the fact that someone is my friend is an institutional fact because friendship carries obligations, rights and responsibilities. But how about the fact that someone is a drunk, a nerd, an intellectual or an underachiever? Are these institutional concepts and are the corresponding terms institutional facts? Not as I am using these expressions, because there is no collectively recognized deontology that goes with these. Of course, if the law establishes criteria under which somebody is a certified drunk and imposes penalties as well as compensation for this status, then being a drunk becomes a status function. X counts as Y. And, again, I might personally feel that as an intellectual I have certain sorts of obligations, but this is still not yet an institutional phenomenon unless there is some collective recognition of these obligations. When I pointed out in a lecture that being a nerd was not a status function, one of my students told me that in his high school it definitely was, because as the class nerd he was expected to help other students with their homework. He was under certain sorts of collectively recognized obligations.

Another sort of "institution" that I am not attempting to describe is massive forms of human practices around certain subject matters that do not as such carry a deontology. So, for example, there are series of practices that go with what we call "science" or "religion" or "education." Does that make science, religion, and education into institutions? Well, we are using "institution" as a technical term anyway, and it is open to us if we want to call these institutions, but I think it is very important that we do not confuse science, education, and religion with such things as money, property, government, and marriage. Within such gross human practices as science, religion, and education there are, indeed, institutions. Thus, for example, the National Science Foundation is an institution, as is the

University of California or the Roman Catholic Church. As I said before, I do not much care whether or not we want to use the word "institution" for both sorts of practices, but the important underlying idea is crucial to emphasize: we need to mark those facts that carry a deontology because they are the glue that holds society together.

ADDENDUM TO CHAPTER 2

I am reluctant to include anything in this volume that does not represent my current thinking on the subject discussed. I think this chapter is acceptable as far as it goes, but since I wrote it, I have had further thoughts that enable me, I believe, to make the analysis wider, simpler, and deeper. I believe there is a simple logical operation by which all of institutional reality is created and also by which it is maintained. The formula that I used in the past to express that operation, "X counts as Y in C," though very general in its application, is a special case and implementation of something even more general. The claim I want to make now is simply this: all of institutional reality (with the one crucially important class of exceptions, language itself) is created by speech acts that have the logical form of Declarations (I will explain this notion in a moment), and indeed they are maintained in existence by speech acts and other sorts of representations that have the logical form of Declarations.

In order to explain what a Declaration is, I have to say a little bit about the nature of language. We use words to relate to reality in different ways. One way is to perform a speech act that purports to represent how things are, such as a statement or an assertion. I call this class Assertives. A characteristic of Assertives is that they are supposed to match reality. They have what I call the word-to-world direction of fit, which I represent with a downward arrow thus: $\downarrow$. But not all speech acts are like that. Some, such as promises, vows, as well as orders and commands, are not supposed to represent an independently existing reality. They are supposed to change reality, either by getting the hearer to do what he is ordered to do or to get the promiser to do what he promised to do. These cases have the world-to-word direction of fit, which I represent with an upward arrow thus: $\uparrow$. I call these cases of the upward or world-to-word direction of fit, in the case of orders and commands, etc., Directives, and in the case of promises, vows, etc, Commissives.

Human beings have evolved a remarkable combination of these where we are able to change reality by representing it as having been so changed.

The most famous of these are the "performative utterances" discovered by J. L. Austin,[2] where we do something simply by saying that we are doing it. Thus the appropriately situated person can adjourn the meeting by saying, "The meeting is adjourned" or can fire an employee by saying, "You are fired." Though performatives are the most famous Declarations, they are not the only kind of Declarations. Religions and supernatural stories are full of Declarations. Thus when God says, "Let there be light," that makes it the case that there is light by Declaration. By definition, Declarations change reality by representing it as being so changed. In changing reality, they achieve the upward or world-to-word direction of fit, but the means by which this is done is by representing the change, thus they achieve the word-to-world direction of fit. These are not two independent directions of fit because one is achieved in virtue of the other: the arrow has to go both ways thus: $\updownarrow$.

The claim I wish to make now is that all status functions, and hence all of institutional reality, with the exception of language, are created by speech acts that have the logical form of Declarations. This is disguised from us by the fact that, of course, rather few institutional facts are created by explicit performative utterances or other explicit Declarations. So we can adjourn a meeting or pronounce somebody husband and wife by Declaration, but we cannot score a touchdown, win an election or get a checkmate just by Declaring ourselves to have made a touchdown, won the election, or made a checkmate. Nonetheless, all these cases can be seen at a deeper level to exemplify the Declarational structure. Thus if we have a constitutive rule, "X counts as Y in C" – for example, crossing a goal line while in possession of the ball counts as a touchdown in American football – we can see that as a *standing* Declaration. It makes it the case into the indefinite future that anything that exemplifies the X term counts as having the Y status function.

Sometimes we just create institutional facts without a preexisting institution, as when a tribe selects someone as a leader without having a standard procedure for selecting leaders. In such a case, the representations function as Declarations creating a new status function. Furthermore, as I remarked in this article, there are cases of the "freestanding Y terms" where you have a Y status function without a corresponding X term. The case of electronic money and the creation of corporations are creations of status functions without some preexisting object or entity on which the status function is

[2] J. L. Austin, *How to Do Things with Words* (Cambridge, Mass.: Harvard University Press, 1962).

imposed. We can now see that all of these exemplify the most general form of the creation of status functions, which is simply:

By Declaration we create the Y status function.

The formula "X counts as Y in C" can then be seen as a very general form of implementation of this structure, but it is nonetheless a special case. Additional cases are provided by the creation of status functions without a preexisting X term, and the creation of status functions without a preexisting constitutive rule.

Just as institutional facts are created by speech acts that have the logical form of Declarations, so the continued maintenance in existence of institutional facts is done by linguistic representations that have the same logical structure, even though they are typically not in the form of an explicit Declaration. For example, simply continuing to represent something as money reinforces its continued status as money. The representations that have the downward or word-to-world direction of fit facilitate the upward or world-to-word direction of fit. So both the creation and the maintenance of institutional facts are done by speech acts or other sorts of representations that have the double direction of fit. Just to have a general term, I will call all such Declarations, both those that create institutional facts and those that maintain them in their existence, "Status Function Declarations."

I said there was a class of exceptions to this general principle, and that class consists of cases of language itself. Declarations themselves are status functions, but they do not in general require further Declarations in order that they can be Declarations. And this is true for linguistic entities in general. The sentence "Snow is white" is such that, according to the constitutive rules of English, it can be uttered to make the statement that snow is white. Its utterance *counts as* a statement that snow is white. Why is it, then, that all of the rest of institutional reality requires Declarational speech acts in order that they can be status functions, and yet language does not? The explanation for this asymmetry requires a deeper analysis of language than I have the space to articulate here. I am writing a book on these matters and I devote considerable space to this issue. For the present, just let me say the following. In creating an institutional reality of money, property, government, marriage, and all the rest, we use semantics to create a set of powers that go beyond the powers of semantics alone. But in the case of language itself, the semantics or meaning of sentences do not have powers that go beyond meaning, and that is why we do not need some Declaration in order to empower sentences to do what they do. The meaning is sufficient. To see this point, look at the interesting cases where we do give extra-linguistic deontic powers to sentences by Declaration, where the Declaration goes beyond the literal meaning of the sentence. In the examples I gave, it isn't enough to have the meaning of the word "adjourn" that you can adjourn the meeting by saying, "The meeting is adjourned." You have to have a special status that goes beyond language and you have to have a special convention that goes beyond the meaning rules of English according to which such and such a person can adjourn the meeting by saying, "The meeting is adjourned." That is not true of all performative utterances. If I say, "I promise" or "I apologize" I do not require any special extra-linguistic institutional structure in order to do that. The institution of language is itself sufficient. Think of language as itself an institution, or if you like, a set of institutions. These institutions, like institutions in general, are matters of status function, and in particular, in the case of language, they are repeated applications of the constitutive rule that X counts as Y in C. Thus, as such and such an utterance counts as a promise, such and such another utterance counts as a statement, etc. But the meaning rules of language themselves are sufficient to guarantee that something will have the deontic powers of a statement or a promise. But they are not sufficient to guarantee that something will have the deontic powers of money or marriage or government or a presidential election. That is what I meant when I said we use semantics to create powers that go beyond the powers of semantics.

To summarize, I am adding two essential points to the article as originally published. First, with the exception of language itself, all status functions, and thus all of human institutional reality, are created by a single type of logical linguistic operation, the Status Function Declaration. These create and maintain a reality in existence by representing that reality as existing. Second, language itself does not require Status Function Declarations in order to exist because the meaning or semantic content of the sentences themselves is sufficient to enable us to perform the speech acts expressed by those meanings. The contrast is that in extra-linguistic status functions, we use semantics to create powers that go beyond the powers of semantics. But the powers of semantics of language itself do not go beyond the powers of semantics, and thus do not require any further representation beyond the literal meaning of the sentences themselves.[3]

---

[3] I am indebted to a rather large number of people for discussion of the matters in this article. I cannot thank all of them, but I do especially want to thank Josef Moural, Barry Smith, and especially my wife, Dagmar Searle. Special thanks also to Roy d'Andrade, who read the first draft and made helpful comments.

REFERENCES

Barash, David P. (1977), *Sociobiology and Behavior* (Amsterdam: Elsevier).

De Soto, Hernando (2003), *The Mystery of Capital: Why Capitalism Triumphs in the West and Fails Everywhere Else* (New York: Basic Books).

Kummer, Hans (1971), *Primate Societies: Group Techniques of Ecological Adaptation* (Worlds of Man series) (Chicago, Ill.: Aldine-Atherton).

Rosaldo, Michelle (1982), "The things we do with words: Llongot, speech acts, and speech act theory in philosophy," *Language and Society* 11: 203–37.

Searle, John R. (1979), "A taxonomy of illocutionary acts," reprinted in John R. Searle, *Expression and Meaning: Studies in the Theory of Speech Acts* (Cambridge: Cambridge University Press).

(1983), *Intentionality: An Essay in the Philosophy of Mind* (Cambridge: Cambridge University Press).

(1990), "Collective Intentions and Actions," in P. Cohen, J. Morgan, and A. Pollack (eds.), *Intentions in Communication* (Cambridge, Mass.: MIT Press), pp. 401–15. Reprinted in John R. Searle (2002), *Consciousness and Language* (Cambridge: Cambridge University Press).

(1995), *The Construction of Social Reality* (New York: Free Press).

Smith, Barry (2003), "John Searle: from speech acts to social reality," in Barry Smith (ed.), *John Searle* (Cambridge: Cambridge University Press), pp. 1–33.

Wilson, Edward O. (1975), *Sociobiology: A New Synthesis* (Cambridge, Mass.: Harvard University Press).

CHAPTER 3

The Turing Test: fifty-five years later

I. DIFFERENT WAYS OF CONSTRUING THE TURING TEST

In spite of the fact that Turing's original article (Turing, 1950) is written in very clear and direct prose, there are a number of different ways to interpret the claims made in it. I am not, in this article, going to discuss what I think Turing's actual intentions were, but instead I will focus on three different ways of construing the results of the Turing Test that have been prominent in its application. I will assume for the sake of this article that the test itself is unambiguous. My discussion concerns the question: How do we interpret a positive result? On one natural construal, the test gives us a way of telling whether or not we have successfully simulated some human cognitive capacity, some human form of intelligent behavior that manifests thinking. If the machine can perform in such a way that an expert cannot distinguish the performance of the machine from the performance of a competent human, then the machine has successfully simulated the intelligent behavior of the human. Indeed, if our aim in Artificial Intelligence is to produce machines that can successfully simulate human intelligence then the Turing Test gives us a criterion for judging our own success and failure. I do not see how one could object to such a test. If the question is whether we have actually simulated, i.e., imitated, human behavior then, so construed, the Turing Test seems trivially right: If you can't tell the difference between the original and the imitation, then the imitation is a successful imitation.

But there is another way of construing the Turing Test which gives results that seem to me much less satisfactory, indeed false. The Turing Test is sometimes construed as an application of philosophical or logical behaviorism. This may indeed be a reasonable interpretation because behaviorism was a dominant theory in psychology and philosophy at the time that Turing wrote. It is customary to distinguish between *logical (or philosophical) behaviorism* and *methodological behaviorism. Logical (or philosophical) behaviorism* is a thesis in philosophy that says mental phenomena are constituted by behavior and dispositions to behavior; *methodological behaviorism* is a research program in psychology claiming that the proper way to study psychology is to study human behavior. When I say "behaviorism" I mean logical behaviorism. According to the behaviorist conception, human mental phenomena simply consist of, are reducible to, behavior and dispositions to behavior. It is a strict logical consequence of behaviorism that if a machine could emit exactly the same sort of behavior that a human emits with regard to some cognitive phenomenon, then the machine has that cognitive phenomenon in exactly the same sense that the human does. On the second construal we should see the Turing Test as an application of behaviorist principles to Artificial Intelligence. So construed, the test shows that machine behavior indistinguishable from human cognitive behavior is not just proof of successful imitation or simulation by the machine, but is conclusive proof of the presence of the appropriate cognition in the machine. How can that be? In its pristine form, behaviorism was the view that the manifestation of the external behavior was not just *evidence for* the presence of cognition on the inside of the system, but rather that the behavior and the disposition to manifest the behavior under appropriate circumstances were *constitutive of* the mental. Where the mind is concerned, there is nothing going on except the behavior and the disposition to the behavior.

Behaviorism flourished when the linguistic mode of philosophizing was at its strongest, and behaviorism was typically stated as a thesis about psychological attributions. Behaviorists typically argued that statements about mental states are entirely translatable into statements, both categorical and hypothetical, about behavior. The introduction of the notion of hypothetical statements was supposed to explain the notion of a disposition. For example, to say that a person has a certain belief is to say that either he/she is now behaving in a certain way (categorical), or if such and such conditions arise he/she would behave in a certain way (hypothetical, dispositional). On this construal, the Turing Test is a consequence of behaviorism, hence if the Turing Test is false then behaviorism is false. To distinguish these two interpretations of the Turing Test, I will use a terminology I introduced years ago to distinguish two corresponding strands in Artificial Intelligence. The first Turing Test, according to which passing the test is conclusive proof of successful imitation or simulation, I will call the Weak Turing Test. The second, or behaviorist Turing Test, according to which passing the test is conclusive proof of the presence of the psychological phenomena, because the behavior that constitutes passing the test constitutes the psychological phenomena, I will call the Strong Turing Test.

Behaviorism is more or less obviously false, as you can see if you give only a moment's reflection to your own mental processes, such mental processes as thinking about where you are going to spend your summer vacation, or feeling a pain. Having the mental state is one thing; exhibiting it in your behavior is something else. It is possible to have the mental state without exhibiting it in behavior and it is possible to have behavior which does not correspond to a mental state. I find it hard to imagine how anyone could fail to see these obvious points. Nonetheless, several well-known philosophers did deny these points and asserted the reducibility of mental life to behavior and dispositions to behavior.

One difficulty that behaviorists often had was accounting for the apparent fact that where intelligent behavior is concerned, there are typically two things going on, the internal mental processes and the expression of these mental processes in behavior. Right now, for example, I am having internal mental processes of thinking about Alan Turing's famous article, and these thought processes are expressed in my behavior of typing my thoughts on a computer. Pure behaviorists, heroically, denied that there were two things going on in such a case, internal mental processes and external behavior. There is just the intelligent behavior, nothing else. If you look at Turing's article, though, it seems that he thinks that the external behavior is a conclusive test for something else, some cognitive process going on inside. But if that is the right way to construe the test, then it is always subject to the objection that the same external behavior might be caused by two quite different internal causal mechanisms. We might build a machine that could duplicate the external behavioral output of a human brain but did so without any thought processes on the inside. (Compare: We can build an electrical engine with the same power output as a gasoline engine, but it does not prove that the electrical engine has internal combustion.) So now we have three different ways of interpreting a positive result of the Turing Test.

(1) The Weak Turing Test: We don't care what is going on inside the system. We just want to duplicate intelligent behavior. If the machine passes the Turing Test, that is conclusive proof that we have succeeded.

(2) The Strong Turing Test: It is a mistake to think that intelligence, thought processes, etc. are something in addition to behavior. There is just the behavior and the tendency or disposition to the behavior. That

is why the Turing Test is conclusive proof of mental processes. There are not two things, mind and behavior; there is just behavior.

(3) The Modified Strong Turing Test: There is a difference between the inner intelligent thought processes and the outer intelligent behavior, but the Turing Test can still give us conclusive proof of the presence of the inner thought processes, once we understand their nature.

This last conception has tacitly proved to be the most influential and will be examined in the following sections.

II. FROM BEHAVIORISM TO STRONG ARTIFICIAL INTELLIGENCE

In one respect, behaviorism was improved after Turing wrote his famous article. Many people in the behaviorist (scientific, anti-dualist) tradition came to the conclusion that the proper analysis of mental contents showed that they consisted not just in behavior and dispositions to behavior, but rather that there had to be a causal component in the analysis. Mental states were to be defined by the causal relations between input stimulus, inner processing, and external behavior. This view came to be called "functionalism," and functionalism was definitely an improvement on behaviorism in that it recognized that mental phenomena in general, and cognition in particular, stand in causal relations to behavior. Indeed functionalists *defined* mental states in terms of these causal relations. However, early functionalists still left the character of the inner mechanism unspecified, and it is subject to an extension of the charge I made against behaviorism. My charge against behaviorism is that you can have the behavior without having the mental states and you can have the mental states without the behavior. Functionalism claims that completely different inner mechanisms, mental or not, could produce the same external behavior in response to the same stimulus; and some of those mechanisms might be mental or not. In the early days of functionalism, its adherents claimed that it did not matter what the inner mechanism was, and that any inner mechanism that produced the right output in response to the right input, and thus satisfied the Turing Test, literally had cognition. This version of functionalism was sometimes called "black box functionalism" because it ignored the character of the mechanism, and just treated the brain as a black box. However, it is intellectually unsatisfying not to have the nature of the mechanism specified; the rise of computer science, together with the rise of Artificial Intelligence within computer science, led to the hypothesis that the essential mechanism that creates behavior that satisfies the Turing Test is computational. This view is sometimes called "computer functionalism" and I have also baptized it "Strong Artificial Intelligence." It seemed like an improvement on both behaviorism and earlier versions of functionalism.

The rise of computer functionalism in philosophy was paralleled by the growth of Artificial Intelligence as a project in computer science. It seemed natural to a number of people in cognitive science (though not to me) to think that the marriage of computer functionalism with the Turing Test might at last give us the key to human cognition. I think this project was aided and not impeded by certain ambiguity in the notion of "Artificial Intelligence," and I want to digress briefly to sort out the ambiguities.

The expression, "Artificial Intelligence" is multiply ambiguous. I think this ambiguity may have been useful in the early days to get funding and to provide a certain openness for the research project. However, it can be a source of intellectual confusion and I want to clarify it. The word "artificial" is systematically ambiguous, because "an artificial X" can mean either a real X, but produced by artifice, or something that is not really an X, but is only an imitation of an X. Thus, for example, artificial dyes are really dyes, but they are produced in factories, unlike vegetable dyes, which are derived from plants of various kinds. But artificial cream is not really cream at all. It is an imitation of cream. So already we have a double ambiguity: "Artificial Intelligence" could be either real intelligence produced artificially, or it could be something that is not really intelligence at all but just an imitation of intelligence. The ambiguity is compounded when we shift over to the word "intelligence." There is a literal use of the word "intelligence" where intelligence does not imply the presence of any thought processes, or any other relevant psychological states, whatever. I can literally say that one book is more intelligent than another book, without implying that either book has consciousness or any other form of cognition. But if I say literally that Sally is more intelligent than Sam, then I am making an attribution of intelligence which implies actual properties of human cognition, it implies actual thought processes and other sorts of exercises of cognitive abilities. Just to have labels for these two different sorts of intelligence, let us use the expression "mental intelligence" in such a way that the presence of mental intelligence implies the presence of actual mental or cognitive processes, and "non-mental intelligence" implies only intelligent processes of some non-mental kind. We attribute mental intelligence to people and some animals, we attribute non-mental intelligence to books and pocket calculators. We need this distinction in any case because it is clear that human beings have both kinds of intelligence. Thus, for example, the stomach is usually said to be a very intelligent organ, but it has no cognitive processes. The ambiguity, then, of each expression allows for at least four different interpretations of the expression "Artificial Intelligence." First, it can mean real mental intelligence, produced artificially (this is the view that I call Strong AI, and it is identical with computer functionalism); second, it can also mean something which is not real mental intelligence but only an imitation. Third, it can mean real non-mental intelligence; and fourth, it can mean an imitation of non-mental intelligence. It is at least arguable that the third and the fourth are identical because where non-mental phenomena are concerned, if you can simulate non-mental intelligence, you produce non-mental intelligence. The strongest of these four interpretations of "Artificial Intelligence" is the claim that in Artificial Intelligence we are artificially producing real mental intelligence, in the sense of "intelligence" that implies real cognitive processes.

In the early days of cognitive science, I did not find many people in AI who were eager to make these distinctions in a precise fashion. Perhaps it was useful to leave the research project open. But if we are going to examine the implications of computer simulations of human cognition, it becomes absolutely crucial to make clear what exactly the aim of the research project is. Are we trying to produce the real mental thing artificially, or are we not? In any case, in the practice of cognitive science, the Strong Turing Test was treated as the Modified Strong Turing Test. The search was not for just any system that could pass the Turing Test, but for *computers* to pass the Turing Test, and the assumption was that such computers would duplicate and not merely simulate human cognition. The tacit assumption was that the human mind is a digital computer program or a set of computer programs. It was typical in the cognitive science textbooks of those days to have an equation that went: "mind is to brain as program is to hardware." If you got the right program, one that can pass the Turing Test, you would have duplicated and not merely simulated human cognition. This is why, for example, even after you got a machine that could perform successfully, there was still a question as to whether or not the program the machine used was the same as the one that humans were using. Psychologists were often asked to perform reaction time experiments to see if we could get evidence for computational equivalence. The idea was that if different reaction times for humans matched differences in the time of the computer operations, then these matching differences were at least evidence that the humans were using the same sort of program as the computer. There was, in short, a marriage between the Strong Turing Test and Strong AI to produce the Modified Strong Turing Test.

III. THE REFUTATION OF STRONG AI AND ITS
PHILOSOPHICAL IMPLICATIONS

Years ago I refuted Strong AI and with it both versions of the Strong Turing Test (Searle, 1980). According to Strong AI, the appropriately programmed digital computer program, programmed so as to be able to pass the Turing Test, literally has the same cognitive capacities as the human being. I refuted this with a now well-known thought experiment called the Chinese Room Argument, wherein a person who does not know Chinese, myself for example, is locked in a room, and, as Turing says, is equipped only with such things as a pencil and a piece of paper, together with other elements that go to make up the data base and the program, in this case Chinese symbols, and a program of instructions as to what to do with the Chinese symbols. In the thought experiment the person in the room, namely me, is able to simulate the behavior of a Chinese person in a way that satisfies the Turing Test, because, for example, he gives the correct answers to Chinese questions, but all the same, he does not understand a word of Chinese. Why not? Because he has no way to get from the manipulation of the symbols to the meanings of the symbols, and if the person in the room does not understand the meanings of the symbols on the basis of implementing the program, then neither does any other computer solely on that basis, because no computer, just in virtue of its computational properties, has anything that the man in the Chinese Room does not have. Furthermore, the whole room has no way of getting meaning from the symbols. The whole system has no way to attach semantics to the syntax of the computer symbols.

However, it is philosophically unsatisfying just to refute a thesis. There has to be an underlying philosophical explanation of why the thesis went wrong. This to me is a more interesting philosophical question and I will say a little more about it. Intelligent human behavior is typically *caused by* inner mental processes and capacities. This causal character of the relation between mind and behavior was ignored by logical behaviorism. Thus, for example, when a native speaker of Chinese can intelligently answer questions in Chinese it is because his/her external behavior is the external expression of his/her inner mental capacities. We saw earlier that this weakness in logical behaviorism was corrected by functionalism. Functionalism, indeed, defined mental states as anything that stood in the right causal relations between external stimulus, other mental states, and external behavior. So a belief is anything that is caused by perceptual inputs, and, together with a desire, causes external behavior. Desires analogously could be defined in terms of input stimulus, other mental states, and external behavior. But this thesis, as I have suggested, left open a terrible weakness: it did not state the specific features of the mental states that enabled them to function causally. This limitation was corrected by computer functionalism to the extent that it at least specified a mechanism: the computer program that mediated the causal relations between the external input stimuli and the external output behavior. But the difficulty with that theory is that the program is defined purely formally or syntactically, and consequently does not, qua program, carry the intrinsic mental or semantic contents that human mental states actually have.

We can now see why the Strong Turing Test gives us a result that is obviously false. If we interpret it in its pristine form as just logical behaviorism we already know that it is false because the presence of the appropriate behavior does not result from the underlying mental states and processes that cause that external behavior in humans. If we augment the logical behaviorist form of the Turing Test with the computer functionalist, or Strong AI form, we still get a result that is obviously false because the external behavior caused by the implementation of an inner computer program, defined entirely formally or syntactically (for example, in terms of Turing's account of a Turing machine as performing such operations as printing o's, erasing 1's, moving one square to the left, moving one square to the right, etc.) is still not sufficient to constitute actual human mental processes, which actually have mental or semantic contents.

Indeed, we typically have such machines for practical purposes because they can give us the same external results without having to go through the kind of internal mental effort that human beings typically require. When I use my adding machine, I use a machine that passes the Turing Test for addition, subtraction, etc., indeed it surpasses even the very best mathematicians in intelligent behavior, but it does not thereby have thought processes about mathematics. How do I know that? How do I know that it is not thinking about long division when it does long division? Because I know how it was designed and built. It contains an electronic circuit designed to carry out the algorithms for addition, subtraction, multiplication, and division. It doesn't think about mathematics, because it doesn't think about anything. And what goes for my pocket calculator goes for more complex forms of commercial computing machinery. They were not designed to be conscious nor to have thought processes, as in the case of Turing machines of the von Neumann architecture. We have designed machines to perform complex operations using only two types of symbols, usually thought of as zeros and ones.

But, one might be inclined to ask, why can't the zeros and ones be sufficient for human mental thought processes? After all, in the very brain itself there are only neurons and they either fire or don't fire, so what is the difference between the binary system of the brain and the binary system of the digital computer? I think that is an intelligent and appropriate question. It has a simple and decisive answer: the neuron firings are part of a causal mechanism that *causes* consciousness and cognition as a higher-level feature of the brain system. The brain is a machine and as such its essential processes are matters of energy transfer. The zeros and ones of the implemented computer program are purely abstract syntactical entities that do not, as such, cause anything. Rather, the program is implemented in the hardware, and the hardware processes that are essential for the implementation are those, and only those, that carry out the formal, syntactical steps of the program. The hardware might cause consciousness for some other reason (for example when I carry out the algorithm for long division, my brain processes also cause me to be conscious), but the program, *qua implemented program*, knows nothing of causing consciousness or anything else except the next state of the program when the machine is running. To put this point slightly more technically: The notion *same implemented program* defines an equivalence class that is specified independently of the physics of the hardware mechanisms in which it is realized. A specific form of hardware, my brain for example, might also cause consciousness while I am carrying out the algorithm for doing long division, but the algorithm itself does not have any causal powers independent of the implementing medium.

It is important to make this point completely clear. The question, "Can a computer think?" is ambiguous. It can mean either "Can something be a computer and also think?" or it can mean "Is computation by itself constitutive of or sufficient for thinking?" If we define computation in Turing's terms, as the manipulation of symbols (zeroes and ones or Chinese symbols, or whatever – it does not matter) then the answer to the first question is obviously yes. Something, me for example, can both think and manipulate symbols. But the answer to the second question is obviously no. Computation so defined – by itself, *qua* computation – is not constitutive of, nor sufficient for, thinking because it is defined entirely syntactically, and thinking has to have something more than just symbols, it has to have a meaning or semantic content attached to the symbols. And that is what the Chinese Room Argument proved: the syntax of the implemented computer program by itself is insufficient for the understanding of the semantics of actual Chinese words and sentences.

Though the sort of computer you buy in a store is also a machine, its computational processes are not defined by energy transfers; rather, they are defined by abstract mathematical processes that we have found ways to implement in the hardware. The problem with the commercial digital computer is not that it is too much of a machine to produce consciousness; rather, it is not enough of a machine because, unlike the brain, its essential operations, its computational operations, are defined in terms of abstract algorithmic processes and not in terms of energy transfers.

In the past, as here, I have found it useful to state this point using the distinction between syntax and semantics. Brain operations cause consciousness that has semantic content. Program operations are purely syntactical, and the syntax by itself does not constitute consciousness, nor is it sufficient to cause consciousness.

Consciousness is a state that the brain is in when it is caused to be in that state by the operations of lower-level neuronal mechanisms. In order to create such a state artificially, you would have to duplicate, and not merely simulate, the actual causal powers of human and animal brains. There is no reason in principle to suppose that we would have to have organic materials to do this, but whatever materials we use we have to duplicate the causal powers of actual brains. We ought to hear the question, "Can you create consciousness with a mechanism other than brains?" in exactly the same way we hear the question, "Can you create the pumping of blood in a mechanism other than human and animal hearts?" In both cases the question is about causal mechanisms and not about syntactical processes. The computer simulation of brain operations stands to the actual brain operations as a computer simulation of a heart stands to the actual pumping of blood.

We can summarize these points in two propositions:

(1) If the Turing Test, is interpreted as either the Strong Turing Test, or in its modified form as the Modified Strong Turing Test, as giving us conclusive proof of the presence of inner mental contents, it fails. It fails because a system, computational or otherwise, can behave as if it were intelligent without having any inner mental processes whatever.

(2) The prospect of creating human thought processes solely by implementing Turing machine programs also fails because the program is defined syntactically. The implemented computer program consists in a set of processes that are specifiable syntactically, in terms of the manipulation of symbols, in a way that is independent of the physics of the implementing medium. Any physics will do provided only that it is rich enough and stable enough to carry out the steps in the program.

And the syntax by itself does not constitute consciousness nor is it by itself sufficient to cause consciousness.

IV. WHY WAS ANYONE EVER A BEHAVIORIST?

I have already made many of these points in a number of other writings. It is worth repeating them briefly because they are sometimes overlooked in these discussions. I now want to turn to a question I have not previously written about: How did it come about that behaviorism persisted for so long since the mistaken character of behaviorism is so obvious, and the Strong Turing Test is itself an expression of behaviorism?

If one looks at the intellectual history of any era, there are likely to be stunning and widespread mistakes that should have been easily avoided, even given the limitations of the knowledge base of the times. An amazing and pervasive mistake throughout the nineteenth century was idealism, the theory that all of reality was mental or spiritual, and that an independent material reality does not exist. It is hard for us today to recover the mode of sensibility that made this view seem not only possible, but indeed compelling, to thinkers of the stature of Berkeley, Royce, Bradley, and Hegel, just to mention a few. In the twentieth century the mirror image of the nineteenth-century mistake of idealism was the mistake of behaviorism, which still exists in some quarters even today. Just as idealism denied the reality of a mind-independent physical world, so behaviorism denies the reality of subjective inner mental states, in favor of an account of the mind according to which mental states consist in external behavior. The black box functionalist and computer functionalist successors to behaviorism inherit the same mistake of denying the irreducible reality of inner, subjective, qualitative mental states. How did we get into this mess?

It is fairly easy to trace the history of post-Cartesian idealism. In its modern form, it begins with Berkeley and is driven by the epistemic obsession that he had inherited from Descartes. The way to overcome the skepticism that seemed to make knowledge of the real world impossible was to deny the gulf between the evidence and the reality that the evidence is supposed to be evidence for. If the material world is supposed to exist independently of experience, and if knowledge of the material world is based on sense experience, then it seems we can never have knowledge of the material world, because we can never get outside the circle of our own experiences to the independent mind reality. We overcome this skepticism by denying the distinction between our experiences and reality. The object is the permanent possibility of sensation (Mill, 1865) and the world is a collection of minds and ideas (Berkeley, 1998). The urge to behaviorism bears an uncanny resemblance to this urge to idealism. If consciousness and intentionality are supposed to exist independently of behavior, and if our only evidence for their existence in other people is the behavior of the other people, then it looks like we are forced to skepticism, because we can never get outside the sequence of the observable behavior of other people to observe the inner mental phenomena that are supposed to lie behind the behavior. But if the mind is just the behavior, and (in the case of functionalism) the observable mechanisms that cause the behavior, then we overcome skepticism about the mind in the same way that idealism overcame skepticism about the external world. In both cases we defeat skepticism by denying that there is a difference between the evidence and the reality that the evidence is evidence for.

Behaviorism is thus best construed as a form of verificationism. Verificationism in turn, is a response to the skeptical tradition that originated with Descartes and received its finest expression in the works of the British empiricists and their twentieth-century followers, the logical positivists. It is no accident that behaviorism was the dominant philosophy of mind of the logical positivists.

V. GIVING UP THE STRONG TURING TEST

If, as I have urged, we should reject the Strong Turing Test and the Modified Strong Turing Test as tests for the presence of mental states, then a natural question is what alternative test do we propose, what alternative to these Strong Turing Tests is there? The correct response to this is that we would be mistaken to suppose that there had to be some single mechanical test for ascertaining the presence of mental states and cognitive capacities in others. There are a variety of ways we can actually find out whether other systems have mental states, and I want to conclude this brief discussion by mentioning some of these. Mental phenomena have a first-person ontology in the sense that they only actually exist when they are experienced by a human or animal agent. That means that the best way to know whether or not a system is having a certain mental process is to be that system. Of course, one often makes mistakes about one's own inner mental states, but all the same, when it comes, for example, to feeling my pains or thinking my thoughts, there is no substitute for being me. However, since there is only one system in the universe that I can be identical with, namely me, I have a problem of how I can know about the thoughts and feelings, capacities and limitations, of other humans and animals. The temptation here is to revert to a type of behaviorism and say, well, the way I know that humans and animals have mental states is by their behavior. I think this answer is incorrect. In the case of my dog, for example, I am completely confident that he has mental states even though he has no language. Now, why am I so confident about that? It is not simply because of his behavior but rather because of the combination of his behavior and the underlying causal mechanisms that I can see are relevantly similar to my own. I do not have to have an elaborate theory of dog physiology to know that that is his nose, these are his ears, that is his mouth, this is his skin, etc. And the way that I am able to infer the presence of mental states on the basis of behavior is that I observe not just a correlation between stimulus and response, but rather that I can see that there are similar causal mechanisms that mediate the relationship between the stimulus and the response. The principle on the basis of which I know that my dog has mental states is not: same behavior therefore same mental states, but rather: similar underlying causal structure, therefore similar cause and effect relationships. This is why, incidentally, though I am confident about dogs and chimpanzees, I am not at all confident about termites and fleas. Well, how would one find out in these cases? Again, I think that the principle is not hard to state, though we do not know enough neurophysiology to apply it in practice. If we understood the actual causal mechanisms that produced consciousness and intentionality in human beings and higher animals, then we would have very good grounds for supposing that these same phenomena occur in other systems. So, for example, let us suppose that there is a certain neurobiological process, the technical name of which we will abbreviate as "ABC," that in human beings and higher animals causes conscious mental phenomena. Now let us suppose that we observe ABC in mice and pigeons, but we do not observe anything like it in fleas and grasshoppers. Let us suppose, furthermore, that we have a causal explanation of the behavior of the fleas and grasshoppers that is quite different from the explanation of the behavior of higher animals, that shows that their causal mechanisms are much more like simple tropisms than they are like complex cognitive phenomena produced by human and animal neurobiology. Then it seems to me we would regard this as conclusive proof that chimpanzees, dogs, mice, and pigeons have conscious mental phenomena in the same way that we do, but that fleas and grasshoppers do not.

I hope that my remarks here will not be misunderstood. I regard Alan Turing as one of the great minds of the twentieth century. It in no way diminishes his achievement to say that the test that he proposed was inadequate if it is understood as an expression of the false philosophical theory of behaviorism.

Behaviorism is a theory for which he was not responsible, and it is now best regarded as obsolete.

REFERENCES

Berkeley, G. (1998), *A Treatise Concerning the Principles of Human Knowledge*, ed. Jonathon Dancy (Oxford: Oxford University Press).

Mill, J. S. (1865), *An Examination of Sir William Hamilton's Philosophy* (London).

Searle, J. R. (1980), "Minds, brains, and programs," *Behavioral and Brains Sciences* 3: 417–424.

Turing, A. (1950), "Computing machinery and intelligence," *Mind* 59 (236): 433–460.

CHAPTER 4

Twenty-one years in the Chinese Room

I

I want to use the occasion of this volume dedicated to the twenty-first anniversary of the Chinese Room Argument to reflect on some of the implications of this debate for cognitive science in general, and indeed, for the current state of our larger intellectual culture. I will not spend much time responding to the many detailed arguments that have been presented. I have already responded to more criticisms of the Chinese Room Argument than to all of the criticisms of all of the other controversial philosophical theses that I have advanced in my life. My reason for having so much confidence that the basic argument is sound is that in the past twenty-one years I have not seen anything to shake its fundamental thesis. The fundamental claim is that the purely formal or abstract or syntactical processes of the implemented computer program could not by themselves be sufficient to *guarantee* the presence of mental content or semantic content of the sort that is essential to human cognition. Of course a system might have semantic content for some other reason. It may be that implementing this program in this particular hardware is sufficient to cause consciousness and intentionality, but such a claim is no longer Strong Artificial Intelligence. It is at the very heart of the Strong AI thesis that the system that implements the program does not matter. Any hardware implementation will do, provided only that it is rich enough and stable enough to carry the program. This is why I can, at least in principle, carry out the steps in the program in the Chinese Room, even though my 'hardware' is quite unlike that of commercial computers. In short, the distinction between the software and the hardware, and the essential point in the whole modern notion of computation that a program is multiply realizable in different hardwares, is sufficient to refute the claim that the implemented software by itself, regardless of the nature of the implementing medium, would be sufficient to guarantee the presence of mental contents.

The Chinese Room Argument, in short, rests on two absolutely fundamental logical truths, and twenty-one years of debate has not in any way shaken either of these. Here they are. First, syntax is not semantics. That is to say, the implemented syntactical or formal program of a computer is not constitutive of, or otherwise sufficient, to guarantee the presence of semantic content; and second, simulation is not duplication. You can simulate the cognitive processes of the human mind as you can simulate rain storms, five alarm fires, digestion, or anything else that you can describe precisely. But it is just as ridiculous to think that a system that had a simulation of consciousness and other mental processes thereby had the mental processes as it would be to think that the simulation of digestion on a computer could thereby actually digest beer and pizza.

I said above that there was no way that the implemented computer program by itself could *guarantee* the presence of mental content or semantic content. But how on earth did the proponents of Strong AI imagine that it could guarantee the presence of mental content? What picture do they have? Actually, the ambiguities in their position are illustrative of certain important failures of reductionist attempts to deal with philosophical issues over the past century, and I want to say a little bit about such reductionist attempts. The typical pattern is to treat the epistemic basis for a phenomenon – behavior in the case of the mind, sense data in the case of material objects – as somehow logically sufficient to guarantee the presence of the phenomenon. The basic urge is a verificationist reductionist urge, and the Turing Test is an expression of this same urge. But the reductionist also wants to continue to track the intuitive idea of the phenomenon that was supposed to be reduced in the first place. The intuitive notion of a mental state or a material object has somehow to be preserved within the reductionist enterprise. This is why the Chinese Room poses such a problem: I implement the program, but I do not understand Chinese. What the Strong AI thesis amounts to in its pure form is that the implemented program is *constitutive* of a mind. A system that implements the right program necessarily has a mind because there isn't anything else to having a mind. The Turing Test gives us a test for the presence of the mind, but the actual thing that it is a test for is a series of computational processes. Now, what is the Strong AI theorist to say in the face of an obvious counter-example such as the Chinese Room? The proponent of Strong AI is committed by the ideology to saying that in the Chinese Room I do in fact understand Chinese because I can pass the Turing Test by carrying out the steps in the computation. But it is simply too preposterous to say that I understand Chinese or that I would understand Chinese by carrying out the steps in the program, because I quite obviously do not, and in the imagined circumstances would not, understand Chinese. What is the reductionist to do? The typical move over the past twenty-one years has been to grant that I do not understand Chinese, but then to say such things as, "Well, it's the whole system that understands Chinese," or sometimes even, "A subsystem in you understands Chinese." But these evasions will not do. The proponent of Strong AI is originally committed to the view that the program is constitutive of mental content, but in the face of obvious counter-examples, retreats to a different position, that the program is somehow *associated with* mental content. That was the whole point of the Systems Reply. The Systems Reply claims that even though there is no semantic content in me alone, there is semantic content somewhere else – in the whole system of which I am a part, or in some subsystem within me. But the same argument that worked originally – namely, I do not have any understanding of Chinese because I do not know what any of the words mean, I have no way to attach meaning to any of the symbols – works for the whole system. The whole system doesn't know what any of the words mean either, because it has no way to attach any mental content to any of the symbols.

What is interesting is not just the evasiveness of the Systems Reply, but the fact that it illustrates the general tendency of twentieth-century reductionist accounts of the mind. Behaviorism was confronted with the same difficulty. The behaviorist is forced to say that the behavior is constitutive of the mental. But in the face of obvious counter-examples the idea was always to suggest that there was some way that, in the system that behaves appropriately, the right mental states would somehow be associated with the behavior.

The problem for all these forms of reductionism is the same: are there really two things or just one? The thesis of reductionism is that there is just one thing – behavior, or computer programs or sense data or whatever – but in the face of the counter-examples the reductionist says that the other thing must be there too. Hence there are two things. The urge of the reductionist to try to hang on to the reduced notion amounts to a quiet abandonment of the reduction. If he really were consistent in the reduction of mental states to program states, he should have said, "There isn't any such thing as understanding in addition to symbol manipulation, there is just the symbol manipulation. Whether that goes on in the individual or in the whole room makes no difference. The symbol manipulation is all there is to understanding." But that is too obviously absurd from the first-person point of view, where I know clearly the distinction between my manipulating symbols in English together with having an understanding of them, and my manipulating symbols in Chinese with no understanding whatever. So the Strong AI theorist makes the desperate move of saying the understanding is somewhere else in the system. It is the whole room that understands, not the person in the room.

There is, in short, a deep contradiction in the reductionist's position. On the one hand, he wants to say there is no such thing as semantic content in addition to symbol manipulation, but on the other hand, when I present a case of symbol manipulation without semantic content, he does not say, "Well, that is all there was in the first place," what he says is, "The semantic content must be somewhere else in the system." This is a straight contradiction. You cannot maintain that there is no such thing as semantic content in addition to symbol manipulation, and then say that there must be semantic content somewhere else in the system in addition to the symbol manipulation. So when I said earlier that the implemented program by itself is insufficient to *guarantee* the presence of mental states, that covered both of the possible moves of the Strong AI theorist. The program by itself is insufficient to *constitute* mental states because of the distinction between syntax and semantics. And it is insufficient by itself to *cause* mental states because the program is defined independently of the physics of its implementation. Any causal power the machine might have to cause consciousness and intentionality would have to be a consequence of the physical nature of the machine. But the program *qua program* hasn't got any physical nature. It consists of a set of formal, syntactical processes that can be implemented in the physics of various kinds of machinery.

To the frequently asked question, "Well, what is the difference between the brain, which, after all, functions by a set of microprocesses such as neuron firings at synapses and the computer with its microprocesses of flip flops, 'and' gates and 'or' gates?", the answer can be given in one word: *causation.* We know that the specific neurobiological processes in the brain are sufficient to cause consciousness, intentionality, and all the rest of our mental life by a form of "bottom-up" causation. Lower-level neuronal processes, presumably at the level of synapses, cause higher-level features of the brain such as consciousness and intentionality. It is no use being told that it is "counter-intuitive" that a kilogram and a half of this gray and white gook in my skull should cause consciousness, because we know in fact that it does. The point I make is not that it is counter-intuitive that computers should be conscious. I have no interest whatever in such intuitions. The point, rather, is that the implemented program is insufficient by itself to guarantee the presence of consciousness. The program is not defined in terms of its powers to cause higher-level features of the system, because it has no such powers. It is defined, rather, in terms of its syntactical or formal structure. Of course, the computer on which I am typing might be conscious for some other reason. Perhaps God has decided to endow all computers that have a label that says "Intel-inside" with consciousness. That is up to Him, and not up to me. My argument is a purely logical argument about the distinction between the syntax of the implemented computer program and the actual semantic content of mental states.

The basic structure of the Chinese Room Argument is rather obvious, and the principles on which it rests – the distinction between syntax and semantics and the distinction between simulation and duplication – are not at all difficult to grasp. I have little or no difficulty in explaining them even to people unsophisticated in any of the technical notions in question. One wonders, therefore, why the debate continues. Well, of course, there are a number of reasons. Many people have a professional commitment to Strong AI. To put the point bluntly, in many cases their careers and the funding of their research projects depend on the continued belief that they are "creating minds" (one Strong AI worker actually assured me that he was "creating minds"). For such people it is psychologically impossible to accept that the project of Strong AI is misconceived in principle. They would like to believe that the failure of Strong AI is due to some temporary limitation of the technology; that if only we had faster computer chips or more complex parallel distributed processing systems, we would be able to overcome the argument. The point of the argument has nothing whatever to do with any state of technology, it has to do with the very concept of computation, a concept that Alonzo Church, Alan Turing, and others explained to us half a century ago.

II

One of the interesting features of contemporary intellectual life that this whole debate has exposed is the persistence of a set of obsolete seventeenth-century categories in which the issues are typically defined and discussed. I am thinking not only of the obsolete contrast of the "mental" and the "physical," of "mind" and "body," but just as important, the obsolete contrast between "man" and "machine." So the issue about Strong AI is often taken to be the same as the question, "Could a machine think?" But of course the whole question is absurd. We are, after all, machines. If "machine" is defined as any physical system capable of performing certain functions, then there is no question that human and animal brains are machines. They are *biological* machines, but so what? There is no logical or philosophical reason why we could not duplicate the operation of a biological machine, using some artificial methods. The whole opposition of man versus machine involves a series of deep philosophical mistakes, and I tried to expose some of them in the original article, but apparently more needs to be said. So I will try to say what I think needs to be said as a series of numbered propositions.

(1) There is no question that machines can think, because human and animal brains are precisely such machines.

(2) There is no question that an artificially made machine could, in principle, think. Just as we can build an artificial heart, so there is no reason why we could not build an artificial brain. The point, however, is that any such artificial machine would have to be able to duplicate, and not merely simulate, the causal powers of the original biological machine. An artificial heart does not merely simulate pumping, it actually pumps. It actually causes the pumping of blood. And an artificial brain would have to do something more than simulate consciousness, it would have to be able to *produce* consciousness. It would have to cause consciousness.

(3) Could we produce consciousness artificially in some medium other than carbon-based organic compounds? The short answer to that question is that we just do not know at present. Since we do not know how the brain does it, we do not know what sorts of chemical devices are necessary for its production. Perhaps it will turn out that consciousness can only be produced using electrochemical phenomena, but does not require organic compounds. It might be that certain types of organic compounds in certain conditions are causally sufficient without it being the case that they are causally necessary. At present we just do not know.

It is important to get clear about what is at issue. When I say that the implemented program by itself is not enough to constitute consciousness and intentionality, that is a logical claim on my part. By definition, the syntax of the program is not constitutive of the semantics of actual thoughts. But when I say that a system composed entirely of beer cans is not sufficient to cause consciousness and intentionality, that is an empirical claim on my part. It is like saying that a system composed entirely of beer cans is not sufficient to digest hamburgers. It is a claim about how nature works. It is logically possible, though not actually possible, that I could be mistaken. But it is not logically possible that syntax by itself should be semantics. Strong AI rests on a logical error. But it is still an open question what sorts of systems are necessary and sufficient to produce consciousness and intentionality. We know at one end that human and animal brains are sufficient to do it. We know at another end that beer cans cannot do it. What sorts of chemistry in between are capable of causing consciousness and intentionality is still an open question, and is likely to remain open until we figure out how brains do it.

(4) Though computers of the sort that you can buy in a store are "machines," computation as standardly defined does not name a machine process. Oddly enough, the problem is not that computational processes are too much machine-like to be conscious, it is rather that they are too little machine-like. The reason for this is that computation is defined purely formally or abstractly in terms of the implementation of a computer algorithm, and not in terms of energy transfer. Let me repeat this point: computation as standardly defined does not name a machine process in the sense in which photosynthesis or internal combustion name machine processes, because photosynthesis and internal combustion necessarily involve energy transfers. Computation does not. Computation is the name of an abstract mathematical process that can be implemented with machines that engage in energy transfer, but the energy transfer is not part of the definition of computation. To state the point with a little more precision: the notion "same implemented program" defines an equivalence class that is specified not in terms of physical or chemical processes, but in terms of abstract mathematical processes. Could a machine process cause a thought process? The answer is: yes. Indeed only a machine process can cause a thought process, and "computation" does not name a machine process; it names a process that can be, and typically is, *implemented* on a machine.

Strong AI is a weird mixture of behaviorism and dualism. It is behaviorist in its acceptance of the Turing Test, but it is at a much more fundamental philosophical level dualist, because it rejects the idea that consciousness and intentionality are ordinary biological phenomena like digestion. In the words of Dennett and Hofstadter, we are to think of the mind as, "an abstract sort of thing whose identity is independent of any particular physical embodiment."[1] I will say more about this point later.

III

There is an interesting series of larger philosophical issues raised by this debate, and I want now to consider at least some of them. I believe that

[1] Hofstadter and Dennett (1981: 15).

future intellectual historians will be puzzled by certain peculiar features of late twentieth- and early twenty-first-century scientific culture. One of the most puzzling of these features is the persistence of certain anti-scientific views masquerading under the guise of science. When I say "masquerading" I do not mean to imply any form of charlatanry or dishonesty on the part of the masqueraders. I think they are quite innocently mistaken about the contrast between their view and a genuinely scientific approach. A few decades ago the most obvious case of an anti-scientific approach masquerading as science was behaviorism in philosophy and psychology. The basic idea of the extreme forms of behaviorism was that there isn't anything to mental life other than our behavior and our dispositions to behavior. But anyone who has ever felt a pain or experienced an emotion knows immediately that this view is false. The pain that I feel is one thing, the behavior that the pain causes me to exhibit is another. What difference could be more obvious? Why wasn't this obvious at the time? Why wasn't it obvious to everybody? Well, let's go a step further, and ask what motivated this peculiar form of anti-scientific view in the midst of a scientific culture. And we find that the mistake of behaviorism was underlain by an even deeper mistake, that of verificationism. People erroneously supposed that the essence of science, and of what they thought of as the "scientific method," was that there must be certain conclusive methods of verifying scientific claims. The extreme version of this view was Logical Positivism, whose adherents claimed that the meaning of any sentence is its method of verification, and therefore that the verification of a sentence about someone's mind gave us the entire meaning of the sentence. Thus, at least where "other minds" are concerned, because the verification of a sentence about another mind allowed only evidence about that person's behavior, it seemed there couldn't be anything else to the mind other than the behavior. I believe that this, like behaviorism itself, is profoundly anti-scientific, but I have not yet said anything about the nature of "science" which would justify that view, and I will delay such an account for a few moments more.

In order to explain exactly why these views – behaviorism and verificationism – were in fact profoundly anti-scientific, though many people thought of them as a natural consequence of something called "scientific method," I need to say something about the history of the development of science and of the scientific world-view in our intellectual culture. The Ancient Greeks did not have science as we now think of it. Perhaps the greatest single achievement of Greek civilization was the invention of the idea of a theory. A theory is a set of systematically logically related propositions that provide an explanation of the phenomena of some domain. One of the earliest examples of a systematic theoretical account of a domain is Euclid's geometry as expounded in his *Elements*. With the invention of the idea of a theory the Greeks arrived at almost everything that is necessary for science, but they did not have the idea of systematic observation and experiment. They never reached the idea of an institutionalized form of systematic observation and experiment. That came really only after the Renaissance. And, as far as I know, it really did not get going until the seventeenth century.

The scientific achievements of the seventeenth century are among the greatest achievements of Western civilization. But the scientific revolution suffered from certain specific local problems that had to do with the intellectual culture of the rest of Western civilization during the seventeenth century, in particular with the enormous intellectual power possessed by organized religion, especially by the Catholic Church.

The intellectual significance of the great conflict between science and religion in the seventeenth century and subsequently is much bigger than anything I can hope to cover in the space of this short chapter. But for the present purposes there are three features to which I would like to call attention. First, most of the philosophers and scientists involved in this dispute did not want to give up on either science or religion; they wanted to pursue their scientific investigations while maintaining their religious convictions. Descartes found a way for them to do that: he divided the world into two, a mental realm of the soul or spirit that was the proper domain of religion, and a physical realm of matter, which was the proper domain of science. This division of the territory seemed to make it possible to have a strict physical science combined with the acceptance of religious doctrines such as the immortality of the soul. Science, in short, was taken to be about matter and the physical world. But there was a realm beyond the reach of science, and that was the realm of the spirit or the soul or mental substance. Descartes's famous distinction between *res cogitans* and *res extensa* is the classic statement of this dualism.

Though this distinction was perhaps politically and sociologically useful in the seventeenth century, it has proved to be unfortunate in the twentieth and twenty-first centuries, because many people still hold the view that consciousness and subjectivity are not proper domains of scientific investigation. Many people believe that the investigation of consciousness and intentionality, phenomena which are inherently subjective and mental, is somehow beyond the reach of an objective science. This is a very deep mistake, with deep historical roots, and I will expose it in more detail shortly.

A second feature of the dispute between science and religion was the obsession with *method.* The idea was that in science there was a special method, and that this method differed from other areas of human investigation. The endless debates about faith and reason were an expression of this great dispute between science and religion, and a consequence of the conviction that what was special about science in attaining the truth was "scientific method." Again, the consequence of this conception, like the consequence of the dualism of Descartes, was to give people a conception of science as more restricted than we have come to think of it today. Science, they thought, is not universal in subject-matter, but has a restricted subject-matter. Some have even said it is restricted to the subject-matter which is mathematically statable. Unless you can measure the phenomena in question, they are not proper scientific phenomena. Furthermore, science is constrained by a particularly narrow notion of method.

A third feature of the conflict between science and religion did not become fully apparent in the seventeenth century, but only emerged in subsequent eras, and indeed has only become fully manifest in the twentieth century. It is this: religion sought absolute and indubitable truths. Science, on the other hand, was much more tentative. Science was a matter of hypotheses that one could test, but these hypotheses were never taken as absolute truths. In the twentieth century the various scientific revolutions, especially the Einsteinian revolution that overthrew the apparent universality of Newtonian physics, and the quantum mechanical revolution that challenges some of our most basic assumptions, seem to make this tentative character of science all the more obvious. The picture that we get is that whatever scientists believe today, they will not believe tomorrow, that there is a continuing evolution from one tentative hypothesis to another. One philosopher who espoused this doctrine explicitly was Karl Popper (Popper, 1959). Popper thought of science as not a matter of attaining the truth, but rather as a matter of putting forward hypotheses and knocking them down. Science never attains the truth, just moves from one hypothesis to another, and the surviving hypotheses, like soldiers in an endless war, are different from earlier hypotheses only because they are still alive and not yet shot down. The move from the pro-science philosophy of Popper to the anti-scientific views of Thomas Kuhn (Kuhn, 1962, 1970)

and Paul Feyerabend (Feyerabend, 1975) is not as great as many philosophers and scientists think. Indeed, many scientists who reject Kuhn, and
would be appalled by Feyerabend's views if they knew anything about
them, profess to admire Popper's philosophy of science. I think they do not
properly understand Popper. They like the fact that Popper praises them
for their originality in putting forward new and original hypotheses, but
they do not understand that Popper rejects the basic assumption behind
their enterprise, namely the assumption that they are getting at the truth.[2]

These three features, dualism, the obsession with method, and the tacit
rejection of truth as the aim of investigation, have exercised a pervasive,
though not always explicit, influence on intellectual life. And these influ-
ences have spilled over into the debate about Strong AI. How exactly? I
mentioned earlier that there is a tacit dualism in the computational conception of the mind. The mind is not an ordinary part of the biological world
like digestion and photosynthesis but is something formal and abstract,
hence we do not have to worry about the specific biochemical mechanisms that produce consciousness and the various forms of intentionality.
Furthermore the key problem is to find a conclusive method for ascertaining the presence of mental phenomena and we have found that in the
Turing Test. The existence of an objective test makes it look as if we are
doing real science. Do we not have an objective method of verification, just
like real sciences? Finally we do not have to worry about what inner facts
correspond to our claims about consciousness and intentionality in real
life. Rather we postulate an abstract mechanism – the computer program –
and we have a test of its success and failure – the Turing Test – and when
our hypotheses are confirmed by the Turing Test that is all the truth we
need. I hope it is obvious that this is a massive tissue of errors, and one of
the virtues of the Chinese Room Argument is that it helps to expose these
errors. Most obviously it refutes the Turing Test. The "system," whether me
in the Chinese Room, the whole room, or a commercial computer, passes
the Turing Test for understanding Chinese but it does not understand
Chinese, because it has no way of attaching any meaning to the Chinese
symbols. The appearance of understanding is an illusion. Furthermore,
when we flesh out the details, the argument reminds us of the necessity of
scientific realism. We are interested in the *fact* of internal mental states, not
in the external appearance. Our claims, if true, have to meet more than an
instrumental test, they have to correspond to facts in the world.

---

[2] For an excellent discussion of these issues, see Stove (1999).

IV

So far I have been calling attention to certain mistakes that people commonly make when they are insufficiently aware of the implications of the scientific world-view. Now I want to turn to three less obvious features of this world-view. These features do not lie on the surface, but, I believe, are readily recognizable.

(1) *The distinction between observer-dependence and observer-independence.* Absolutely essential to our understanding of the world is to be able to distinguish between those features of the world that exist independently of our attitudes and purposes, and those that exist only relative to us. I have at various times characterized this as the distinction between those features of the world that are "intrinsic" and those that are observer-dependent, but the word "intrinsic" is a frequent source of confusion, so to avoid confusion I sometimes characterize the distinction as between observer-dependence and observer-relativity on the one hand, and observer-independence on the other. Typically the natural sciences study features that are observer-independent: force, mass, gravitational attraction, photosynthesis, tectonic plates, molecules, and planets, are all observer-independent. If we all cease to exist tomorrow, these would go on existing, and indeed, if we had never existed, these would still have existed. I realize that in physics it is common to identify some of these parameters relative to coordinate systems, but it is also essential to see that even though the physics textbooks sometimes call this "relative to an observer," they do not mean that in my sense. They do not think, for example, that in order for an object to have a mass, somebody has to be consciously thinking about it, or indeed that anybody ever has to consciously think about it.

The social sciences typically deal with phenomena that are observer-dependent. I am thinking of phenomena like political parties, marriage, money, elections, nation states, property, and organized sports. As usual, psychology falls somewhere in between. Most of psychology deals with observer-independent phenomena such as perception and memory, but sometimes in social psychology, we deal with observer-dependent phenomena, such as social organizations. With these distinctions in mind it is absolutely crucial to distinguish between those attributions of mental phenomena that are observer-dependent, and those attributions that are observer-independent. My present state of consciousness is entirely observer-independent. No matter what anybody thinks, I am now conscious. But the attributions of mental states that I make to my computer are observer-dependent. If I say the computer now has more *memory* than it used to have or that it *knows how* to run more word-processing programs than it used to be able to do, both of these mental attributions are obviously observer-dependent. Literally speaking, the computer does not remember anything, and it does not know anything, it is just a machine that we use for certain purposes. I think these attributions started out as metaphors, but they are evolving new literal meanings as the metaphors become dead metaphors.

Once we recognize the distinction between observer-dependent and observer-independent phenomena, then we can see that we need to distinguish three different phenomena where intentionality is concerned.

(a) Observer-independent intentionality. Example: I am now thirsty or I am now hungry.
(b) Observer-dependent intentionality, where the ascription of the intentionality is literal. Example: The French sentence "J'ai faim" means "I am hungry." Notice in this case there is nothing metaphorical about the attribution of a meaning to a French sentence. It is quite literal. But the French sentence construed as a purely formal, syntactical object has no meaning in itself, the meaning that it has is only relative to French speakers, that is, it is in my sense observer-dependent.
(c) Metaphorical attributions of intentionality. These are cases where we say, "My car is thirsty for gasoline," or "My lawn is thirsty for water." In such cases the attributions are not intended literally, and as long as no one takes them literally, there is no confusion. As I remarked earlier, attributions of intentionality to computers are passing from the non-literal metaphorical to the literal observer-dependent. But in both cases, both in the metaphorical and in the literal ascriptions, the attributions are observer-dependent. There is nothing intrinsic to the computer that makes a phenomenon a case of remembering, in the way that it is intrinsic to me and not observer-relative that I can now remember a picnic that I attended last week.

(2) *Success and failure are observer-dependent.* Computer science is correctly regarded as a branch of engineering. Engineering is, taken collectively, the set of disciplines that seek to use the results of the natural sciences to try to improve the life of human beings and improve their control over nature. Physics tells us how the world works, engineering tells us how to use that knowledge to build bridges, airplanes, and computers. This seems to me the exactly right way to understand these disciplines. However, this leads to a persistent error in the philosophical interpretations of the results of

computer science. The error is to suppose that, somehow or other, success and failure are natural categories. In the simplest terms, the assumption is that if the computer can do something as well as humans can do it, or do it better than humans can do it, that somehow or other these successes and failures are psychologically relevant. This is true both of people who are sympathetic to Artificial Intelligence, and people who are not sympathetic. Both make the same error. Thus, for example, Ray Kurzweil (Kurzweil, 1999) supposes that increased computational power by itself is evidence of psychological relevance; and Roger Penrose (Penrose, 1994) assumes that the failure of computer algorithms to match human performance in seeing the truth of unprovable sentences, as shown by Gödel, is relevant to appraising the project of Strong AI. Both of these involve a very deep mistake. The mistake is supposing that nature is about succeeding and failing. So I want to emphasize this point. Nature knows nothing of success and failure. In nature, events just happen. What we think of as succeeding and failing is relative to our consciousness, relative to our interests. And we can assume that other conscious animals also have some kind of idea of success and failure, which again is relative to their interests.

It might seem that evolutionary biology gives us examples that are exceptions to this principle. After all, is it not an objective scientific fact that certain species *succeed* in surviving and that others *fail?* Is it not also an objective scientific fact that individual members of a species can succeed from an evolutionary point of view in reproducing their genes and that other animals fail in this reproductive function? The facts of survival and extinction are, indeed, facts like any others. But the fact that we think of one as success and the other as failure is up to us. The discipline of evolutionary biology does indeed proceed *as if* organisms were trying to survive and reproduce, and were succeeding and failing in doing so. But it has to be remembered that the apparent intentionality of the success and failure involved is entirely observer-dependent. I do not believe we could do evolutionary biology as a subject without thinking in terms of inclusive fitness and corresponding success in surviving and failure to survive of species. But it does not follow from evolutionary biology that success and failure are intrinsic to nature. A plant that survives and reproduces has only "succeeded" relative to our conception of success and failure. The plant knows nothing of success and failure. The plant just has blind biochemical processes that either produce certain effects or do not produce those effects.

This is the deep fallacy embodied in the whole idea of the Turing Test. The objection of the Turing Test is not just the one I made earlier, namely that you could have the same external behavior without having the same internal processes. That I take it is an obvious point, and I hardly need to belabor it any further. But there is a more interesting error involved in the Turing Test, and that is that somehow or other succeeding and failing in our technological projects is, by itself, of scientific significance. It is not.

Nowhere was this confusion about success and failure more blatant than in all the hype that surrounded the success of the IBM team in building and programming a machine, Deep Blue, that could beat the World Chess Champion. Using new hardware that could calculate over 200 million chess moves per second, and developing a tree that could go to twelve places before assigning numerical values to the terminus points, the IBM engineers built a machine that could beat Gary Kasparov. This was a tremendous engineering achievement. Of what scientific significance, for understanding human psychology, was this result? As far as I can tell, it was of no significance whatever.

Because commercial computers were designed as labor-saving artifacts, and because we have come to measure our success and failure in designing computers in terms of their greater or lesser successes in carrying out tasks that humans can carry out, we tend to think that somehow or other the scientific significance of computation is measured in its success or failure in competing with human beings. This whole theory is a nest of mistakes. Human success and failures exist only relative to human interests. And indeed computer success and failures exist only relative to human interests. And indeed computer success and failures exist only relative to human interests because the machine does not have any psychologically real or observer-independent interests. In the case of Deep Blue, the machine did not know that it was playing chess, evaluating possible moves, or even winning and losing. It did not know any of these things, because it does not know anything. All psychological attributions made of it were observer-dependent. Indeed it did not even know that it was number-crunching or carrying out a program. In an observer-independent sense, the only things going on in the machine were very rapid state transitions in electronic circuits.

(3) *Objectivity and subjectivity.* There is a persistent mistake that pervades much of our intellectual culture, and the debates that I have had with some people in the AI community have brought it out; it is a mistake in our conception of objectivity and subjectivity. The claim is that science is by definition objective, and the implication is supposed to be that because the mental phenomena of our ordinary experience seem to be subjective, their study cannot be part of a science properly construed. This is an error. There are at least two distinctions of objectivity and subjectivity that are being

confused with each other. First there is a distinction between epistemic objectivity and subjectivity. If I say, "Calvin Coolidge was born in the United States," that claim is epistemically objective because its truth or falsity can be ascertained as a matter of fact independent of the attitudes of the observers. But if I say, "Calvin Coolidge was a great president," that claim is epistemically subjective because its truth or falsity cannot be ascertained objectively, the claim can only be made relative to people's interests and evaluations. In addition to this sense of the objective/subjective distinction, there is another sense having to do with ontology, having to do with the mode of existence of entities. In that sense, mountains and molecules, as well as planets and tectonic plates, are ontologically objective. Pains, tickles, and itches, on the other hand, are ontologically subjective. They exist only as they are experienced by human or animal subjects. The point of this distinction for the present discussion is that the ontological subjectivity of the domain of human mental life does not preclude an epistemically objective science of this domain. It is one of the many mistakes involved in a certain conception of cognitive science, that the subjectivity of our commonsense notion of the mental precludes it from being a proper subject-matter for science. This is the error of confusing ontological subjectivity and objectivity with epistemic subjectivity and objectivity. Once we recognize the existence of an ontologically subjective domain, then there is no obstacle in having an epistemically objective science of that domain.

v

What have these three points – about observer-dependence and observer-independence, the observer dependence of success and failure, and the different distinctions hiding in the objective/subjective distinction – got to do with Strong AI and the debate about the Chinese Room Argument? I think they are used to buttress the mistakes that I pointed out earlier. I pointed out that Strong AI is a weird mixture of behaviorism and dualism. It is behavioristic in accepting the Turing Test, which is a straight expression of behaviorism. If it walks like a duck and talks like a duck, etc., then it is a duck, and if it behaves exactly as if it understood Chinese then it does understand Chinese. I used to think it strange that this mistake was married to dualism, but I now see that they are a natural match. Here is how. If you accept the behavioristic criterion for the presence of the mental, then the mental is unlikely to be anything truly substantive of a biological nature. It is unlikely to be like digestion or photosynthesis or the secretion of bile, or any other natural human biological process. So the behaviorism of the Turing Test goes well with the idea that the mind is something formal and abstract. Now, the obvious falsity of this ought to strike everybody. There is nothing formal or abstract about wanting to throw up or to feeling a surge of anger. But if you accept the weird mixture of dualism and behaviorism that emerged in the twentieth century, then it will seem perfectly natural to think that the mind is not a substantive physical process, but is rather something formal and abstract. And we all know which piece of modern technology can produce things that are formal and abstract. That is precisely what computer science does. It implements formal and abstract computer programs in concrete physical hardwares. And what matters is not the hardware, since any hardware will do; what matters is the formal, abstract program.

But now, what fact about the physical system makes it the case that it has psychological properties? At this point the failure to distinguish the observer-independent and the observer-dependent features comes into play. We all feel completely comfortable in saying that our present computers have bigger memories and are much more intelligent than the computers we had ten years ago. What we are inclined to forget is that none of these attributions attributes any observer-independent features to the system. In each case the psychology is in the eye of the beholder.

And if we go deeper we can see that the failure to see the distinction between observer-dependent and observer-independent features of the world is fatal to the claims that Artificial Intelligence could ever be a branch of the natural sciences. The crucial question to ask is: what about computation? Is it observer-independent, or is it observer-dependent? Remember, of course, that the fact that something is observer-dependent, and hence to that extent ontologically subjective, does not render it epistemically subjective. But, to repeat the question, what about computation? Well, there are computations that I actually do consciously, where there is no question that the computation is observer-independent. If I add two plus two to get four, that computation goes on in me regardless of what anybody thinks. But if I say of this pocket calculator that it is computing two plus two equals four, that is only relative to our interests. We have designed it, used it, programmed it, etc., in such a way that we can use it to compute with. In short, the computation of the pocket calculator is entirely observer-dependent. And what goes for the pocket calculator goes for the commercial computer. The commercial computer has a whole lot of observer-independent features, indeed that is why we pay so much money for it. It has electrical state transitions of incredible rapidity, and we can control those and program them. But in addition to the electrical state transitions, the computation that we attribute to the computer is observer-dependent. It is only relative to our interests that we can identify those state transitions as os and 1s etc. Now, to repeat, when I say that it is observer dependent, I do not mean that it is arbitrary. You cannot use just any piece of circuitry as an and-gate or an or-gate, but it is nonetheless not a natural phenomenon.

Furthermore, we have the added mistake of supposing that success and failure are somehow or other relevant to science. That is, it is assumed, as I mentioned earlier, that increased computational capacities, Moore's Law in action, will somehow get us closer to producing a conscious computer. But this again is a mistake that comes from not understanding the basic character of the natural sciences. They investigate nature, and nature as such knows nothing of success and failure. In order to create consciousness you have to create mechanisms which can duplicate and not merely simulate the capacity of the brain to create consciousness. And by itself, the production of observer-relative success in competing with humans is no evidence at all for the presence of consciousness.

Finally, the quest for epistemic objectivity, a legitimate quest in science, is mistakenly supposed to preclude ontological subjectivity as a domain of investigation. This is such a massive error that one is amazed to see it in real life, but there it is. Rather than investigating the inner, qualitative, ontologically subjective character of human mental life, investigators in AI find the objective physical character of the computer systems, the physical symbol systems, reassuring. It seems we can only be doing real science if we change the subject and talk not about mental reality but about our electronic systems and their programs. This error is based on not seeing that you can have an epistemically objective science of a domain that is ontologically subjective. Indeed such sciences already exist. Any textbook of neurology moves without philosophical qualms between discussion of the patients' (ontologically subjective) pains, anxieties, and fears and the underlying (ontologically objective) neuronal structures that both cause these symptoms and in which they are realized.

CONCLUSION

One of the main morals to be drawn from this entire discussion is that an epistemically objective science of the mind will have to account for the existence of ontologically subjective phenomena such as consciousness and intentionality. In this science the computer will play the same role that it plays in any other science. It is a useful tool for investigation, and it is especially useful for producing simulations of natural phenomena. But the simulation should not be confused with duplication, whether the subject-matter is the mind, or anything else.

In the twenty-one years since the original publication of "Minds, brains, and programs" a remarkable development has taken place. We have come to understand a great deal more about how brains function and we are beginning to understand how they might produce consciousness. We have a long way to go and I would not wish to overestimate the progress that has been made. But it is not out of the question that we will within the lifetimes of people living today come to understand how brain processes cause consciousness and how conscious states are realized in the brain. With an understanding of the biological mechanisms of consciousness most of the problems of intentionality will also be solved, because the intentionality of vision, hearing, memory, etc. are in the first instance all cases of conscious intentionality. The unconscious forms are derivative from the conscious forms. In cognitive science there is an inexorable paradigm shift taking place: we are moving from computational cognitive science to cognitive neuroscience. To the genuine science of the brain, the fantasy of Strong Artificial Intelligence, the fantasy that simply by designing the right computer program you could create consciousness and intentionality, is irrelevant.

REFERENCES

Feyerabend, P. K. (1975), *Against Method* (London: New Left Books).

Hofstadter, D., and Dennett, D. C. (eds.) (1981), *The Mind's I: Fantasies and Reflections on Self and Soul* (New York: Basic Books).

Kuhn, T. S. (1962), *The Structure of Scientific Revolutions* (Chicago: University of Chicago Press).

(1970), *The Structure of Scientific Revolutions*, 2nd edn. (Chicago: University of Chicago Press).

Kurzweil, R. (1999), *The Age of Spiritual Machines* (New York: Viking).

Penrose, R. (1994), *Shadows of the Mind: A Search for the Missing Science of Consciousness* (Oxford: Oxford University Press).

Popper, K. R. (1959), *The Logic of Scientific Discovery* (London: Hutchinson).

Stove, D. C. (1999), *Against the Idols of the Age*, ed. R. Kimball (New Brunswick: Transaction Publishers).

CHAPTER 5

Is the brain a digital computer?

Presidential Address delivered before the Sixty-fourth Annual Pacific Division Meeting of the American Philosophical Association in Los Angeles, California, March 30, 1990.

I. INTRODUCTION, STRONG AI, WEAK AI AND COGNITIVISM

There are different ways to present a Presidential Address to the APA; the one I have chosen is simply to report on work that I am doing right now, on work in progress. I am going to present some of my further explorations into the computational model of the mind.[1]

The basic idea of the computer model of the mind is that the mind is the program and the brain the hardware of a computational system. A slogan one often sees is "the mind is to the brain as the program is to the hardware."[2]

Let us begin our investigation of this claim by distinguishing three questions:

(1) Is the brain a digital computer?
(2) Is the mind a computer program?
(3) Can the operations of the brain be simulated on a digital computer?

I will be addressing 1 and not 2 or 3. I think 2 can be decisively answered in the negative. Since programs are defined purely formally or syntactically and since minds have an intrinsic mental content, it follows immediately that the program by itself cannot constitute the mind. The formal syntax of the program does not by itself guarantee the presence of mental contents.

---

[1] For earlier explorations see Searle (1980) and Searle (1984).
[2] This view is announced and defended in a large number of books and articles many of which appear to have more or less the same title, e.g. *Computers and Thought* (Feigenbaum and Feldman, 1963), *Computers and Thought* (Sharples *et al.*, 1988), *The computer and the Mind* (Johnson-Laird, 1988), *Computation and Cognition* (Pylyshyn, 1985), "The computer model of the mind" (Block, 1990), and of course, "Computing machinery and intelligence" (Turing, 1950).

I showed this a decade ago in the Chinese Room Argument (Searle, 1980). A computer, me for example, could run the steps of the program for some mental capacity, such as understanding Chinese, without understanding a word of Chinese. The argument rests on the simple logical truth that syntax is not the same as, nor is it by itself sufficient for, semantics. So the answer to the second question is obviously "No."

The answer to 3, seems to me equally obviously "Yes," at least on a natural interpretation. That is, naturally interpreted, the question means: Is there some description of the brain such that under that description you could do a computational simulation of the operations of the brain? But since according to Church's thesis, anything that can be given a precise enough characterization as a set of steps can be simulated on a digital computer, it follows trivially that the question has an affirmative answer. The operations of the brain can be simulated on a digital computer in the same sense in which weather systems, the behavior of the New York stock market or the pattern of airline flights over Latin America can. So our question is not, "Is the mind a program?" The answer to that is, "No." Nor is it, "Can the brain be simulated?" The answer to that is, "Yes." The question is, "Is the brain a digital computer?" And for purposes of this discussion I am taking that question as equivalent to: "Are brain processes computational?"

One might think that this question would lose much of its interest if question 2 receives a negative answer. That is, one might suppose that unless the mind is a program, there is no interest to the question whether the brain is a computer. But that is not really the case. Even for those who agree that programs by themselves are not constitutive of mental phenomena, there is still an important question: Granted that there is more to the mind than the syntactical operations of the digital computer; nonetheless, it might be the case that mental states are *at least* computational states and mental processes are computational processes operating over the formal structure of these mental states. This, in fact, seems to me the position taken by a fairly large number of people.

I am not saying that the view is fully clear, but the idea is something like this: At some level of description brain processes are syntactical; there are so to speak, "sentences in the head." These need not be sentences in English or Chinese, but perhaps in the "Language of Thought" (Fodor, 1975). Now, like any sentences, they have a syntactical structure and a semantics or meaning, and the problem of syntax can be separated from the problem of semantics. The problem of semantics is: How do these sentences in the head get their meanings? But that question can be discussed independently of the question: How does the brain work in processing these sentences? A typical answer to that latter question is: The brain works as a digital computer performing computational operations over the syntactical structure of sentences in the head.

Just to keep the terminology straight, I call the view that all there is to having a mind is having a program Strong AI, the view that brain processes (and mental processes) can be simulated computationally Weak AI, and the view that the brain is a digital computer Cognitivism.

This paper is about Cognitivism, and I had better say at the beginning what motivates it. If you read books about the brain (say Shepherd, 1983 or Kuffler and Nicholls, 1976) you get a certain picture of what is going on in the brain. If you then turn to books about computation (say Boolos and Jeffrey, 1989) you get a picture of the logical structure of the theory of computation. If you then turn to books about cognitive science (say Pylyshyn, 1985) they tell you that what the brain books describe is really the same as what the computability books were describing. Philosophically speaking, this does not smell right to me and I have learned, at least at the beginning of an investigation, to follow my sense of smell.

II. THE PRIMAL STORY

I want to begin the discussion by trying to state as strongly as I can why Cognitivism has seemed intuitively appealing. There is a story about the relation of human intelligence to computation that goes back at least to Turing's classic paper (1950), and I believe it is the foundation of the Cognitivist view. I will call it the Primal Story:

We begin with two results in mathematical logic, the Church-Turing thesis (sometimes called Church's thesis) and Turing's theorem. For our purposes, the Church-Turing thesis states that for any algorithm there is some Turing machine that can implement that algorithm. Turing's theorem says that there is a Universal Turing Machine which can simulate any Turing machine. Now if we put these two together we have the result that a Universal Turing Machine can implement any algorithm whatever.

But now, what made this result so exciting? What made it send shivers up and down the spines of a whole generation of young workers in Artificial Intelligence is the following thought: Suppose the brain is a Universal Turing Machine.

Well, are there any good reasons for supposing the brain might be a Universal Turing Machine? Let us continue with the Primal Story.

It is clear that at least some human mental abilities are algorithmic. For example, I can consciously do long division by going through the steps of an algorithm for solving long division problems. It is furthermore a consequence of the Church-Turing thesis and Turing's theorem that anything a human can do algorithmically can be done on a Universal Turing Machine. I can implement, for example, the very same algorithm that I use for long division on a digital computer. In such a case, as described by Turing (1950), both I, the human computer, and the mechanical computer are implementing the same algorithm; I am doing it consciously, the mechanical computer non-consciously. Now it seems reasonable to suppose there might also be a whole lot of mental processes going on in my brain non-consciously which are also computational. And if so, we could find out how the brain works by simulating these very processes on a digital computer. Just as we got a computer simulation of the processes for doing long division, so we could get a computer simulation of the processes for understanding language, visual perception, categorization, etc.

"But what about semantics? After all, programs are purely syntactical." Here another set of logico-mathematical results comes into play in the Primal Story.

The development of proof theory showed that within certain well-known limits the semantic relations between propositions can be entirely mirrored by the syntactic relations between the sentences that express those propositions. Now suppose that mental contents in the head are expressed syntactically in the head, then all we would need to account for mental processes would be computational processes between the syntactical elements in the head. If we get the proof theory right the semantics will take care of itself; and that is what computers do: they implement the proof theory.

We thus have a well-defined research program. We try to discover the programs being implemented in the brain by programming computers to implement the same programs. We do this in turn by getting the mechanical computer to match the performance of the human computer (i.e. to pass the Turing Test) and then getting the psychologists to look for evidence that the internal processes are the same in the two types of computer.

Now in what follows I would like the reader to keep this Primal Story in mind – notice especially Turing's contrast between the conscious implementation of the program by the human computer and the non-conscious implementation of programs, whether by the brain or by the mechanical computer; notice furthermore the idea that we might just *discover* programs running in nature, the very same programs that we put into our mechanical computers.

If one looks at the books and articles supporting Cognitivism one finds certain common assumptions, often unstated, but nonetheless pervasive.

First, it is often assumed that the only alternative to the view that the brain is a digital computer is some form of dualism. The idea is that unless you believe in the existence of immortal Cartesian souls, you must believe that the brain is a computer. Indeed, it often seems to be assumed that the question whether the brain is a physical mechanism determining our mental states and whether the brain is a digital computer are the same question. Rhetorically speaking, the idea is to bully the reader into thinking that unless he accepts the idea that the brain is some kind of computer, he is committed to some weird anti-scientific views. Recently the field has opened up a bit to allow that the brain might not be an old-fashioned von Neumann-style digital computer, but rather a more sophisticated kind of parallel processing computational equipment. Still, to deny that the brain is computational is to risk losing your membership in the scientific community.

Second, it is also assumed that the question whether brain processes are computational is just a plain empirical question. It is to be settled by factual investigation in the same way that such questions as whether the heart is a pump or whether green leaves do photosynthesis were settled as matters of fact. There is no room for logic chopping or conceptual analysis, since we are talking about matters of hard scientific fact. Indeed I think many people who work in this field would doubt that the title of this paper poses an appropriate philosophic question at all. "Is the brain really a digital computer?" is no more a philosophical question than "Is the neurotransmitter at neuro-muscular junctions really acetylcholene?"

Even people who are unsympathetic to Cognitivism, such as Penrose and Dreyfus, seem to treat it as a straightforward factual issue. They do not seem to be worried about the question what sort of claim it might be that they are doubting. But I am puzzled by the question: What sort of fact about the brain could constitute its being a computer?

Third, another stylistic feature of this literature is the haste and sometimes even carelessness with which the foundational questions are glossed over. What exactly are the anatomical and physiological features of brains that are being discussed? What exactly is a digital computer? And how are the answers to these two questions supposed to connect? The usual procedure in these books and articles is to make a few remarks about 0's and 1's, give a popular summary of the Church-Turing thesis, and then get on with the more exciting things such as computer achievements and failures. To my surprise in reading this literature I have found that there seems to be a peculiar philosophical hiatus. On the one hand, we have a very elegant set of mathematical results ranging from Turing's theorem to

Church's thesis to recursive function theory. On the other hand, we have an impressive set of electronic devices which we use every day. Since we have such advanced mathematics and such good electronics, we assume that somehow somebody must have done the basic philosophical work of connecting the mathematics to the electronics. But as far as I can tell that is not the case. On the contrary, we are in a peculiar situation where there is little theoretical agreement among the practitioners on such absolutely fundamental questions as, What exactly is a digital computer? What exactly is a symbol? What exactly is a computational process? Under what physical conditions exactly are two systems implementing the same program?

III. THE DEFINITION OF COMPUTATION

Since there is no universal agreement on the fundamental questions, I believe it is best to go back to the sources, back to the original definitions given by Alan Turing.

According to Turing, a Turing machine can carry out certain elementary operations: It can rewrite a 0 on its tape as a 1, it can rewrite a 1 on its tape as a 0, it can shift the tape one square to the left, or it can shift the tape one square to the right. It is controlled by a program of instruction and each instruction specifies a condition and an action to be carried out if the condition is satisfied.

That is the standard definition of computation, but, taken literally, it is at least a bit misleading. If you open up your home computer you are most unlikely to find any 0s and 1s or even a tape. But this does not really matter for the definition. To find out if an object is really a digital computer, it turns out that we do not actually have to look for 0s and 1s, etc.; rather we just have to look for something that we could *treat as* or *count as* or *could be used to* function as 0s and 1s. Furthermore, to make the matter more puzzling, it turns out that this machine could be made out of just about anything. As Johnson-Laird says, "It could be made out of cogs and levers like an old fashioned mechanical calculator; it could be made out of a hydraulic system through which water flows; it could be made out of transistors etched into a silicon chip through which an electrical current flows. It could even be carried out by the brain. Each of these machines uses a different medium to represent binary symbols – the positions of cogs, the presence or absence of water, the level of the voltage and perhaps nerve impulses" (Johnson Laird, 1988: 39).

Similar remarks are made by most of the people who write on this topic. For example, Ned Block (1990), shows how we can have electrical gates where the 1s and 0s are assigned to voltage levels of 4 volts and 7 volts respectively. So we might think that we should go and look for voltage levels. But Block tells us that 1 is only "conventionally" assigned to a certain voltage level. The situation grows more puzzling when he informs us further that we did not need to use electricity at all but we could have used an elaborate system of cats and mice and cheese and make our gates in such a way that the cat will strain at the leash and pull open a gate which we can also treat as if it were a 0 or 1. The point, as Block is anxious to insist, is "the irrelevance of hardware realization to computational description. These gates work in different ways but they are nonetheless computationally equivalent" (p. 260). In the same vein, Pylyshyn says that a computational sequence could be realized by "a group of pigeons trained to peck as a Turing machine!" (Pylyshyn, 1985: 57).

But now if we are trying to take seriously the idea that the brain is a digital computer, we get the uncomfortable result that we could make a system that does just what the brain does out of pretty much anything. Computationally speaking, on this view, you can make a "brain" that functions just like yours and mine out of cats and mice and cheese or levers or water pipes or pigeons or anything else provided the two systems are, in Block's sense, "computationally equivalent." You would just need an awful lot of cats, or pigeons, or water pipes, or whatever it might be. The proponents of Cognitivism report this result with sheer and unconcealed delight. But I think they ought to be worried about it, and I am going to try to show that it is just the tip of a whole iceberg of problems.

IV. FIRST DIFFICULTY: SYNTAX IS NOT INTRINSIC TO PHYSICS

Why are the defenders of computationalism not worried by the implications of multiple realizability? The answer is that they think it is typical of functional accounts that the same function admits of multiple realizations. In this respect, computers are just like carburetors and thermostats. Just as carburetors can be made of brass or steel, so computers can be made of an indefinite range of hardware materials.

But there is a difference: The classes of carburetors and thermostats are defined in terms of the production of certain *physical* effects. That is why, for example, nobody says you can make carburetors out of pigeons. But the class of computers is defined syntactically in terms of the *assignment* of 0s and 1s. The multiple realizability is a consequence not of the fact that the same physical effect can be achieved in different physical substances, but that the relevant properties are purely syntactical. The physics is irrelevant except insofar as it admits of the assignments of os and 1s and of state transitions between them.

But this has two consequences which might be disastrous:

(1) The same principle that implies multiple realizability would seem to imply universal realizability. If computation is defined in terms of the assignment of syntax then everything would be a digital computer, because any object whatever could have syntactical ascriptions made to it. You could describe anything in terms of os and 1s.

(2) Worse yet, syntax is not intrinsic to physics. The ascription of syntactical properties is always relative to an agent or observer who treats certain physical phenomena as syntactical.

Now why exactly would these consequences be disastrous?

Well, we wanted to know how the brain works, specifically how it produces mental phenomena. And it would not answer that question to be told that the brain is a digital computer in the sense in which stomach, liver, heart, solar system, and the state of Kansas are all digital computers. The model we had was that we might discover some fact about the operation of the brain which would show that it is a computer. We wanted to know if there was not some sense in which brains were *intrinsically* digital computers in a way that green leaves intrinsically perform photosynthesis or hearts intrinsically pump blood. It is not a matter of us arbitrarily or "conventionally" assigning the word "pump" to hearts or "photosynthesis" to leaves. There is an actual fact of the matter. And what we were asking is, "Is there in that way a fact of the matter about brains that would make them digital computers?" It does not answer that question to be told, yes, brains are digital computers because everything is a digital computer.

On the standard textbook definition of computation,

(1) For any object there is some description of that object such that under that description the object is a digital computer.

(2) For any program there is some sufficiently complex object such that there is some description of the object under which it is implementing the program. Thus, for example, the wall behind my back is right now implementing the Wordstar program, because there is some pattern of molecule movements which is isomorphic with the formal structure of Wordstar. But if the wall is implementing Wordstar then if it is a big enough wall it is implementing any program, including any program implemented in the brain.

I think the main reason that the proponents do not see that multiple or universal realizability is a problem is that they do not see it as a consequence of a much deeper point, namely that the "syntax" is not the name of a physical feature, like mass or gravity. On the contrary they talk of "syntactical engines" and even "semantic engines" as if such talk were like that of gasoline engines or diesel engines, as if it could be just a plain matter of fact that the brain or anything else is a syntactical engine.

I think it is probably possible to block the result of universal realizability by tightening up our definition of computation. Certainly we ought to respect the fact that programmers and engineers regard it as a quirk of Turing's original definitions and not as a real feature of computation. Unpublished works by Brian Smith, Vinod Goel, and John Batali all suggest that a more realistic definition of computation will emphasize such features as the causal relations among program states, programmability and controllability of the mechanism, and situatedness in the real world. But these further restrictions on the definition of computation are no help in the present discussion because the really deep problem is that syntax is essentially an observer-relative notion. The multiple realizability of computationally equivalent processes in different physical media was not just a sign that the processes were abstract, but that they were not intrinsic to the system at all. They depended on an interpretation from outside. We were looking for some facts of the matter which would make brain processes computational; but given the way we have defined computation, there never could be any such facts of the matter. We can't, on the one hand, say that anything is a digital computer if we can assign a syntax to it and then suppose there is a factual question intrinsic to its physical operation whether or not a natural system such as the brain is a digital computer.

And if the word "syntax" seems puzzling, the same point can be stated without it. That is, someone might claim that the notions of "syntax" and "symbols" are just a manner of speaking and that what we are really interested in is the existence of systems with discrete physical phenomena and state transitions between them. On this view we don't really need 0s and 1s; they are just a convenient shorthand. But, I believe, this move is no help. A physical state of a system is a computational state only relative to the assignment to that state of some computational role, function, or interpretation. The same problem arises without 0s and 1s because notions such as computation, algorithm, and program do not name intrinsic physical features of systems. Computational states are not *discovered within* the physics, they are *assigned* to the physics.

This is a different argument from the Chinese Room Argument and I should have seen it ten years ago but I did not. The Chinese Room Argument showed that semantics is not intrinsic to syntax. I am now making the separate and different point that syntax is not intrinsic to physics. For the purposes of the original argument I was simply assuming that the syntactical characterization of the computer was unproblematic. But that is a mistake. There is no way you could discover that something is intrinsically a digital computer because the characterization of it as a digital computer is always relative to an observer who assigns a syntactical interpretation to the purely physical features of the system. As applied to the Language of Thought hypothesis, this has the consequence that the thesis is incoherent. There is no way you could discover that there are, intrinsically, unknown sentences in your head because something is a sentence only relative to some agent or user who uses it as a sentence. As applied to the computational model generally, the characterization of a process as computational is a characterization of a physical system from outside; and the identification of the process as computational does not identify an intrinsic feature of the physics, it is essentially an observer-relative characterization.

This point has to be understood precisely. I am not saying there are a priori limits on the patterns we could discover in nature. We could no doubt discover a pattern of events in my brain that was isomorphic to the implementation of the vi program on this computer. But to say that something is *functioning as* a computational process is to say something more than that a pattern of physical events is occurring. It requires the assignment of a computational interpretation by some agent. Analogously, we might discover in nature objects which had the same sort of shape as chairs and which could therefore be used as chairs; but we could not discover objects in nature which were functioning as chairs, except relative to some agents who regarded them or used them as chairs.

V. SECOND DIFFICULTY: THE HOMUNCULUS FALLACY IS ENDEMIC TO COGNITIVISM

So far, we seem to have arrived at a problem. Syntax is not part of physics. This has the consequence that if computation is defined syntactically then nothing is intrinsically a digital computer solely in virtue of its physical properties. Is there any way out of this problem? Yes, there is, and it is a way standardly taken in cognitive science, but it is out of the frying pan and into the fire. Most of the works I have seen in the computational theory of the mind commit some variation on the homunculus fallacy. The idea always is to treat the brain as if there were some agent inside it using it to compute with. A typical case is David Marr (1982), who describes the task of vision as proceeding from a two-dimensional visual array on the retina to a three-dimensional description of the external world as output of the visual system. The difficulty is: Who is reading the description? Indeed, it looks throughout Marr's book, and in other standard works on the subject, as if we have to invoke a homunculus inside the system in order to treat its operations as genuinely computational.

Many writers feel that the homunculus fallacy is not really a problem, because, with Dennett (1978), they feel that the homunculus can be "discharged." The idea is this: Since the computational operations of the computer can be analyzed into progressively simpler units, until eventually we reach simple flip-flop, "yes-no," "1-0" patterns, it seems that the higher-level homunculi can be discharged with progressively stupider homunculi, until finally we reach the bottom level of a simple flip-flop that involves no real homunculus at all. The idea, in short, is that recursive decomposition will eliminate the homunculi.

It took me a long time to figure out what these people were driving at, so in case someone else is similarly puzzled I will explain an example in detail: Suppose that we have a computer that multiplies six times eight to get forty-eight. Now we ask, "How does it do it?" Well, the answer might be that it adds six to itself seven times.[3] But if you ask, "How does it add six to itself seven times?", the answer might be that, first, it converts all of the numerals into binary notation, and second, it applies a simple algorithm for operating on binary notation until finally we reach the bottom level at which the only instructions are of the form, "Print a zero, erase a one." So, for example, at the top level our intelligent homunculus says, "I know how to multiply six times eight to get forty-eight." But at the next lower level he is replaced by a stupider homunculus who says, "I do not actually know how to do multiplication, but I can do addition." Below him are some stupider ones who say, "We do not actually know how to do addition or multiplication, but we know how to convert decimal to binary." Below these are stupider ones who say, "We do not know anything about any of this stuff, but we know how to operate on binary symbols." At the bottom level are a whole bunch of homunculi who just say, "Zero one, zero one." All of the higher levels reduce to this bottom level. Only the bottom level really exists; the top levels are all just *as-if.*

---

[3] People sometimes say that it would have to add six to itself *eight* times. But that is bad arithmetic. Six added to itself eight times is fifty-four, because six added to itself zero times is still six. It is amazing how often this mistake is made.

Various authors (e.g. Haugeland, 1981, Block, 1990) describe this feature when they say that the system is a syntactical engine driving a semantic engine. But we still must face the question we had before: What facts intrinsic to the system make it syntactical? What facts about the bottom level or any other level make these operations into zeros and ones? *Without a homunculus that stands outside the recursive decomposition, we do not even have a syntax to operate with.* The attempt to eliminate the homunculus fallacy through recursive decomposition fails, because the only way to get the syntax intrinsic to the physics is to put a homunculus in the physics.

There is a fascinating feature to all of this. Cognitivists cheerfully concede that the higher levels of computation, e.g. "multiply 6 times 8," are observer relative; there is nothing really there that corresponds directly to multiplication; it is all in the eye of the homunculus/beholder. But they want to stop this concession at the lower levels. The electronic circuit, they admit, does not really multiply 6×8 as such, but it really does manipulate 0s and 1s and these manipulations, so to speak, add up to multiplication. But to concede that the higher levels of computation are not intrinsic to the physics is already to concede that the lower levels are not intrinsic either. So the homunculus fallacy is still with us.

For real computers of the kind you buy in the store, there is no homunculus problem; each user is the homunculus in question. But if we are to suppose that the brain is a digital computer, we are still faced with the question "And who is the user?" Typical homunculus questions in cognitive science are such as the following: "How does the visual system compute shape from shading; how does it compute object distance from size of retinal image?" A parallel question would be, "How do nails compute the distance they are to travel in the board from the impact of the hammer and the density of the wood?" And the answer is the same in both sorts of case: If we are talking about how the system works intrinsically neither nails nor visual systems compute anything. We as outside homunculi might describe them computationally, and it is often useful to do so. But you do not understand hammering by supposing that nails are somehow intrinsically implementing hammering algorithms and you do not understand vision by supposing the system is implementing, e.g., the shape from shading algorithm.

VI. THIRD DIFFICULTY: SYNTAX HAS NO CAUSAL POWERS

Certain sorts of explanations in the natural sciences specify mechanisms which function causally in the production of the phenomena to be explained. This is especially common in the biological sciences. Think of the germ theory of disease, the account of photosynthesis, the DNA theory of inherited traits, and even the Darwinian theory of natural selection. In each case a causal mechanism is specified, and in each case the specification gives an explanation of the output of the mechanism. Now if you go back and look at the Primal Story it seems clear that this is the sort of explanation promised by Cognitivism. The mechanisms by which brain processes produce cognition are supposed to be computational, and by specifying the programs we will have specified the causes of cognition. One beauty of this research program, often remarked, is that we do not need to know the details of brain functioning in order to explain cognition. Brain processes provide only the hardware implementation of the cognitive programs, but the program level is where the real cognitive explanations are given. On the standard account, as stated by Newell, for example, there are three levels of explanation, hardware, program, and intentionality (Newell calls this last level the knowledge level), and the special contribution of cognitive science is made at the program level.

But if what I have said so far is correct, then there is something fishy about this whole project. I used to believe that as a causal account the cognitivist's theory was at least false; but I now am having difficulty formulating a version of it that is coherent even to the point where it could be an empirical thesis at all. The thesis is that there is a whole lot of symbols being manipulated in the brain, 0s and 1s flashing through the brain at lightning speed and invisible not only to the naked eye but even to the most powerful electron microscope, and it is these which cause cognition. But the difficulty is that the 0s and 1s as such have no causal powers at all because they do not even exist except in the eyes of the beholder. The implemented program has no causal powers other than those of the implementing medium because the program has no real existence, no ontology, beyond that of the implementing medium. Physically speaking there is no such thing as a separate "program level."

You can see this if you go back to the Primal Story and remind yourself of the difference between the mechanical computer and Turing's human computer. In Turing's human computer there really is a program level intrinsic to the system and it is functioning causally at that level to convert input to output. This is because the human is consciously following the rules for doing a certain computation, and this causally explains his performance. But when we program the mechanical computer to perform the same computation, the assignment of a computational interpretation is now relative to us, the outside homunculi. And there is no longer a level of intentional causation intrinsic to the system. The human computer is consciously following rules, and this fact explains his behavior, but the mechanical computer is not literally following any rules at all. It is designed to behave exactly as if it were following rules, and so for practical, commercial purposes it does not matter. Now Cognitivism tells us that the brain functions like the commercial computer and this causes cognition. But without a homunculus, both commercial computer and brain have only patterns and the patterns have no causal powers in addition to those of the implementing media. So it seems there is no way Cognitivism *could* give a causal account of cognition.

However there is a puzzle for my view. Anyone who works with computers even casually knows that we often do in fact give causal explanations that appeal to the program. For example, we can say that when I hit this key I got such and such results because the machine is implementing the vi program and not the emacs program; and this looks like an ordinary causal explanation. So the puzzle is, how do we reconcile the fact that syntax, as such, has no causal powers with the fact that we do give causal explanations that appeal to programs? And, more pressingly, would these sorts of explanations provide an appropriate model for Cognitivism, will they rescue Cognitivism? Could we, for example, rescue the analogy with thermostats by pointing out that just as the notion "thermostat" figures in causal explanations independently of any reference to the physics of its implementation, so the notion "program" might be explanatory while equally independent of the physics?

To explore this puzzle let us try to make the case for Cognitivism by extending the Primal Story to show how the Cognitivist investigative procedures work in actual research practice. The idea, typically, is to program a commercial computer so that it simulates some cognitive capacity, such as vision or language. Then, if we get a good simulation, one that gives us at least Turing equivalence, we hypothesize that the brain computer is running the same program as the commercial computer, and to test the hypothesis we look for indirect psychological evidence, such as reaction times. So it seems that we can causally explain the behavior of the brain computer by citing the program in exactly the same sense in which we can explain the behavior of the commercial computer. Now what is wrong with that? Doesn't it sound like a perfectly legitimate scientific research program? We know that the commercial computer's conversion of input to output is explained by a program, and in the brain we discover the same program, hence we have a causal explanation.

Two things ought to worry us immediately about this project. First, we would never accept this mode of explanation for any function of the brain where we actually understood how it worked at the neurobiological level. Second, we would not accept it for other sorts of system that we can simulate computationally. To illustrate the first point, consider for example, the famous account of "What the Frog's Eye Tells the Frog's Brain" (Lettvin *et al.*, 1959 in McCulloch, 1965). The account is given entirely in terms of the anatomy and physiology of the frog's nervous system. A typical passage, chosen at random, goes like this:

1. Sustained Contrast Detectors

An unmyelinated axon of this group does not respond when the general illumination is turned on or off. If the sharp edge of an object either lighter or darker than the background moves into its field and stops, it discharges promptly and continues discharging, no matter what the shape of the edge or whether the object is smaller or larger than the receptive field. (p. 239)

I have never heard anyone say that all this is just the hardware implementation, and that they should have figured out which program the frog was implementing. I do not doubt that you could do a computer simulation of the frog's "bug detectors." Perhaps someone has done it. But we all know that once you understand how the frog's visual system actually works, the "computational level" is just irrelevant.

To illustrate the second point, consider simulations of other sorts of systems. I am, for example, typing these words on a machine that simulates the behavior of an old-fashioned mechanical typewriter.[4] As simulations go, the word-processing program simulates a typewriter better than any AI program I know of simulates the brain. But no sane person thinks: "At long last we understand how typewriters work, they are implementations of word processing programs." It is simply not the case in general that computational simulations provide causal explanations of the phenomena simulated.

So what is going on? We do not in general suppose that computational simulations of brain processes give us any explanations in place of or in addition to neurobiological accounts of how the brain actually works. And we do not in general take "X is a computational simulation of Y" to name a symmetrical relation. That is, we do not suppose that because the computer simulates a typewriter that therefore the typewriter simulates a computer. We do not suppose that because a weather program simulates a hurricane, that the causal explanation of the behavior of the hurricane is provided by the program. So why should we make an exception to

---

[4] The example was suggested by John Batali.

these principles where unknown brain processes are concerned? Are there any good grounds for making the exception? And what kind of a causal explanation is an explanation that cites a formal program?

Here, I believe, is the solution to our puzzle. Once you remove the homunculus from the system, you are left only with a pattern of events to which someone from the outside could attach a computational interpretation. Now the only sense in which the specification of the pattern by itself provides a causal explanation is that if you know that a certain pattern exists in a system you know that some cause or other is responsible for the pattern. So you can, for example, predict later stages from earlier stages. Furthermore, if you already know that the system has been programmed by an outside homunculus, you can give explanations that make reference to the intentionality of the homunculus. You can say, e.g., this machine behaves the way it does because it is running vi. That is like explaining that this book begins with a bit about happy families and does not contain any long passages about a bunch of brothers, because it is Tolstoy's *Anna Karenina* and not Dostoevsky's *The Brothers Karamazov*. But you cannot explain a physical system such as a typewriter or a brain by identifying a pattern which it shares with its computational simulation, because the existence of the pattern does not explain how the system actually works *as a physical system*. In the case of cognition the pattern is at much too high a level of abstraction to explain such concrete mental (and therefore physical) events as the occurrence of a visual perception or the understanding of a sentence.

Now, I think it is obvious that we cannot explain how typewriters and hurricanes work by pointing to formal patterns they share with their computational simulations. Why is it not obvious in the case of the brain?

Here we come to the second part of our solution to the puzzle. In making the case for Cognitivism we were tacitly supposing that the brain might be implementing algorithms for cognition, in the same sense that Turing's human computer and his mechanical computer implement algorithms. But it is precisely that assumption which we have seen to be mistaken. To see this, ask yourself what happens when a system implements an algorithm. In the human computer the system consciously goes through the steps of the algorithm, so the process is both causal and logical; logical, because the algorithm provides a set of rules for deriving the output symbols from the input symbols; causal, because the agent is making a conscious effort to go through the steps. Similarly in the case of the mechanical computer, the whole system includes an outside homunculus, and with the homunculus the system is both causal and logical; logical, because the homunculus provides an interpretation to the processes of the machine; and causal, because the hardware of the machine causes it to go through the processes. But these conditions cannot be met by the brute, blind non-conscious neurophysiological operations of the brain. In the brain computer there is no conscious intentional implementation of the algorithm as there is in the mechanical computer either, because that requires an outside homunculus to attach a human computer, but there can't be any non-conscious implementation as there is in the computational interpretation to the physical events. The most we could find in the brain is a pattern of events which is formally similar to the implemented program in the mechanical computer, but that pattern, as such, has no causal powers to call its own and hence explains nothing.

In sum, the fact that the attribution of syntax identifies no further causal powers is fatal to the claim that programs provide causal explanations of cognition. To explore the consequences of this, let us remind ourselves of what Cognitivist explanations actually look like. Explanations such as Chomsky's account of the syntax of natural languages or Marr's account of vision proceed by stating a set of rules according to which a symbolic input is converted into a symbolic output. In Chomsky's case, for example, a single input symbol, S, is converted into any one of a potentially infinite number of sentences by the repeated application of a set of syntactical rules. In Marr's case, representations of a two-dimensional visual array are converted into three-dimensional "descriptions" of the world in accordance with certain algorithms. Marr's tripartite distinctions between the computational task, the algorithmic solution of the task and the hardware implementation of the algorithm has (like Newell's distinctions) become famous as a statement of the general pattern of the explanation.

If you take these explanations naively, as I do, it is best to think of them as saying that it is just as if a man alone in a room were going through a set of steps of following rules to generate English sentences or 3D descriptions, as the case might be. But now, let us ask what facts in the real world are supposed to correspond to these explanations as applied to the brain. In Chomsky's case, for example, we are not supposed to think that the agent consciously goes through a set of repeated applications of rules; nor are we supposed to think that he is unconsciously thinking his way through the set of rules. Rather the rules are "computational" and the brain is carrying out the computations. But what does that mean? Well, we are supposed to think that it is just like a commercial computer. The sort of thing that corresponds to the ascription of the same set of rules to a commercial computer is supposed to correspond to the ascription of those rules to the brain. But we have seen that in the commercial computer the ascription is always observer relative, the ascription is made relative to a homunculus who assigns computational interpretations to the hardware states. Without the homunculus there is no computation, just an electronic circuit. So how do we get computation into the brain without a homunculus? As far as I know, neither Chomsky nor Marr ever addressed the question or even thought there was such a question. But without a homunculus there is no explanatory power to the postulation of the program states. There is just a physical mechanism, the brain, with its various real physical and physical/mental causal levels of description.

VII. FOURTH DIFFICULTY: THE BRAIN DOES NOT DO INFORMATION PROCESSING

In this section I turn finally to what I think is, in some ways, the central issue in all of this, the issue of information processing. Many people in the "cognitive science" scientific paradigm will feel that much of my discussion is simply irrelevant and they will argue against it as follows:

There is a difference between the brain and all of these other systems you have been describing, and this difference explains why a computational simulation in the case of the other systems is a mere simulation, whereas in the case of the brain a computational simulation is actually duplicating and not merely modeling the functional properties of the brain. The reason is that the brain, unlike these other systems, is an *information-processing* system. And this fact about the brain is, in your words, "intrinsic." It is just a fact about biology that the brain functions to process information, and since we can also process the same information computationally, computational models of brain processes have a different role altogether from computational models of, for example, the weather. So there is a well-defined research question: "Are the computational procedures by which the brain processes information the same as the procedures by which computers process the same information?"

What I just imagined an opponent saying embodies one of the worst mistakes in cognitive science. The mistake is to suppose that in the sense in which computers are used to process information, brains also process information. To see that that is a mistake, contrast what goes on in the computer with what goes on in the brain. In the case of the computer, an outside agent encodes some information in a form that can be processed by the circuitry of the computer. That is, he or she provides a syntactical realization of the information that the computer can implement in, for example, different voltage levels. The computer then goes through a series of electrical stages that the outside agent can interpret both syntactically and semantically even though, of course, the hardware has no intrinsic syntax or semantics: It is all in the eye of the beholder. And the physics does not matter provided only that you can get it to implement the algorithm. Finally, an output is produced in the form of physical phenomena which an observer can interpret as symbols with a syntax and a semantics.

But now contrast that with the brain. In the case of the brain, none of the relevant neurobiological processes are observer relative (though of course, like anything, they can be described from an observer-relative point of view) and the specificity of the neurophysiology matters desperately. To make this difference clear, let us go through an example. Suppose I see a car coming toward me. A standard computational model of vision will take in information about the visual array on my retina and eventually print out the sentence, "There is a car coming toward me." But that is not what happens in the actual biology. In the biology a concrete and specific series of electro-chemical reactions are set up by the assault of the photons on the photo receptor cells of my retina, and this entire process eventually results in a concrete visual experience. The biological reality is not that of a bunch of words or symbols being produced by the visual system, rather it is a matter of a concrete, specific, conscious visual event; this very visual experience. Now, that concrete visual event is as specific and as concrete as a hurricane or the digestion of a meal. We can, with the computer, do an information-processing model of that event or of its production, as we can do an information-processing model of the weather, digestion, or any other phenomenon, but the phenomena themselves are not thereby information-processing systems.

In short, the sense of information processing that is used in cognitive science is at much too high a level of abstraction to capture the concrete biological reality of intrinsic intentionality. The "information" in the brain is always specific to some modality or other. It is specific to thought, or vision, or hearing, or touch, for example. The level of information process-ing which is described in the cognitive science computational models of cognition, on the other hand, is simply a matter of getting a set of symbols as output in response to a set of symbols as input.

We are blinded to this difference by the fact that the same sentence, "I see a car coming toward me," can be used to record both the visual intentionality and the output of the computational model of vision. But this should not obscure from us the fact that the visual experience is a concrete event and is produced in the brain by specific electro-chemical biological processes. To confuse these events and processes with formal symbol manipulation is to confuse the reality with the model. The upshot of this part of the discussion is that in the sense of "information" used in cognitive science, it is simply false to say that the brain is an information-processing device.

VIII. SUMMARY OF THE ARGUMENT

This brief argument has a simple logical structure and I will lay it out:

(1) On the standard textbook definition, computation is defined syntactically in terms of symbol manipulation.

(2) But syntax and symbols are not defined in terms of physics. Though symbol tokens are always physical tokens, "symbol" and "same symbol" are not defined in terms of physical features. Syntax, in short, is not intrinsic to physics.

(3) This has the consequence that computation is not discovered in the physics, it is assigned to it. Certain physical phenomena are assigned or used or programmed or interpreted syntactically. Syntax and symbols are observer relative.

(4) It follows that you could not *discover* that the brain or anything else was intrinsically a digital computer, although you could assign a computational interpretation to it as you could to anything else. The point is not that the claim "The brain is a digital computer" is false. Rather, it does not get up to the level of falsehood. It does not have a clear sense. You will have misunderstood my account if you think that I am arguing that it is simply false that the brain is a digital computer. The question "Is the brain a digital computer?" is as ill defined as the questions "Is it an abacus?", "Is it a book?", "Is it a set of symbols?", "Is it a set of mathematical formulae?"

(5) Some physical systems facilitate the computational use much better than others. That is why we build, program, and use them. In such cases we are the homunculus in the system interpreting the physics in both syntactic and semantic terms.

(6) But the causal explanations we then give do not cite causal properties different from the physics of the implementation and the intentionality of the homunculus.

(7) The standard, though tacit, way out of this is to commit the homunculus fallacy. The homunculus fallacy is endemic to computational models of cognition and cannot be removed by the standard recursive decomposition arguments. They are addressed to a different question.

(8) We cannot avoid the foregoing results by supposing that the brain is doing "information processing." The brain, as far as its intrinsic operations are concerned, does no information processing. It is a specific biological organ and its specific neurobiological processes cause specific forms of intentionality. In the brain, intrinsically, there are neurobiological processes and sometimes they cause consciousness. But that is the end of the story.[5]

REFERENCES

Block, Ned (1990), "The computer model of the mind," in E. Smith and D. N. Osherson (eds.), *An Invitation to Cognitive Science, III: Thinking* (Cambridge, Mass.: MIT Press): 247–289.

Boolos, George S. and Jeffrey, Richard C. (1989), *Computability and Logic* (Cambridge: Cambridge University Press).

Dennett, Daniel C. (1978), *Brainstorms: Philosophical Essays on Mind and Psychology* (Cambridge, Mass.: MIT Press).

Feigenbaum, E. A. and Feldman, J. (eds.) (1963), *Computers and Thought* (New York and San Francisco: McGraw-Hill Company).

Fodor, J. (1975), *The Language of Thought* (New York: Thomas Y. Crowell).

Haugeland, John (ed.) (1981), *Mind Design* (Cambridge, Mass.: MIT Press).

Johnson-Laird, P. N. (1988), *The Computer and the Mind* (Cambridge, Mass.: Harvard University Press).

Kuffler, Stephen W. and Nicholls, John G. (1976), *From Neuron to Brain* (Sunderland, Mass.: Sinauer Associates).

Lettvin, J. Y., Maturana, H. R., McCulloch, W. S., and Pitts, W. H. (1959), "What the frog's eye tells the frog's brain," *Proceedings of the Institute of Radio Engineers*, 47 (1940–1951), reprinted in McCulloch, 1965, pp. 230–255.

Marr, David (1982), *Vision* (San Francisco: W. H. Freeman and Company).

McCulloch, Warren S. (1965), *The Embodiments of Mind* (Cambridge, Mass.: MIT Press).

Pylyshyn, Z. (1985), *Computation and Cognition* (Cambridge, Mass.: MIT Press).

Searle, John R. (1980), "Minds, brains and programs," *The Behavioral and Brain Sciences* 3: 417–424.

   (1984), *Minds, Brains and Science* (Cambridge, Mass.: Harvard University Press).

Sharples, M., Hogg, D., Hutchinson, C., Torrance, S., and Young, D. (1988), *Computers and Thought* (Cambridge, Mass. and London: MIT Press).

Shepherd, Gordon M. (1983), *Neurobiology* (New York and Oxford: Oxford University Press).

Turing, Alan (1950), "Computing machinery and intelligence," *Mind* 59: 433–460.

---

[5] I am indebted to a remarkably large number of people for discussions of the issues in this paper. I cannot thank them all, but special thanks are due to John Batali, Vinod Goel, Ivan Havel, Kirk Ludwig, Dagmar Searle, and Klaus Strelau.

CHAPTER 6

The phenomenological illusion

I was asked to lecture at the Wittgenstein conference in Kirchberg in 2004 on the subject of phenomenology. This request surprised me somewhat because I am certainly not a scholar on the writings of phenomenological philosophers, nor have I done much work that I consider phenomenological in any strict sense. However, I was glad to accept the invitation because I have had some peculiar experiences with phenomenology. Also, it seemed worth discussing this issue at a Wittgenstein conference because the recent revival of interest in consciousness among analytic philosophers has lead to a renewed interest in phenomenological authors, since, of course, phenomenology is in large part concerned with consciousness.

I presented a lecture on the subject, the general thesis of which was that there is a type of idealism present in some of the leading phenomenologists, specifically later Husserl, Heidegger, and Merleau-Ponty. It is idealism of a specific kind that I tried to define semantically – somewhat different from the traditional idealism of Berkeley, which is defined metaphysically, but close enough in family resemblance to the traditional conceptions of idealism to merit the term. The definition I used was this: A view is idealist in this semantic sense if it does not allow for irreducibly *de re* references to objects. All references to objects are interpreted as being within the scope of some phenomenological operator, such as Dasein or transcendental consciousness. I also argued that this form of idealism leads to certain structural limitations on what these phenomenological authors can achieve. The problem with the discussion in Kirchberg is that too much time was spent arguing about whether it is correct to interpret later Husserl and Heidegger as idealists in the traditional sense. For me that is not the interesting question. The mere fact of an ambiguity or unclarity in their position on the issue of idealism, the fact that it is not obvious that they are resolutely anti-idealistic and resolutely realistic, is sufficient for me to make the points that I want to make. In any case, the definition I gave of idealism lead to confusion with traditional conceptions of idealism, so I am now for the most part abandoning the use of that term. Instead of "idealism" I introduce the notion of "perspectivalism" to mark the tendency of some authors to treat the perspective from which something is regarded – transcendental consciousness, Dasein, ready-to-hand, present-at-hand, etc. – as somehow part of its ontology. I have recast the article so as to make the issues about the interpretation of Husserl, Heidegger, and Merleau-Ponty – issues of textual interpretation of the sort that is usually boring – secondary to the main philosophical points. I want the substantive philosophical points to seem quite obvious. Whenever there is a non-obvious point about the interpretation of a text I will mark it as such. I want to emphasize at the start that *if phenomenology is defined as the examination of the structure of consciousness, I have no objections whatever to phenomenology.* My misgivings are about some specific authors and their practice of this method.

I. THE CURRENT SITUATION IN PHILOSOPHY

Before beginning my discussion of phenomenology, I want to say a little bit about how I see the contemporary philosophical scene. There is exactly one overriding question in contemporary philosophy. As a preliminary formulation, we can say the question is: How do we account for our conceptions of ourselves as a certain sort of human being in a universe that we know consists entirely of physical particles in fields of force. More precisely: Given that any sort of Cartesianism or other form of metaphysical dualism is out of the question, how do we give an account of ourselves as conscious, intentionalistic, rational, speech-act performing, ethical, free-will-possessing, political, and social animals in a world that consists *entirely* of mindless, meaningless brute physical particles. Most of the important questions of philosophy are variations on this single question. So, the question of free will and determinism is: How can we have free action in a universe that is determined in accordance with causal laws? The problem of ethics is: How can there be an ethical right and wrong in a world of meaningless physical particles? The question of consciousness is: How can unconscious bits of matter in the skull cause consciousness, and how can irreducibly subjective states of consciousness exist in an entirely "physical" world? The question in the philosophy of language is: How can brute physical sounds that come out of a speaker's mouth constitute the performance of meaningful speech acts? The question for society is: How can there be an objective reality of money, property, government, and marriage when all of these phenomena only exist, in some sense, because we believe that they exist? How is it possible that human beings can, by their subjective thought processes, create an objective social reality? And so on with other philosophical questions that are variations on the central question. I am deliberately putting these points in a very crude fashion; and, as analytic philosophers, you will all recognize that before we go to work on them, they would need much more careful statement. How, then, can we and should we approach this question or this set of questions?

Our question is, how does the human reality fit into the basic reality? And what is the basic underlying reality? Well, that is a complicated story, but two central features of it can be stated quite simply. We know that the basic structure of the entire universe consists in entities that we find it convenient (if not entirely accurate) to call "particles," and these exist in fields of force and are typically organized into systems. We know furthermore that we and all living systems have evolved over a period of somewhere between three and five billion years by processes of Darwinian natural selection. It is a deep mistake to think that these two propositions are just theories of science. "Science" is the name of a set of procedures by which we have identified the truth, but once identified, the truth is public property. It does not belong to some special domain; indeed "science" does not name an ontological domain. These two propositions are now so widely accepted that it is hardly necessary for me to belabor them. I also want to add a third. In addition to the atomic theory of matter and the evolutionary theory of biology, we have to add the neurobiological basis of all human and animal mental life. All of our consciousness, intentionality, and all the rest of our mental life are caused by neurobiological processes and realized in neurobiological systems. This is not as universally accepted as the first two propositions; but it will be, and for the purposes of this discussion I am going to take it for granted. These three propositions taken together – atomic physics, evolutionary biology, and embodied brain neurobiology – I will call propositions that describe "the basic facts" or "the basic reality." So now our philosophical question can be posed more precisely: What are the relations between the human reality and the basic reality.

A preliminary difficulty with phenomenology is that the phenomenologists that I know cannot hear the question I am asking. They think it expresses some kind of Cartesianism, that I am opposing the human realm to the physical realm, *res cogitans* to *res extensa*. Indeed, Hubert Dreyfus had said over and over that I am a Cartesian. This misunderstanding is so breathtaking that I hardly know how to answer it. The human world is part of one world, not something different. The question, how does the human reality relate to the more fundamental reality, is no more Cartesian than the question how does chemistry relate to the more fundamental atomic physics. In a recent article Dreyfus writes "we should adopt a richer ontology than the Cartesian one of minds and nature assumed by Husserl, and Searle." He adds that we should follow Merleau-Ponty in postulating "a third kind of being."[1] This is not just a misunderstanding of my views on Dreyfus's part, it reveals a very deep misconception. The assumption is that there are already two different kinds of being, mind and nature, and that we need to postulate "a third kind of being." I do not have the space here to expose the full inadequacy of this conception, and for purposes of this discussion I can only say that the very terminology of "minds and nature" and "a third kind of being" makes it impossible to address the fundamental questions of philosophy. There is no opposition between minds and nature, because mind is part of nature, and there are not three kinds of being, because there are not two kinds of being or even one kind of being, because the whole notion of "being" is confused.

Paradoxically, Wittgenstein helped to make possible a type of philosophy that I think he would have abominated. By taking skepticism seriously, and by attempting to show that it is based on a profound misunderstanding of language, Wittgenstein helped to remove skepticism from the center of the philosophical agenda and make it possible to do a type of systematic, theoretical, constructive philosophy of the sort that he thought was impossible. Skepticism has been removed from the center of the philosophical agenda for two main reasons. First, linguistic philosophy has convinced many people that skepticism of the traditional kind cannot be intelligibly stated (this is where Wittgenstein comes in); and second, more importantly, we know too much. The single most important intellectual fact about the present era is that knowledge grows. We now have a huge body of knowledge that is certain, objective and universal. You cannot, for example, send men to the moon and back and then seriously doubt whether the external world exists. The decline of epistemology as the central subject in philosophy has made possible a type of post-skeptical, post-epistemic, post-foundationalist philosophy. This is the type of philosophy that I have always practiced. The theory of speech acts, the theory of intentionality, the theory of consciousness, and the theory of social reality (all of which are areas I have worked in) are precisely areas in which we seek general, theoretical accounts of a large philosophically puzzling domain. Notice, also, that there is no sharp boundary between philosophy and science in these domains. For example,

---

[1] Dreyfus, 1999: 21.

the advent of cognitive science and the development of neurobiology have produced all sorts of cooperative endeavors between philosophers and scientists. In fact, cognitive science was invented in large part by philosophers and philosophically minded psychologists who got sick of behaviorism in psychology.

That is the question or set of questions. What is the appropriate method for attacking these questions? The answer about methodology is always the same. Use any method you can lay your hands on, and stick with any method that works. The methods that I have found most useful in my work are what I call the methods of logical analysis, and I will contrast those with other methods in a few moments.

II. MY EXPERIENCES WITH PHENOMENOLOGY

Before launching into the main argument, I want to say a bit more of an autobiographical nature. When I first began work on a book on intentionality, I read some of the huge literature on the subject. The literature in analytic philosophy seemed to me feeble. The best work was supposed to be an exchange between Chisholm and Sellars on the topic of intentionality,[2] but that exchange seemed to me to have a persistent confusion between intentionality-with-a-t and intensionality-with-an-s. Many sentences about intentional-with-a-t states, that is, many sentences about beliefs, desires, hopes, and fears, for example, are themselves intensional-with-an-s sentences; because, for example, they fail the tests of substitutability (Leibniz's Law) and existential generalization. These are the two standard tests for extensionality. But the fact that sentences about intentional-with-a-t states are typically intensional-with-an-s sentences does not show that there is something inherently intensional-with-an-s about intentional-with-a-t states. It is typical among people who use linguistic methods to confuse features of the description of a phenomenon with features of the phenomenon being described. So I did not learn anything from the Chisholm–Sellars correspondence or, indeed, from Chisholm's collection, which purports to make a connection between phenomenology and the issues that I was interested in.[3]

So I turned to the phenomenologists, and the book that I was urged to read was Husserl's *Logical Investigations*.[4] Well, I read the *First Logical Investigation*, and, frankly, I was very disappointed. It seemed to me that it was in no way an advance on Frege and was, in fact, rather badly

---

[2] Chisholm and Sellars, 1958.   [3] Chisholm, 1960.   [4] Husserl, 1970.

written, unclear, and confused. So I abandoned the effort to try to learn something about intentionality from previous writers and just went to work on my own. It turned out to be a rather difficult task, the hardest I have ever undertaken in philosophy. After several years I produced the book *Intentionality: An Essay in the Philosophy of Mind.*[5] When that book was published, I was flabbergasted to discover that a lot of people thought it was Husserlian, that I was somehow or other following Husserl and adopting a Husserlian approach to intentionality. As a matter of my actual history, that is entirely false. I learned nothing from Husserl, literally, nothing, though, of course, I did learn a lot from Frege and Wittgenstein. There is a special irony here in that in the course of writing the book, I had several arguments with experts on Husserl, especially Dagfinn Føllesdal, who argued that Husserl's version of intentionality was superior to mine in various respects. No doubt there are interesting overlaps between my views and Husserl's. Indeed it would be surprising if there were no overlaps, because we are talking about the same subject. Such similarities are certainly worth exploring. But I want to call attention to crucial differences in method.

Another brush I had with phenomenology was with my colleague Hubert Dreyfus. Though he knew that I had read very little of Husserl, he became convinced that I was essentially repeating Husserl's views. Dreyfus tells me that he hates Husserl with a passion, and that he was, in his words, "playing Heidegger" to what he supposed was my Husserl.[6] The result was a series of published criticisms of my various theories that went on for years and years. Dreyfus has now conceded that my views are not like Husserl's, but the published criticisms continue and I will mention some of them later. Dreyfus has published at least half a dozen criticisms of my views,[7] including numerous objections in his book on Heidegger. Most of my interpretation of Husserl, Heidegger, and Merleau-Ponty has been heavily influenced by Dreyfus. He has spent his entire professional life studying these and other authors in that tradition, and as we have taught various seminars on these and related issues, I have been exposed to his reading of these authors more than those of any other commentator. In what follows, a perhaps disproportionate amount of space is devoted to Dreyfus because I understand his work much better than I understand the authors he is writing about.

[5] Searle, 1983.   [6] Dreyfus, 1999: 3.
[7] Among them are Dreyfus, 1993, 1991, 2001; Dreyfus and Wakefield, 1990.

III. THE TRANSCENDENTAL REDUCTION, THE WESENSCHAU, AND HOW THEY DIFFER FROM LOGICAL ANALYSIS

Two crucial features of Husserl's method are what he calls the transcendental reduction (or bracketing or the Epoché) and the intuition of essences (or Wesenschau). In the transcendental reduction you suspend judgment about how the world actually is; you bracket the real world and just describe the structure of your conscious experiences. But there are two ways to describe the structure of your conscious experiences. One would be a kind of naive naturalistic account where you just describe how things seem to you. That is not Husserl's method. Husserl proposes that when we describe the results of the transcendental reduction, we should transcend naturalism and try to intuit the essence of what it is that we are describing. So we do not just describe how this particular shade of red seems to me, but we try to get at the essence of redness. That is the intuition of essences. So there are two features to the Husserlian methods: the transcendental reduction and the intuition of essences. These are not equivalent, and indeed they are independent; we could have one without the other.

These methods and logical analysis are somewhat related, but they are by no means identical. Let me describe logical analysis as I understand it and practice it. The paradigm case of logical analysis, the one that had provided us with a model for literally a century, is Russell's theory of descriptions (first published in 1905).[8] In the theory of descriptions, Russell does not ask himself what it consciously feels like when he utters the sentence, "The king of France is bald"; and as I interpret him, he is not seeking a Husserlian Wesenschau either. He does not ask himself what his state of consciousness is; rather, he tries to describe the conditions under which the sentence would be true. He arrives at his famous analysis by analyzing *truth conditions*, not by analyzing his experience. This has provided the model for analytic philosophy since, and the way that I have applied it involves significant extensions beyond the Russellian paradigm. In the theory of speech acts, I asked not under what conditions are speech acts true, but, rather, under what conditions is a speech act of a certain type, such as promising, *successfully and non-defectively performed*. As in Russell's case, the idea was to get an analysis in terms of a set of conditions, ideally a set of necessary and sufficient conditions, for such concepts as promising, ordering, stating, or any other of the fundamental speech act notions. By the time I did that, I was fully aware, of course, of important doubts,

[8] Russell, 1905.

raised by Wittgenstein and others, about the possibility of getting necessary and sufficient conditions because of vagueness, family resemblance, open texture, and other well-known phenomena. These, however, do not make the project of logical analysis impossible; they simply make it more difficult and more interesting. So, for example, the fact that there are marginal and dubious cases of promising or requesting, etc. does not make the project of logical analysis impossible, but it makes it more interesting and more complex.

When I went on to analyze intentionality, my method there, again, was to state conditions, in this case *conditions of satisfaction*. To understand what a belief is, you have to know under what conditions it is true. In the case of a desire, under what conditions it is satisfied. In the case of an intention, under what conditions it is carried out, and so on with other intentional states. But, once again, the analysis is in terms of conditions. Intentional states represent their conditions of satisfaction, and like all representation, intentional representation is under *aspects*, what Frege called "modes of presentation." Notice the contrast with Husserl, who wants to get an intuition of essences by examining the structure of his consciousness. For me, many of the conditions of satisfaction are not immediately available to consciousness; they are not phenomenologically real. I suspect also that Husserl had an ontological conception of representations as certain kinds of occurent mental events. My conception is purely logical. Representations for me are not to be thought of as always like pictures or sentences, but rather anything at all that can have conditions of satisfaction is a representation.

Though I did not realize it at the time, one of the effects of my book *Intentionality* was to take the subject of intentionality away from the introspectionism of the Continental tradition and try to make it a respectable subject for analytic philosophers. Previous analytic discussions of intentionality either tended to be behavioristic, like Ryle's, or linguistic, like Chisholm's and Sellars's. Traditionally, analytic philosophers are reluctant to accept any irreducibly first-personal account of anything. I presented a first-person account of intentionality, real instrinsic intentionality, using the resources of logical analysis. Unlike Husserl, whose method is introspective and transcendental, my conception of intentionality is resolutely naturalistic. Intentionality is a biological feature of the world, on all fours with digestion or photosynthesis. It is caused by and realized in the brain.

In the case of social reality, my analysis is also in terms of conditions, though it is less obviously so. There, the question is: What are the constitutive features that make up institutional facts? What sort of facts about the world make it the case that I am married, or that I am a citizen of the United States, or that I have a certain amount of money, or that I am a professor at the University of California, Berkeley? All of those are institutional facts, and the idea is to uncover the ontology of those facts by uncovering what conditions are necessary and sufficient to constitute those facts as such. It is important to emphasize that the analysis is in no sense a causal analysis. I am not asking what *caused* these bits of paper to be money, but rather what facts about them *constitute* their being money. My investigation of social ontology is a continuation of the methods of analysis that I have described earlier.

So, as a preliminary formulation, we can say that the method of Husserlian phenomenology is to describe the noema by giving its essential structure. The method of logical analysis is to state conditions – truth conditions, performance conditions, conditions of constitution, etc.

I said there was an overlap between the Husserlian methods of transcendental reduction and Wesenschau and the methods of logical analysis. The overlap arises simply because sometimes the intuition of essences gives the same result as the analysis of conditions. For example, I think both would give similar analyses of belief, at least of beliefs as they occur in conscious thought processes. The problem, however, is that sometimes they give different analyses. This came out years ago in my arguments with Føllesdal, where I claimed that there are certain causal conditions on various kinds of intentional phenomena, but he denied those on the grounds that there was no immediate phenomenological reality to the causal conditions. An obvious example is the causal self-referentiality of many intentional phenomena such as perception, memory, and voluntary action. I will say more about these cases in detail later, but for the present the point is: *some of the most important logical features of intentionality are beyond the reach of phenomenology because they have no immediate phenomenological reality.*

Well, what, then, is the method of logical analysis by which it gets at these conditions, if it is not one of just describing the structure of experience? The answer is that it is an extension of the methods of linguistic philosophy. You ask, "What would we say if . . .?" or "What would be the case if . . .?" Grice gives a classic instance of this in his proof that there is a causal condition on seeing, even in cases where that causal condition is not experienced as part of the phenomenology of the visual experience.[9] Thus, suppose I see an object, but a mirror is then inserted in such a way that I have exactly the

[9] Grice, 1989.

same type of experience I had before, and I still take myself to be seeing the same object; but, in fact, the mirror image is reflecting a different but type-identical object. I am no longer seeing the object I was originally seeing because that object is not causing my visual experience. The proof is that we *would not describe* this as a case of seeing the original object. This is straight, linguistic philosophy; it is not phenomenological analysis. This is a crucial and decisive distinction between my notion of intentional content and Husserl's notion of noema. The noema can only contain things that are phenomenologically real. *On my view, phenomenology is a good beginning on the analysis of intentionality, but it cannot go all the way because there are all sorts of conditions which simply have no immediate phenomenological reality.*

It seems to me that the right attitude to this whole discussion is that we should use phenomenological methods where they are appropriate, and analytic methods where they are appropriate. It is as simple and trivial as that. *Properly understood, there is no conflict between analytic philosophy and phenomenology.* They offer non-competing and complementary methods of investigation and anybody prepared to do serious work should be ready to use both. I think that is exactly the right attitude to have and if everyone agreed to it we could all go home.

IV. SOME EXAMPLES OF THE PHENOMENOLOGICAL ILLUSION

But if we look at the actual practices of phenomenologists, there is a deep disagreement between the sort of philosophy I do and phenomenology. In discussing these issues with phenomenologists I have found that in the study of the philosophy of mind, where something is not phenomenologically real they suppose it is not real at all, in the sense that it has no mental, intentionalistic, or logical reality. And where it is phenomenologically real, then that is real enough. I call this the phenomenological illusion, and I will give several examples of it, beginning with problems in the philosophy of language.

(1) *The problem of meaning.* The problem of meaning in its starkest form is to explain the relation of the physics of the utterance to the semantics. What fact about the acoustic blast that comes out my mouth makes it a speech act? This is the linguistic expression of the fundamental problem I mentioned earlier: how do we account for the human reality given the basic facts? This problem is the main problem in the philosophy of language: How do the (observer-independent) processes in the mind create an (observer-dependent) meaning? How do we get from the acoustic blast

to the full-blown speech act? I try to answer this by presenting a theory of speech acts that includes an account of meaning. On Dreyfus's reading, Husserl's answer to that question is that we first identify meaningless brute phenomena and then consciously impose meaning upon them. This account seems obviously false, because normally no such prior identification or conscious imposition takes place.

So let us turn to Heidegger. According to Dreyfus,

> Heidegger holds that there is no way to account for referring and truth starting with language as occurent sounds coupled with occurent representations. We saw in Ch 11 that Heidegger thinks that all sounds, from motorcycle roars to words, are directly experienced as meaningful. So if we stick close to the phenomenon we *dissolve* [my italics] the Husserl/Searle problem of how to give meaning to mere noises, so that we can then refer by means of mere noises.[10]

So the problem which forms the basis of philosophy of language and linguistics, simply *dissolves*. There is no such problem. If Heidegger is right, 150 years of discussion of this problem from Frege through Russell, Wittgenstein, Grice, and Searle would be rendered irrelevant, by a dissolution of the problem. But wait a minute. We know before we ever get started on philosophy that when I speak, acoustic blasts are coming out of my mouth and larynx. This is just a fact of physics, one of the basic facts I referred to earlier. We know also that I am performing meaningful speech acts. We know, again, before we ever get started on philosophy, that there must be an answer to the question, what is the relation between the acoustic blast and the speech act, because, initially at least, the relation is one of identity. The production of that acoustic blast just is the performance of that speech act. We know, again before we ever get going on the investigation, that the production of meaning is entirely observer relative, entirely done by humans, because we know that without intentional human thought and action there is no meaning. Now why do Heidegger/Dreyfus fail to see these obvious points? The answer is that they are suffering from the phenomenological illusion. Because the creation of meaningfulness out of meaninglessness is not consciously experienced as such (at least not typically) then it does not exist. This is a clear example of the phenomenological illusion.

Let us state this point precisely. Because of the phenomenological illusion, the existential phenomenologist cannot state the problem of meaning nor hear the answer. According to Heidegger, there is no problem. The

[10] Dreyfus, 1991: 268.

problem *dissolves* because we always already experience all sounds as meaningful. The Heideggerians suppose that if there is an imposition of meaning it would have to be done consciously by first identifying the meaningless element and then consciously imposing meaning on it. Unless the imposition of meaning is phenomenologically real, it does not exist.

(2) *The problem of social reality.* Let us turn now from language to society. The problem for language was how do we get from sound to meaning. The problem (or one problem) for society is parallel. How do we get from the brute facts to the social and institutional facts? To the first question the phenomenologist cannot hear the question because he or she thinks it is a phenomenological question, when it is not. The same difficulty afflicts the discussion of social reality. Just as the question of language was how do we get from the brute facts of sounds and marks to the semantic facts of meaningful speech acts, so the question for society is how do we get from, for example, the brute fact that this is a sheet of paper with ink marks to the institutional fact that this is a twenty dollar bill? I try to answer that question; as far as I can tell, the existential phenomenologists literally cannot hear the question. For Heidegger the question dissolves, because the object was "always already" a twenty dollar bill. So the objections I made to Heidegger's account of meaning apply also to the account of social reality. Indeed, I cannot find a distinction in Heidegger between the role of tools such as hammers, where there is no deontology involved, and the role of tools such as money, which only makes sense given a deontology.

(3) *The problem of functions.* Let us pursue this line of thought further. Once you take the basic facts seriously you are struck by an important distinction: Some features of the world exist regardless of our feelings and attitudes. I call these *observer independent.* And they include such things as force, mass, gravitational attraction, photosynthesis, etc. Other things are dependent on us because they are our creations. These include money, property, government, hammers, cars, and tools generally. I call these *observer dependent* or *observer relative.* All functions, and hence all tools and equipment generally, are observer relative. Obviously, the observer-dependent facts of the world are dependent on the observer independent, because the observer-dependent facts are created as such out of an observer-independent or brute reality by human consciousness and intentionality, both of which are themselves observer independent. Thus meaningful utterances, tools, governments, money, and equipment generally are human creations out of meaningless observer-independent materials. So, a piece of paper is money or an object is a hammer only because we have imposed functions on them, the functions of being money or a hammer.

The observer independent is ontologically primary, the observer dependent is derivative. Now here is the interest of all this for the present discussion: *Heidegger has the ontology exactly backwards, one hundred percent wrong.* He says the ready-to-hand is prior, the present-at-hand is derivative. The hammers and the dollar bills are prior to the sheets of paper and the collection of metal molecules. Why does he say this? I think the answer is clear; phenomenologically the hammer and the dollar bill typically are prior. We don't when using the hammer or the dollar bill think much about the basic atomic structure or other observer-independent features of each. In short, Heidegger is subject to the phenomenological illusion in a clear way: he thinks that because the ready-to-hand is phenomenologically prior it is ontologically prior. What is even worse is that he denies that the ready-to-hand is observer relative. He thinks that something is a hammer *in itself,* and he denies that we create a meaningful social and linguistic reality out of meaningless entities. Rather he says we are "always already" in a meaningful world. Here is what he says:

The kind of Being which belongs to these entities is readiness-to-hand. But this characteristic is not to be understood *as merely a way of taking them,* [my italics] as if we were taking such "aspects" into the "entities" which we proximally encounter, or as if some world-stuff which is proximally present-at-hand in itself were "given subjective colouring" in this way.[11]

This seems plainly wrong. If you take away the rhetorical flourishes in his prose, the view that he says is false is the correct view. The characteristic of being money or a hammer is precisely a "way of taking them." Such features as being money or being a hammer are observer relative and in that sense the object is "given subjective coloring" when we treat it as a hammer. Heidegger's views are expressions of his rejection of the basic nature of the basic facts.

(4) *Causal self-referentiality as it is manifested in perception, memory, and intentions.* As I mentioned earlier, if you examined the conditions of satisfaction of several forms of cognition, especially perception, memory, prior intention, and intention in action, you find that they all have a causal condition. They will not be satisfied unless they are caused by (in the case of perception and memory) or themselves cause (in the case of prior intention and intention in action) the rest of their conditions of satisfaction. To take the example I mentioned earlier, I do not see the object unless the presence and features of the object cause the experience

---

[11] Heidegger, 1962: 101.

of seeing the object with those features. Now this causal self-referentiality is generally not available to phenomenological analysis, because you don't typically consciously experience the object as causing you to see it or experience your prior intentions as causing your subsequent actions. It is this causal self-referentiality of perception and action that comes out in logical analysis but is not typically revealed under phenomenological analysis, because it is not phenomenologically real, in the sense that it is not always present to consciousness at the time of the actual experience. But it is obviously real as a condition, because it is part of the conditions of satisfaction of the intentional phenomena in question. Of course, you can indirectly bring the causal conditions of satisfaction to consciousness. In the case of perception there is an experienced contrast between the voluntary character of visual imagination, where my intention causes the visual image, and my actual visual perception, where I experience the visual experience as caused by objects in the external world. In the case of action there is an experienced contrast between a normal action, where I am in causal control of my bodily movements, and cases where the bodily movements are caused by stimulation of the motor cortex, as was done by the neurosurgeon Wilder Penfield in some famous experiments.[12] So you can consciously get at the causal self-referentiality, but only indirectly. The causal condition of seeing something red does not jump out at you the way that the redness does.

(5) *Skillful coping.* Another example of the phenomenological illusion comes out in Merleau-Ponty's discussion of skillful coping, which he calls "motor intentionality."[13] The idea is that because there are all kinds of routine actions such as walking or driving a car that do not have the concentrated focused consciousness of intentionality, of the kind you get, for example, when you are giving a lecture, that therefore they have a different kind of intentionality altogether. If it feels different then it must be different. But if you look at the actual conditions of satisfaction there is no difference in the logical structure. To see this, contrast doing a type of action as skillful coping and doing it as concentrated deliberate action. For example, normally when I get up and walk to the door I do it without special concentration or deliberation. Skillful coping. But now I do it and concentrate my attention on doing it. Deliberate action. But in the cases as described, though they feel different, they are logically similar. In both cases I am acting intentionally and in both there are causally self-referential

---

[12] Penfield, 1975: 76.   [13] Merleau-Ponty, 1962.

conditions of satisfaction. I succeeded in what I was trying to do only if my intentions in action caused the bodily movements.

The fact that the actions feel different does not imply that they are logically different. It is a clear case of the phenomenological illusion to suppose that different phenomenology implies a different kind of intentionality with a different logical structure.

(6) *Propositional representations, conditions of satisfaction and subject/object intentionality.* Dreyfus, following Merleau-Ponty, continually criticizes my conception of intentionality on the grounds that, according to him, it cannot account for motor intentionality, because, he says, such intentionality does not consist in propositional representations, does not have conditions of satisfaction, and is not "subject/object" intentionality. Rather, he says, it has "conditions of improvement" which are non-representational and non-propositional; and because the agent is in a skilled involvement with the world, it is not subject/object intentionality. An example of the sort of thing he has in mind, indeed an example he gives repeatedly when criticizing me, is this: when playing tennis I might have the "conditions of improvement," concerning my tennis stroke. Such conditions of improvement, he says, are not propositional, they do not have conditions of satisfaction, and they are not cases of "subject/object intentionality." I find this account confused, not to say self-contradictory; and I think once again, for reasons I will explain, it reveals the phenomenological illusion.

Let us go through it step by step. First step: he says skillful coping has conditions of improvement that are not propositional. But the notion of a condition is already propositional, simply because a condition is always a condition *that such and such is the case.* Second step: the notion of a representation, as I use it, trivially applies to anything in this domain that has conditions, because a representation is simply anything at all that has conditions of satisfaction, such as truth conditions, obedience conditions, conditions of improvement, etc. As I remarked earlier, representation for me is a logical, not a phenomenological, notion. The expression "mental representation" does not imply "sentences or pictures in the head." So both the cases of conditions of satisfaction and conditions of improvement are cases of propositional representation. Third step: all intentionality by definition is "subject/object intentionality" because all intentionality is a matter of a human or animal engaged with the world where the human's or animal's thoughts, perceptions, and behavior have conditions of satisfaction. The fact that conscious intentionality does not feel like a subject engaged with an object is irrelevant. How it feels phenomenologically has no necessary bearing on its logical structure. Fourth step: all conditions of improvement are by definition conditions of satisfaction, because I can succeed or fail in achieving conditions of improvement. Conditions of improvement are simply a subclass of conditions of satisfaction, i.e. cases of my succeeding in doing what I am trying to do. In short, as I use these expressions, Dreyfus's account is self-contradictory. You cannot say that motor intentionality has conditions of improvement but is not representational, not propositional, not subject/object and has no conditions of satisfaction, because the very notion of intentional conditions of improvement implies: propositional, representational, conditions of satisfaction, and subject/object intentionality.

Why are these points not obvious? I think the answer is the phenomenological illusion. In general these features are not present to the phenomenology. The phenomenology is systematically misleading. We do not, when playing tennis have a conscious experience of having propositional representations of conditions of satisfaction (e.g. improvement) and we do not consciously think of ourselves as embodied consciousnesses in interaction with the world. The phenomenological illusion can even give us the impression that the tennis racket is somehow part of our body, and indeed when we are playing tennis or skiing, the tennis racket or the skis seem more like an extension of the body than they seem like instruments. But this, of course, is a phenomenological illusion. In fact there are no nerve endings in the tennis racket, nor in the skis; but if you get good at skiing or playing tennis it will seem almost as if there are. It does not seem as if you are an embodied brain engaged with a world; rather it seems as if you and the world form a single unity, and of course there is no propositional content running consciously through your head. But all the same, the entire logical apparatus of intentionality applies. One could only miss the logical point if one was suffering the phenomenological illusion. If you describe the phenomenology and stop there, you miss the underlying logical structures.

From a biological point of view, what seems to be going on in these cases is this. It is simply more economical biologically, more efficient, and consequently has an evolutionary advantage, that we should engage with the world in ways that disguise the actual logical relations. Indeed, some recent work in neurobiology supports the view that lots of intentionality, even in vision, is unconscious.[14] There is nothing wrong with the lived phenomenology that leaves out many of the logical features. On the

---

[14] Milner and Goodale, 1995.

contrary leaving out all sorts of logical features has an enormous evolutionary advantage for us. What is wrong is mistaking the phenomenology for the totality of the actual facts. The phenomenological theory is based on an illusion generated by the fact that my skillful coping does not seem to involve a distinction between me and the world, does not seem to involve propositional content, and does not seem to involve representations. But to repeat, phenomenology fails us, because we are trying to get at the underlying reality that lies beyond the reach of the conscious phenomenology. Dreyfus frequently points out that we need not know in advance what a perfect tennis swing is going to feel like. Quite so. Similarly we need not know in advance what a perfect turn is going to feel like in skiing, but all the same we have conditions of satisfaction whose content is that they are satisfied only if I make a perfect or at least a better turn, or only if I make a perfect or at least a better tennis swing.

(7) *Causation and constitution.* There is an interesting misunderstanding of my whole approach to these issues which I think also reveals the phenomenological illusion. I am not sure that this is general to phenomenology because the only case that I know is Dreyfus, but anyway here is how it goes. I gave a "causal account" of the structure of action by finding that the conditions of satisfaction of both prior intentions and intentions in action had to contain a causal component. The prior intention causes the whole action, the intention in action causes the bodily movement, etc. (Though to repeat, in typical cases this will not be phenomenologically available. You need not be conscious when you are carrying out your prior intention that your action was in part caused by that prior intention.) Now, interestingly, Dreyfus supposes that, when I give an account of the structure of social reality, it must also be causal. He thinks that I am giving a causal account of the fact that this piece of paper in front of me is a twenty dollar bill. But there is nothing in my text that would lead to such a misunderstanding. I am giving a constitutive account. The question I am asking is, What fact about this piece of paper and other similar pieces of paper makes them into money? I do not ask the question, What caused this piece of paper to be money? (I am not even sure what such a question would mean) but rather, What fact about it constitutes its being money?

It was surprising to me that anyone could have this misunderstanding but I now believe that it follows from the phenomenological illusion. If there were a logical structure then it would have to be phenomenologically real, but if it is phenomenologically real then the brute part of the phenomenology, thinking that this is a piece of paper, would have to be the causal basis for the institutional part of the phenomenology, thinking that it is a twenty dollar bill. So the object is caused to be a twenty dollar bill by thinking that it is a twenty dollar bill. I now see that if you are subject to the phenomenological illusion it follows quite naturally.

V. A DIAGNOSIS OF THE PHENOMENOLOGICAL ILLUSION

So far I am reasonably confident that what I am identifying as mistakes are genuine mistakes, and that I have not misunderstood the authors that I am criticizing. But now I turn to a more speculative part of this article: What is the diagnosis of the phenomenological illusion?

I have said that any sane philosophy dealing with these issues in our epoch has to start with the basic facts. (This does not, of course, imply that there cannot be philosophical investigations of, and challenges to, the basic facts themselves.) Now, why exactly are they basic? Why, for example, are the facts of physics more basic than those of literary criticism or sociology? That is a question that is legitimately asked, and it has a clear answer. Literary and social facts are dependent on the facts of physics in a way that the facts of physics are not dependent on literature or society. Take away all the literature and all the social institutions, and you still have physics. Take away all the physical particles, and you lose literature, society and everything else.

One possible diagnosis of the sources of the phenomenological illusion is simply this: The phenomenologists I am discussing do not start with the basic facts. And given their presuppositions it is hard to see how they could. The actual approach they adopt is to treat the human reality as in some sense more fundamental, or, as some of them would like to say, more "primordial," than the basic reality. The way this manifests itself in their writings is that they tend not to make *de re* references. References to objects are interpreted as inside the scope of some phenomenological operator, such as transcendental consciousness or Dasein. This failure to take the basic reality as basic and primordial, and to suppose that somehow or other the human reality is more basic than the basic reality, gives rise to what I have called the phenomenological illusion. Several people whose opinions I respect think it is unfair to characterize the result as "idealism," but in practice at least it comes out as a kind of perspectivalism. Reality exists but only from a perspective.

In the case of late Husserl, all of his talk about the transcendental ego and the primacy of consciousness is, I believe, a part of his rejection of the idea that what I have been calling the basic facts are really basic. Consciousness for Husserl has an absolute existence and is not dependent on brain processes or anything else in nature.[15] Here are some fairly typical passages from *The Crisis of the European Sciences and Transcendental Phenomenology*: "This greatest of all revolutions must be characterized as the transformation of scientific objectivism – not only modern objectivism but also that of all the earlier philosophies of the millennia – into a transcendental subjectivism."[16] Again, "rather, what is primary in itself is subjectivity, understood as that which naively pregives the being of the world and then rationalizes it or (what is the same thing) objectifies it."[17] Transcendental subjectivity for Husserl does not depend on the basic facts; rather, it is the other way round. Another statement of this point occurs in the *Cartesian Meditations*: "the objective world, the world that exists for me, that always has and always will exist for me, the only world that ever can exist for me – this world, with all its objects, I said, derives its whole sense and its existential status, which it has for me, from me myself, *from me as the transcendental Ego*, the Ego who comes to the fore only with transcendental-phenomenological epoché."[18]

I think that Merleau-Ponty is an idealist in a rather traditional sense. Merleau-Ponty talks a great deal about what he calls the body and the importance of the body, but it turns out that the body he is talking about is not the flesh and blood hunk of matter that constitutes each of us but, rather, *le corps vécu*, the lived-body, by which he means the set of phenomenological experiences we have of our own bodies. Merleau-Ponty thinks the brain and the rest of the physical body are arrived at by a kind of abstraction from the *corps vécu*, but the *corps vécu* is basic and primary.

Well what about Heidegger? It ought to arouse our suspicions that people who spend enormous efforts on interpreting his work disagree on the fundamental question whether he was an idealist.[19] For the purposes of this discussion, his lack of a resolute commitment to the basic facts is enough. Suppose you took the notion of Dasein seriously, in the sense that you thought it referred to a real phenomenon in the real world. Your first question would be: How does the brain cause Dasein and how does it exist in the brain? Or if you thought the brain was not the right explanatory level you would have to say exactly how and where Dasein is located in the space-time trajectory of the organism and you would have to locate the right causes, both the micro causes that are causing Dasein and its causal effects on the organic processes of the organism. There is no escaping the fact that we all live in one space-time continuum, and if Dasein exists it

---

[15] Cf. Moran, 2000: 136.   [16] Husserl, 1970b: 68.   [17] Husserl, 1970b: 69.   [18] Husserl, 1960: 26.
[19] Blattner (1999) says he is an idealist; Carman (2003) says he is not.

has to be located and causally situated in that continuum. Furthermore, if you took Dasein seriously you would then have to ask, How does Dasein fit into the biological evolutionary scheme? Do other primates have it? Other mammals? What is its evolutionary function? I can't find an answer to these questions in Heidegger or even a sense that he is aware of them or takes them seriously. But taking these questions seriously is the price of taking Dasein seriously, unless of course you are denying the primordiality of the basic facts.

A recent book by Richard Polt is very revealing in this regard. He tells us, "Heidegger will not even consider a number of questions that the scientifically minded reader will want to ask." These are the sorts of questions I have just mentioned. Why will he not consider these questions? "For Heidegger the ontological question is more fundamental than these ontical questions."[20] I think Polt is right in his reading of Heidegger and it reveals the inadequacy of Heidegger's approach. Once you accept the basic facts, then Dasein has to be a derivative, dependent, higher-level feature of nervous systems. You would have to say beings are primordial, Dasein and Being are derivative.

I want to emphasize this point. Given what we know about how the universe works, any human reality at all has to be derivative, and dependent on, or in my jargon *caused by and realized in*, the more basic reality of particle physics, organic molecules, and cellular biology. This is not an optional way of looking at things, it is just how the universe works. So if you are going to talk seriously about the human reality of *Dasein*, *Geworfenheit, Befindlichkeit, Sorge* and all the rest of it you have to start with the primordial facts, what I have called the basic facts. But as Polt correctly observes, Heidegger rejects this approach from the start. His rejection is only intelligible given that he is not accepting the basic facts as basic.

As far as I can tell (and I may be mistaken about this) *because of their failure to recognize the primacy of the basic facts, the phenomenologists seem to be unable to give a* de re *reading of references to objects.* They hear the references to the basic facts, about molecules, for example, as always already inside the scope of the "present-at-hand" (or some other phenomenological) operator, and they hear the references to hammers and money, etc. as always already inside the scope of the "ready-to-hand" (or some other phenomenological) operator. Look at the quote from Dreyfus above. "Heidegger holds that there is no way to account for referring and truth

[20] Polt, 1999: 43.

starting with language as *occurent sounds . . .*" But that is precisely how one has to account for meaning, reference, truth, etc. because we know before we ever start on the philosophical problems that the speech act is performed by making "occurent sounds," marks, etc. The inadequacy of existential phenomenology could not be stated more clearly: Dreyfus is in effect saying that the Heideggerian cannot state the solution because he cannot hear the question.

Perhaps the most subtle way the failure to give a *de re* reading emerges in Dreyfus's commentary is in the recurring puzzling references to something he calls a "stance." A typical passage is this, "but then, like Husserl but unlike Heidegger, Searle switches to a *detached logical stance* [my italics] and tells us: 'The important thing to see at this point is that functions are never intrinsic to the physics of any phenomenon . . .'"[21] The puzzling thing about Dreyfus's comment is that I did not switch from one stance to another at all; I just described the facts. It is a fact that an object is both a material object and a car, that a piece of paper is both a piece of paper and a dollar bill and so on. No difference in *stance* is required. When I say the piece of paper in my hand is a twenty dollar bill I am not switching from the "detached logical stance" (piece of paper) to the "concerned participant" stance (twenty dollar bill). I am just reporting a fact. To think I must be switching stances is as implausible in this case as to suppose that when I say "my friend owes me twenty dollars," I must be switching from the personal relation stance (my friend) to the economic stance (owes me twenty dollars). Why this talk about stances and switching stances? It took me a long time to see this but once you see it, it seems obvious: because of the primordiality of Dasein, the stance becomes part of the ontology. The point of view becomes part of what is described. This is the point of all the puzzling talk about what things "show up" and it leads to a kind of relativism, as we will see.

On the same page, the following sentence occurs: "It seemed to me that both the external, logical, god-like claim that, for there to be a social world, the brute facts in nature must somehow acquire meaning, and the internal phenomenological description of human beings as always already in a meaningful world, were both correct but in tension." The reference to "god-like" reveals that once again he thinks that the stance is part of the phenomenon, that the brute facts only *exist* from a certain stance or from a point of view, either god-like or "detached, logical," as the case might

---

[21] Dreyfus, 1999: 12.

be. Now, this is a very deep mistake, and it is a foundational mistake, as I just suggested: the point of view becomes part of the ontology. But where brute, observer-independent facts are concerned there is no point of view built into their ontology. *The basic facts exist apart from any stance or point of view.* The picture that Dreyfus seems to have is that institutional facts exist from one point of view and brute facts exist from another point of view. But that is wrong. Brute facts simply exist. No point of view is necessary. Institutional facts exist from a point of view of the participants in the institution and their participation in the institution creates the facts. But where Dreyfus cites a "tension" there is no tension. There is no tension at all in supposing that the piece of paper in my hand is both a piece of paper and a ten dollar bill. There is a philosophical problem, as to how human beings create an institutional reality by imposing status functions on brute facts. Notice that when I said that, I did not do any shifting of stances or anything of the sort. But the form of perspectivalism, the phenomenologists' presupposition that every reference is in the scope of a phenomenological operator, is deep, and it is radical. The form of their perspectivalism is to suppose that the point of view from which the phenomena are described becomes part of the ontology of the phenomena. I ask the question, How do we get from the brute facts to the institutional facts? How does the mind impose status functions on the phenomena? The logical form of that question is: Given that there is a brute reality of observer-independent phenomena, phenomena that have an absolute existence, independent of any human attitudes, stances, etc., how do such phenomena acquire status functions? The reference to brute phenomena is *de re*, it has wide-scope occurrence. The problem is that the phenomenologist cannot hear the *de re* occurrence. Everything must be within the scope of some phenomenological operator. Thus Dreyfus hears the question as asking: From the detached logical point of view there exist brute facts, from the active participant's point of view there exist institutional facts. What is the relation between them? But now there does seem to be a "tension" because the point of view is part of the ontology. There is now a problem about reconciling the detached logical point of view with the active participant's point of view. Nothing has wide scope or *de re* occurrence. That is the perspectivalism that I have I tried to identify.

VI. PERSPECTIVALISM AND RELATIVISM IN HEIDEGGER

The perspectivalism, which is the basis of the phenomenological illusion, comes out even more strongly in Heidegger's discussion of realism. Here is a strange passage from Dreyfus's book on Heidegger: "The Greeks stood in awe of the gods their practices revealed, and we have to discover the elementary particles – we do not construct them."[22] He also talks about how the Christian practices of the Middle Ages revealed saints. All of this is designed to show that Heidegger is not a relativist or an idealist, but rather that he "holds a subtle and plausible position beyond metaphysical realism and antirealism." And what exactly is that position?

Nature is what it is and has whatever causal properties it has independently of us. Different questions such as Aristotle's and Galileo's reveal different natural kinds and different kinds of causal properties. Different cultural interpretations of reality reveal different aspects of the real too. But there is no right answer to the question. What is the ultimate reality in terms of which everything else becomes intelligible?[23]

This has some strange consequences: "it follows from Heidegger's account that several incompatible lexicons can be true, i.e., can reveal how things are in themselves." There can even be "incompatible realities."[24]

What are we to make of all this? If you try to take it literally, it comes out as a mixture of falsehood and nonsense. It is just false to say that the Greek gods were revealed by Greek practices, because there weren't any gods to get revealed. The Ancient Greeks were mistaken. (I speak with some epistemic authority here. I have actually been on Mount Olympus.) One might as well say that Santa Claus is revealed by children's practices on Christmas Eve. And it is nonsense to speak of "incompatible realities" or "incompatible lexicons." If by "incompatible" is meant "inconsistent" then only propositions, statements, etc. can be compatible or incompatible; and inconsistent statements cannot both be true. Not surprisingly Dreyfus gives no examples of how inconsistent statements can both be true. He speculates that Aristotelian final causes might be more "revealing," but that does not give us what we need. If Aristotelian final causes exist, then theories that deny their existence are just plain false. It is not a case of incompatible statements both being true.

So what is going on here? I think what makes apparent nonsense seem like philosophical insight is a relativism that derives from the underlying perspectivalism. The picture is that from the point of view (stance, practices, Dasein) of the Greeks, their gods really existed. From our point of view (stance, practices, Dasein), they do not exist. Similarly from our point of view, elementary particles exist, but maybe from some other point of

[22] Dreyfus, 1991: 268.   [23] Dreyfus, 1991: 264.   [24] Dreyfus, 1991: 279–280.

view, they do not exist. But there is no ultimately right point of view from which we can say that one is right and the other is wrong. There is only Dasein, "the being in terms of whose practices all aspects of reality show up."[25]

But we need not rely on Dreyfus's interpretation. Here is Heidegger's text itself.

The proposition "2 times 2 = 4" as a true assertion is true only as long as Dasein exists. If in principle no Dasein any longer exists, then the proposition is no longer valid, not because the proposition is invalid as such, not because it would have become false and 2 times 2 = 4 would have changed into 2 times 2 = 5, but because the uncoveredness of something as truth can only co-exist with the existing Dasein that does the uncovering. There is not a single valid reason for presupposing eternal truths.[26]

This is perspectivalism with a vengeance. The reference to numbers is not *de re*, to the numbers themselves, but only within the scope of the phenomenological operator Dasein. So everything becomes relative to Dasein and "There is not a single valid reason for presupposing eternal truths." The correct thing to say is this. Numbers are not temporal entities. Simple arithmetical equations are timeless and in that sense "eternal." There is nothing exciting about this. It is trivial. I believe the fact that Heidegger denies such trivialities is a symptom of the perspectivalism I have been trying to identify.

In his book on Heidegger, Dreyfus tells us that the problems that I have been discussing dissolve, that there are no such problems. But here is what he says in a subsequent work: "That, thanks to human beings, a meaningful world somehow devolves upon a meaningless universe, is a contemporary given, accepted by analytic philosophers and phenomenologists alike."[27] I believe this sentence requires close attention. We were told earlier that there was no such problem as how meaningfulness was imposed on the meaningless brute reality, because it did not happen. We are always already in a meaningful world and so the problem "dissolves." But in this sentence, we are expressing gratitude, "thanks to human beings." But what is it, *exactly*, that we are thankful for if nothing happened in the first place, if the problem dissolved because there never was anything to be thankful for? And what does "devolves" mean? (Actually, it is a translation of Heidegger's "Zufall.") And why "somehow"? Isn't it the job of the philosopher to tell us exactly how? Are Heidegger/Dreyfus giving up on the philosophical

---

[25] Dreyfus, 1991: 264.   [26] Heidegger, 1982: 221.   [27] Dreyfus, 1999: 20.

question when they tell us it happens "somehow"? I give an answer to the question of how it happens, Dreyfus tells us first that it never happened and now that it happened "somehow." What does he think is wrong with my answer as to how it happened? He does not tell us. And why are the basic facts just a "contemporary" given and not an absolute permanent fact? "Contemporary" suggests contingent, not absolute. What needs to be said is the following: There exists a meaningless universe and human beings are products of evolution in that universe. Human beings, by their individual and collective efforts, create the part of the world that contains linguistic, social, and institutional reality. Now, why do existential phenomenologists seem unable to say this? And why can't he tell us exactly what human beings did, for which we are now expressing gratitude, that enabled the ready-to-hand to "devolve" upon the present-at-hand?

Any representation of anything is always from a certain point of view so, for example, if I represent something as water, I represent it at a different level than if I represent it as H_2O molecules. Same stuff, different levels of description. One of the sources of perspectivalism (the other one is epistemic) is to try to read the point of view back into the reality represented. From the fact that all representation is from a point of view, from a certain stance, it does not follow that the stance, point of view, etc. are part of the reality represented. The mistake of the phenomenologists, at least in the writings that I am familiar with, is that they do not seem to get this point. The stance, point of view, etc. become part of the ontology, so when Dreyfus speaks of a "contemporary given," he means, given, but only from our contemporary point of view. He does not mean it is an absolute timeless truth that we contemporaries happen to have discovered.

The correct picture, I believe, is the following: We live in a world of the basic facts, as described by atomic physics, evolutionary biology, and neurobiology. All our lives, including all of our mental lives, are dependent on the basic facts. Given that, we have an interesting set of questions about how human beings are able to create a meaningful set of semantic, institutional, social, etc., facts out of the basic facts using their consciousness and intentionality. The institutional, social, and other similar facts, etc. have a relative existence. They exist only relative to human beings. But the basic facts do not in that way have a relative existence. They have an absolute existence. They are there regardless of what we think. Now, this is the point that the phenomenologists I am discussing do not acknowledge. All facts have to be relative to some point of view, some stance. In the case of the existential phenomenologist, it is relative to Dasein. In the case of the late Husserlians, it is relative to the transcendental Ego. But the reference to the basic facts is never wide scope; it is never *de re*. It is always inside one of the phenomenological operators. One favorite of these operators, by the way, is "show up." Nothing ever has an absolute existence, not even planets or hydrogen atoms. They just "show up." It is that point, the syntactical-semantic point, that makes it impossible for phenomenology to address the most important contemporary philosophical problems.

There is an objection one frequently hears that goes as follows: What I call the basic facts are just what happens to be widely believed at a certain point in history, a "contemporary given," as Dreyfus calls them. But they were not always believed in the past and it is quite likely that they will be superseded in the future. So there are no timeless absolute basic facts; there are just beliefs that people think are true relative to their time and place. This mistake is prominent in Thomas Kuhn, for example.[28] But the answer to it is this. It is only on the assumption of a non-relative, absolute reality that it is worthwhile to change our opinions in the first place. We are trying to get absolute non-relative truths about an absolute non-relative reality. The fact that we keep changing our opinions as we learn more only makes sense given the assumption that our aim is the description of an absolute non-relative world. The fact of opinion change is an argument against relativism, not an argument for it. It is quite likely that our conception of what I have been calling the basic facts will be improved on, and at least some of our present conceptions will become obsolete. This shows not that there are no basic facts, nor that the basic facts only have a relative existence, but that their absolute existence does not by itself guarantee that at any point in our history we have accurately stated them. The facts don't change, but the extent of our knowledge does.

VII. REPLY TO DREYFUS

I will conclude this discussion by showing how Dreyfus's latest attacks on my views exemplify the phenomenological illusion that I have been trying to expose. I have implicitly answered some of his objections in the previous pages, but I would like to make the answers explicit now.

He makes two criticisms of my views. First, he says that in my account of intentionality, I fail to note the existence of "absorbed coping," which is unlike the intentionality that I do discuss in that it is non-propositional, non-representational and not subject-object intentionality. Second, he says that in my account of social reality I fail to take account of what he

---

[28] Kuhn, 1962.

calls "social norms," and that these are more basic and somehow prior to the institutional facts that I do discuss. One of the many remarkable things about this article is that each of the examples designed to show the superiority of phenomenology show exactly the opposite. What he presents as counter-examples are precisely the sorts of examples I considered when I presented my original views, and in each case he misdescribes the examples, and the misdescription is a result of the phenomenological illusion. In the case of absorbed coping, he says that I have reluctantly conceded that such cases exist. On the contrary, I discussed these cases in my earliest accounts of intentionality, where I talked about such examples as skiing, driving a car, or just getting up and pacing around. And about social reality, he says that I have failed to take account of such things as a tribe treating someone as a leader, or gender differences marked by such terms as "lady" and "gentleman." On the contrary, the case of leadership is one that I discussed explicitly, and the gender differences fit my account more or less exactly as I will now show.

Let us consider each of these in turn. I agree with Dreyfus that there are phenomenological differences in different kinds of intentionality, though I do not agree with what he says about the differences. For example, there is clearly a difference between the kind of concentrated attention that I need to devote to the expression of my thoughts in giving a lecture, and the various subsidiary gestures and movements that I make as part of giving the lecture. I do not regard this difference as in any way an objection or a difficulty. On the contrary, as I said earlier, it seems to me an obvious advantage that evolution has given us that not everything we do intentionally needs to be at the focus of our attention; and, indeed, many of the things we do intentionally, we do quite unconsciously. The answer to Dreyfus can be stated explicitly: the phenomenological difference does not show a logical difference. He would have to show difference in the conditions of satisfaction, or some other important logical difference, and he does not do that. Indeed, he misdescribes the situation. He says, for example, that when people move to a comfortable distance from other people in an elevator, they do so *unintentionally*; they have no intentions. I do not think that can be a correct description. This is a typical case of intentional action. It is not premeditated; there is no prior intention. And it may be done without even the agent's awareness that he is doing it, but all the same, it is not like the peristaltic contraction of the gut. It is clearly intentional.

The point about the structure of intentionality is that all intentionality by definition is propositional. It is all representational, and it is all subject-object. These are not phenomenological points. They are points about the logical structure of intentionality. It is a phenomenological illusion to suppose that different phenomenology implies different logical structure.

Dreyfus's second objection is to my account of social reality, where he says I neglect something he calls social norms. He thinks there is a difference between social norms, such as how far apart one stands from people when one engages in conversation, or how we treat someone as a leader, or as a lady, or gentleman (gender differences), and institutional facts, such as the fact that I have a twenty dollar bill in my hand. But then, unfortunately, he lists as social norms a series of things which are institutional facts. Indeed, some of them are my examples of institutional facts. His most important example is the case where someone is selected as a leader by a tribe without any conscious act or procedure of selecting a leadership but just by treating the person with a certain deference, authority, respect, etc. His other examples are gender differences by which we create "ladies and gentlemen." On my account "leader," "lady," and "gentleman" are all names of status functions and thus describe institutional facts. Indeed, I give the example of the selection of a leader as a paradigm case of an institutional fact.[29] So-and-so in our tribe counts as our leader; *X counts as Y*. The fact that Dreyfus presents my examples as if they were counterexamples to me suggests that there is something radically wrong with his account. What is wrong with his account is the phenomenological illusion. There was no conscious thought of the form X counts as Y, so it could not have happened.

Why does he not see that there is a crucial difference between gradually selecting someone as a leader, or treating people as ladies and gentlemen, on the one hand, and how far apart one stands in conversation, on the other. The crucial difference is a logical difference. That is, there is no deontology to how far apart you stand. No rights, duties, obligations, authority, or power accrues to distance-standing in a way that it does accrue to leaders, ladies, and gentlemen. The source of the problem is the phenomenological illusion. In both distance standing and deference, one may behave in a way that just seems appropriate. But the two cases, logically speaking, are radically different, because in the distance standing, there is no deontology involved, whereas, where status functions are concerned, the deontology is essential. The phenomenological method cannot access the deontology because, in general, it is not phenomenologically real.

[29] Searle, 1995.

VIII. CONCLUSION: THE ROLE OF PHENOMENOLOGY

I have for the most part been discussing particular authors in the phenomenological tradition. But suppose we forget about these authors and ask, What is the right role of phenomenology in contemporary philosophy? It seems to me that phenomenology has an important role to play. Once we accept the basic facts, and once we see that the mind, with all of its phenomenology, is derivative of, dependent on, the basic facts, then, it seems to me, phenomenology plays an essential role in the analysis of the sorts of problems that I have been addressing. First of all, we begin with the phenomenology of our ordinary experience when we talk about dealing with money, property, government, and marriage, not to mention belief, hope, fear, desire, and hunger. But the point is that the phenomenological investigation is only the beginning. You then have to go on and investigate logical structures, most of which are not often accessible to phenomenology. And, of course, in the course of the investigation, phenomenology plays another role: it sets conditions of adequacy. You cannot say anything that is phenomenologically false. You cannot say, for example, that every intentional state is conscious or that every intentional action is consciously intended, because that is phenomenologically false. These mistakes that I have been alleging should not be attributed to phenomenology as a research program but to particular misconceptions of that research program.[30]

REFERENCES

Blattner, William D. (1999), *Heidegger's Temporal Idealism* (New York: Cambridge University Press).

Carman, Taylor (2003), *Heidegger's Analytic* (Cambridge: Cambridge University Press).

Chisholm, Roderick (ed.) (1960), *Realism and the Background of Phenomenology* (Glencoe, Ill.: Free Press).

and Sellars, W. (1958), "Chisholm–Sellers correspondence on intentionality," in Herbert Feigl, Michael Scriven and, Grover Maxwell (eds.), *Minnesota Studies in the Philosophy of Science: Concepts, Theories and the Mind-Body Problem* (Minneapolis: University of Minnesota Press), 2: 521–539.

Dreyfus, Hubert L. (1991), *Being-in-the-World: A Commentary on Heidegger's* Being and Time, *Division I* (Cambridge, Mass.: MIT Press).

---

[30] In preparing this article, I was helped immensely by several people who read earlier drafts. I especially want to thank Taylor Carman, Hubert Dreyfus, Sean Kelly, Jennifer Hudin, Josef Moural, Kevin Mulligan, Dagmar Searle, and Barry Smith.

(1993), "Heidegger's critique of the Husserl/Searle account of intentionality," *Social Research* 60: 17–38.

(1999), "The primacy of phenomenology over logical analysis," *Philosophical Topics* 27, 2: 3–24.

(2001), "Phenomenological description versus rational reconstruction," *La Revue Internationale de Philosophie* 55, 217: 181–196.

and Wakefield, Jerome (1991), "Intentionality and the phenomenology of action," in Ernest Lepore and Robert van Gulick (eds.), *Searle and his Critics* (Cambridge, Mass.: Basil Blackwell).

Grice, H. P. (1989), "The Causal Theory of Perception," reprinted in Grice, H. P., *Studies in the Way of Words* (Cambridge, Mass.: Harvard University Press), 224–247.

Heidegger, Martin (1962), *Being and Time* (New York: Harper and Row).

(1982), *The Basic Problems of Phenomenology* (Bloomington, Ind.: Indiana University Press).

Husserl, Edmund (1960), *Cartesian Meditations* (The Hague: Martinus Nijhoff).

(1970a), *Logical Investigations*, 2 vols. (New York: Humanities Press).

(1970b), *The Crisis of the European Sciences and Transcendental Phenomenology* (Evanston: Northwestern University Press).

Kuhn, Thomas (1962), *The Structure of Scientific Revolutions* (Chicago: University of Chicago Press).

Merleau-Ponty, Maurice (1962), *Phenomenology of Perception* (London: Routledge).

Milner, A. D. and Goodale, M. A. (1995), *The Visual Brain in Action* (Oxford: Oxford University Press).

Moran, Dermot (2000), *Introduction to Phenomenology* (London and New York: Routledge).

Penfield, Wilder (1975), *The Mystery of the Mind: A Critical Study of Consciousness and the Human Brain* (Princeton: Princeton University Press).

Polt, Richard (1999), *Heidegger: An Introduction* (Ithaca: Cornell University Press).

Russell, Bertrand (1905), "On Denoting," *Mind*.

Searle, John R. (1983), *Intentionality: An Essay in the Philosophy of Mind* (Cambridge: Cambridge University Press).

CHAPTER 7

The self as a problem in philosophy and neurobiology

I. THE PHILOSOPHICAL PROBLEM OF THE SELF

There are a large number of different problems concerning the self in psychology, neurobiology, philosophy, and other disciplines. I have the impression that many of the problems of the self studied in neurobiology concern various forms of pathology – defects in the integrity, coherence, or functioning of the self. I will have nothing to say about these pathologies because I know next to nothing about them. I will only mention those pathologies, such as the split-brain patients, that are directly relevant to the philosophical problems of the self.

In philosophy, the traditional problem of the self is the problem of personal identity. Indeed, in the standard *Encyclopedia of Philosophy*, (Edwards, 1967) the entry "self" just says "see personal identity." The problem of personal identity is the problem of stating the criteria by which we identify someone as the same person through changes. Thus, for example, the problem of personal identity arises in such a question as, What fact about me, here and now, makes me the same person as the person who bore my name and lived in my house twenty years ago? There are a number of criteria of personal identity and they do not always yield the same result. I will get to these shortly.

I think that in fact there are at least two philosophical problems concerning the self. Besides the problem of personal identity, there is the problem of whether it is necessary to postulate the existence of a self that goes beyond the recognition of the body and of the sequence of experiences that occur in the body. In our philosophical tradition, and especially in our religious tradition, it is common to suppose that in addition to our bodies we also possess souls, that the souls are the essence of ourselves, and that, therefore, for each of us, his or her self consists of a soul. On this view, what we think of as our mental life, both conscious and unconscious, is something that goes on not in our bodies but in our souls, which can also be called our selves, or our minds. According to Descartes, an influential exponent of this tradition, each of us is identical, not with a body, but with an entity we can call mind, soul, or self; and we only happen to be contingently attached to a body during the course of a lifetime. Once we die, the soul will depart from the body and have a separate existence. I think the temptation to confuse the problem of personal identity with this second problem of the self derives from the fact that we suppose that if we had an affirmative solution to the second problem it would automatically provide a solution to the first. If we knew that in addition to our bodies we each had a soul, or self, or mind, and this entity was the very essence of our being, then the continuation of the self, so described, would immediately provide a solution of the problem of personal identity. You are identical with the person who lived here twenty years ago because you are the same soul or self.

So much for the tradition. Where are we today? Well, I don't know any-body who believes in the existence of an immortal soul except those who do so for some religious reason. A famous neurobiologist who believed in the soul was Sir John Eccles. And there are a number of philosophers who also believe in the existence of an immortal soul, but like Eccles their belief is part of their general religious conviction. From my experience, most philosophers do not believe in the existence of the soul. Furthermore, what is more important for the purposes of our present discussion, most philoso-phers do not believe in the existence of the self as something in addition to the sequence of our experiences, conscious and unconscious, and the body in which these experiences occur. I think most philosophers accept Hume's skepticism about the existence of the self (Hume, 1951: 251 ff). Hume asked himself the following question, When I turn my attention inward and focus on what is going on in my mind, what do I find? Hume says that I do not find any self or soul or person in addition to the sequence of my experiences. If, for example, I clutch my forehead and concentrate very seriously on what is happening in a way that will try to locate my self, what I locate will be the pressure of my hand on my forehead and a whole lot of other such experiences, "impressions" and "ideas" as Hume calls them. Hume's view, which has been very influential and probably the most common view in philosophy about the self, is that each of us consists in a physical body, and each of us has a sequence of experiences within that body.[1] But that is it, as far as human life is concerned. There

---

[1] Strictly speaking, Hume did not believe that we were justified in supposing that bodies had a "separate and distinct" existence, but that is another issue that is independent of his skepticism about the self.

is no self or soul left over, nor is there any need to postulate any such an entity.

Well, what about personal identity? There are a variety of criteria that we do in fact employ in deciding questions of the identity of a person across time and change.

It seems to me that, in fact, we employ at least four different criteria for deciding questions of identity. The first and most important is the identity of the body. I am the same person as the person who bore my name decades ago because my present body is spatio-temporally continuous with the body that existed under my name at that time. Of course, there are philosophical puzzles: None of the molecules in my body today is the same as those in my body of decades ago, so how can the body be the same if all the microparts are different? Furthermore, philosophers are good at inventing puzzling science-fiction thought experiments. Suppose that bodily fusion and fission were common. What would we say if humans routinely split into two or three or five bodies, as amoebae now split into two? But in spite of these puzzles, we have a pretty clear notion of bodily identity that works across time and change. Well why isn't that enough? Unlike the identity of material objects such as cars and houses, we are convinced that the identity of the body is not enough to constitute my personal identity. We all understand Kafka's story of Gregor Samsa who wakes to find *himself* in the body of a giant insect. And it is easy to imagine science-fiction scenarios of brain transplants in which I might find myself having a different body. Furthermore, possession of the same brain might not by itself be enough for personal identity. Suppose that I had the same brain but that all the information in my brain were transferred to another person's brain and the information in his brain were transferred to mine. We might feel that I now inhabit his body, and he inhabits mine. I am not saying that these science-fiction fantasies are sufficiently clear, or even coherent. I only point to them because they indicate that where our own personal identity is concerned, we think there is more to it than just the body. Well, what more? Locke said that the essential thing to personal identity is what he called "consciousness" (Locke, 1924: 182–201). Most interpreters think that by "consciousness" he meant our present memory experiences of a continuity between our present self and the earlier self that had the experiences on which our present memories are based. In short, Locke's consciousness criterion is usually, and I think correctly, interpreted as a memory criterion. The idea is that in addition to the continuity of the body we need a continuity of consciousness as recorded in memory. In addition to the third-person criterion of bodily continuity, we need the first-person criterion of the experience of the personal identity of the self. And this is how all human personal identity differs from the identities of cars and houses, etc.

A third criterion, commonly used in ordinary life, is relative stability and continuity of personality. In cases where we feel that a person's personality has altered dramatically and drastically, we are inclined to feel "he is not the same person any more." To take a famous case, when an iron bar went through the skull of the nineteenth-century railway worker Phineas Gage, he miraculously survived, but his personality was totally different. Before, he had been friendly, gregarious, and reliable; afterwards, he became hostile, surly, and capricious. From a purely practical point of view we would continue to regard him as the same person. For example, he would still owe the taxes of Phineas Gage and still own the property of Phineas Gage. But from a neurobiological point of view, and a philosophical point of view, we want to know very much what had changed in Phineas Gage so as to render him a totally different personality from what he had been before.

A fourth criterion is the relative coherence of the spatio-temporal continuity of the physical body through change. There is a standard pattern by which one and the same body grows and ages until eventual death. But suppose that the entity, though spatio-temporally continuous, varies wildly and unpredictably in its physical form. Suppose my body might change into that of a car or a house or a mountain. We think we understand Gregor Samsa's body changing into that of a large insect, but how far are we prepared to go? I do not think we need to answer that question in advance. The point I am making now is that we in fact employ four different sets of criteria in our concept of personal identity – spatio-temporal continuity of body, continuous memory, continuity of personality, and coherence of physical change – and that the everyday concept works well enough because these hang together to give consistent answers in real life.

So far so good, or so it might seem. It seems there is no such thing as the self in addition to all that stuff I have been talking about – continuity and coherence of the living body together with continuous memory sequences and coherent personalities. But I don't think this conclusion is correct. I have reluctantly come to the conclusion that the nature of human consciousness requires the postulation of a non-Humean self, and this postulation poses problems for neurobiology that go beyond the standard neurobiological problems of consciousness but will enable us to repose the question of consciousness in important ways.

II. THE NEUROBIOLOGICAL PROBLEM OF CONSCIOUSNESS

Sometimes, but unfortunately not very often, we can get a scientific solution to a longstanding philosophical problem. A famous case is the problem of life. The problem was, How can mere inert, inanimate matter be alive? Traditionally, there were two possible answers, the mechanist answer, according to which life could be reduced to mechanical processes, and the vitalist answer, according to which something more was needed, an *élan vital*, a vital force, that infused life into inert matter. We cannot take this problem seriously any more, and it is hard for us to recover the passion with which it was debated a mere century ago. The point is not that the mechanists won and the vitalists lost, but rather we got a much richer conception of biochemical mechanisms – a conception that did not exist when the debate raged in the nineteenth and early twentieth centuries.

I hope something like this is also happening to the problem of consciousness. The problem here is, How can mere unconscious bits of matter in the brain cause consciousness? On this problem we have a head start over the problem of life because we know before we ever get started on the investigation that processes in the brain do in fact cause consciousness. All the same, much, though not all, current neurobiological research suffers from a mistaken conception of the problem and that in turn derives from a mistaken conception of the self. In order to work up to the self, I have to say a little bit about consciousness.

I sometimes still hear it said that "consciousness" is hard to define. But if we are just talking about a definition that gives us not a scientific analysis, but rather locates the target of our investigation, then it seems to me that consciousness is not hard to define. Here is a definition: consciousness consists of those states of feelings, sentience, or awareness that typically begin when we wake from a dreamless sleep and continue throughout the day until those feelings stop, until we go to sleep again, go into a coma, die, or otherwise become "unconscious." On this account, dreams are a form of consciousness that occur to us during sleep. What, then, are the features of consciousness that we would like to be able to explain on this definition? Conscious states, so defined, are *qualitative* in the sense that there is always a certain qualitative feel to what it is like to be in one conscious state rather than another. We all know the difference between listening to Beethoven's Ninth Symphony and drinking cold beer. The difference is precisely the kind of qualitative difference that I am talking about. We know furthermore that all such conscious states are *subjective* in the sense that they only exist as experienced by a human or animal subject. Conscious states require a subject for their very existence. They do not exist in a neutral or third-person fashion, they have an existence that depends on their first-person subjective qualities, and that is just another way of saying that a conscious state must always be someone's conscious state. In philosophy this point is sometimes put by saying consciousness has a "first-person ontology." "First-person" here means there must be an *I*, some subject that experiences the consciousness, and "ontology" just refers to the mode of existence that something has. A third feature of consciousness is less frequently remarked on, but I think it is absolutely essential to understanding the other two. Conscious states always come to us as part of a unified conscious field. So when I am listening to Beethoven's Ninth Symphony while drinking beer, I do not just have the experience of listening and the experience of drinking, rather I have the experience of drinking and listening as part of one total conscious experience, and this is characteristic of consciousness generally, that consciousness always and only occurs as part of a unified conscious field. This is why, by the way, the split-brain experiments are so important to the study of consciousness. As far as we can tell from the experiments of Sperry and Gazzaniga (Gazzaniga, 1985), the patient whose corpus collosum has been cut gives all the external symptoms of having two separate conscious fields, one in each hemisphere, and that these are only imperfectly united into a single conscious field, and sometimes they exist as separate conscious fields.

Among philosophers, Immanuel Kant attached a great deal of importance to the unity of the conscious field. He called it "the transcendental unity of apperception" (Kant, 1997). I think the unity of our conscious field is going to be important to our analysis of the concept of the self and I will say more about it later. For the moment, I just want to call attention to the fact that these three features, qualitativeness, subjectivity, and unity, are not independent of each other. Each implies the next. You cannot have a qualitative experience such as tasting beer without that experience occurring as part of some subjective state of awareness, and you cannot have a subjective state of awareness except as part of a total field of awareness, even if the only thing in this particular impoverished field is the state of awareness itself. So we might say, initially at least, the problem of consciousness is precisely the problem of qualitative, unified subjectivity. The three features are simply different aspects of the one common essential trait of consciousness. Now there are lots of other traits of consciousness that should be investigated, and I have investigated the philosophical aspects of them at some length in a number of books (Searle, 1984, 1992, 1997, 2004). But for the purposes of this article, I am going to focus only on these three, and particularly on the last one, because they are most relevant for our examination of the problem of the self.

Notice an interesting feature of the unified conscious field. Within the field we can change our attention at will. Without moving my head, or even my eyes, I can focus my attention on this or that feature of my visual field. And even with my eyes closed I can think now about this problem, now that problem, moving the focus of my attention, again, entirely at will. This ought to seem puzzling to us. The brain creates a conscious field just as the stomach and digestive tract create digestion. So what has conscious *will* got to do with it? To put a question crudely, when I say I can shift my attention at will, who does the shifting? Why should there be anything more to my conscious life than the existence of a conscious field? Where is there anything more? I will come back to these questions because I think they are essential to understanding the problem of a self.

How can we solve the problem of consciousness as a problem in neurobiology? Well, first of all we have to state exactly what the problem we wish to be able to solve is. And here I think the answer can be stated quite simply. The neurobiological problem of consciousness is: How exactly do brain processes cause our conscious states in all of their enormous richness and variety, and how exactly are these conscious states realized in the brain? Why do conscious states exist at all, and where and how do they exist in the brain? It took a long time for many neurobiologists to see that this was a crucial question in neurobiology, indeed I would say it is the number one question in the biological sciences today. Right now there is a great deal of research on precisely this topic.

Most researchers are searching for the Neuronal Correlate of Consciousness (NCC). The idea is this: in order to solve the problem of consciousness, we should find out first what is going on in the brain at the neurobiological level at a time when a subject is conscious. What neurobiological features are correlated with the conscious features? We now think, perhaps with too much optimism, that recent improvements in our investigative techniques, especially single cell recording and fMRI, will give us a richer research apparatus for discovering the NCC. The idea, though often not explicitly stated, is that the investigation will proceed according to a pattern that has been fairly common in the history of science. The first step is to find a neuronal correlate of conscious states. This would be the NCC. The second stage is to investigate whether the NCC is actually a *causal* correlation, and we do this by the usual tests. In an otherwise unconscious subject, can you produce consciousness by producing the NCC? In an otherwise conscious subject, can you shut off consciousness by shutting off the NCC? If you have affirmative answers to these questions, then it is a reasonable supposition that the correlation is more than accidental; it is, in all likelihood, a causal correlation.

The third stage, and we are a long way from reaching this stage, is to get a general theory, a general statement of the laws or principles by which the correlation functions causally in the life of the organism. This research, as I said, is off and running. I am quite optimistic about its long-term prospects, though I have to admit, progress has been very slow. In general there are two lines of research that go on in this field, one of which seems to me much more promising than the other, though the more promising, unfortunately, is less easy to conduct as an actual research project. The most common line of research is what I call the "building block approach" (Searle, 2000). The idea of this approach is to think of the unified conscious field as made up of all of its different components. Right now, for example, I am experiencing the color red as I look at a red box on my table, I am hearing the sound of my voice, I am feeling a slight aftertaste of coffee in my mouth, etc. Now the idea of the building block approach is to think of the entire conscious field as made up of such building blocks: the experiences of color, of sound, of taste, etc. On this view, if we could find the NCC for even one building block, and understand the mechanisms by which that NCC caused consciousness, that presumably would give us an entering wedge that would enable us to crack the whole problem of consciousness. The mechanisms by which the NCC for a particular conscious state produce that conscious state will presumably be generalizeable to other conscious states. The analogy with genetics is obvious: you do not have to know how every phenotypical trait is the expression of some gene or set of genes in order to appreciate the power of the DNA conception of genetics. You have to understand the general mechanisms involved, and then you can apply them to particular cases. Most research on consciousness that I am aware of follows the building block approach.

Another approach, pursued by a minority of investigators, is what I call the "unified field approach." We want to know not so much what causes the experience of red, though that is part of our overall investigation, but rather how the brain becomes conscious in the first place. What exactly is the difference between the unconscious brain and the conscious brain, and how exactly do those differences cause the brain to be in a state of consciousness? The state of consciousness, as I have argued earlier, is a matter of a unified conscious field. So the question for this approach is: How does the brain produce the unified conscious field?

I said that I think the unified field approach is superior. Why? Science typically has proceeded by the practice of breaking larger problems down to smaller problems, by seeking an atomistic approach to large problems. Why wouldn't this work for consciousness? Perhaps it will, but there is an immediate objection: the building block approach identifies building blocks that can only exist in a subject who is already conscious. But if that is right then it looks like the NCC for the experience of the color red does not give us the NCC for the experience of consciousness, rather it gives us the NCC for a particular mode *within a preexisting conscious field.* On the unified field approach we should think of perception *not as creating* consciousness, but as *modifying* the preexisting conscious field (Rodolfo Llinás, 2001). On the building block approach, perception creates consciousness just like that, out of nothing except neuronal processes. On the unified field approach, perception does not create consciousness but modifies the consciousness of the preexisting conscious field.

Why am I so convinced that the building block approach is the wrong approach? The answer is that if we take the building block approach as giving us the NCC for consciousness and not for particular modifications of the conscious field, then it would make predictions that seem implausible. The approach would predict that in an otherwise unconscious subject, if you could introduce the NCC for the experience of the color red, the subject would suddenly have a conscious flash of red, and then lapse back into total unconsciousness. That seems to me extremely unlikely. From what we know about the experience of red, it occurs only in subjects who have a preexisting consciousness, who are conscious already when they experience red. And so on with perception in general. Alarm clocks, for example, do not create just a single percept, but rather create a field in which that percept is the central entity.

Whether the building block or the unified field approach is better is an empirical question not to be settled by philosophical analysis, and I am prepared to be proven wrong. Perhaps the building block approach will succeed in the end. But right now I think it is a source of difficulty. In fact, it turns out it is not at all hard to find various kinds of NCCs for particular sorts of experiences and many researchers have done that (Kinwasher, 2001). But we still have not solved the problem of consciousness by these findings because we still do not have an answer to the question, What makes the brain conscious?

The reason I have belabored this point is because I think that there are lessons to be learned about the neurobiological problem of the self from reflecting on the neurobiological problem of consciousness.

III. THE REQUIREMENT OF THE SELF AS A FORMAL FEATURE OF THE UNIFIED CONSCIOUS FIELD AND ITS IMPLICATIONS FOR NEUROBIOLOGY

There are famous objections to Locke's criterion of memory as the essential criterion for personal identity. One objection is this: it would be circular to make memory a criterion for the identity of the self, because in order to establish that the memories in question are correct memories, one first has to establish that the person who has these memories is really identical with the person whose experiences he claims to remember. Thus, if I now sincerely claim that I remember writing the *Critique of Pure Reason*, that by itself goes no way at all towards showing that I am in fact identical with the actual author of the *Critique of Pure Reason*, because one would first have to establish that I did write the *Critique* before one could know that the memories are accurate. But for exactly the same reason the fact that I now claim to remember writing *Speech Acts* by itself goes no way at all toward showing that I am identical with the actual author of *Speech Acts*. So it looks like memory is no good as a criterion of the self because to establish that the memory is an accurate memory as opposed to an illusory one, one first has to establish the very identity that the memory was supposed to establish. I think this is a fair objection if we treat memory as a criterion of personal identity, but that need not be our only interest in memory. It seems to me, for this discussion, what we are interested in is not how to establish conclusively that I am identical with such and such a person who lived so many years ago, but rather, what facts about my conscious states give me a sense of myself as a single continuing entity through time? It is this sense of the self that is more relevant to problems in neurobiology.

I now think that with the introduction of memory I am prepared to state the philosophical problem of the self, and how it bears on neurobiology, a little more precisely. It is a remarkable feature of the conscious field, that I identified earlier, that the elements of the conscious field are not, so to speak, neutral. They are not just given to me as independent phenomena, but rather they exhibit certain special traits which I now want to specify further. First, it is an absolutely astounding thing about the conscious field that given the same conscious field I can shift my attention at will. Even without changing the direction of my eyes, I can focus my attention now on the coffee cup on the table, now at the computer screen in front of me, now at the bookcase on my right. The shift of attention within a constant conscious field is something I can do at will. A second feature, which derives from the first, is that I can change the entire conscious field at will, simply by doing something different, such as moving my head or closing my eyes, or standing up and leaving the room. The fact that I have the ability to do things seems to be an essential part of the normal human conscious field, and we can easily imagine a different mode of existence where I was utterly passive, where I simply experienced events occurring to me but had no sense whatever of having any control over them. When I engage in conscious voluntary action, I have a sense of my own freedom. I have the sense that I am doing this, but I could, right here and now, be doing something different. In such cases I have the impression that the causes of my action, in the form of the reasons on which I am acting, are not causally sufficient to determine the action. In normal non-pathological cases, the action is *motivated but not determined*, because there is a *gap* between the perceived causes and the action. This gap has a name in philosophy, it is called the freedom of the will. It does not matter for our present purposes whether the sense of freedom is a mark of real freedom or only an illusion. I cannot think the gap away, for even if I become a convinced determinist and refuse to make any choices on the grounds that everything is determined anyway, my refusal to make any choices is intelligible to me as my action only under the presupposition of freedom. I have freely chosen not to make any free choices. The third feature of the conscious field is that I do in fact have a sense of myself as a particular person situated at a particular time and place in history, with a certain set of particular experiences and memories. We need to put these various features together into a unified account of the self before we can state questions that could be addressed by neurobiology.

The sequence of conscious experiences (as identified by Hume) together with the fact that these experiences come to us as part of a unified conscious field (as identified by Kant) is still not enough to give us the characteristic experiences that constitute our idea of the self. Even if we add to the Hume–Kant story the idea that some of these experiences are memories of earlier experiences (as identified by Locke), we still do not have our conception of the self. What is missing? Let us go back to the point I made earlier, that we can shift our attention at will, and indeed initiate actions at will. Who does the shifting and who does the initiating? One thing I have noticed in teaching these matters to undergraduates, and discussing them with high-powered professionals, is that *everybody* feels the attraction of the homunculus fallacy. It is very tempting to think that there is a little guy in my head who does my thinking, perceiving, and acting. Of course, the homunculus fallacy is a fallacy, because it leads to an infinite regress. If my vision can only occur because the little man in my head watches the TV screen in my head, then who watches the TV screen in the little man's head? But, and this is the crucial point, though the homunculus is a fallacy, the urge to postulate the homunculus is powerful and well founded. The problem is that we cannot make sense of our conscious experiences if we think of them as just a sequence of events (impressions and ideas à la Hume) related by present memory experiences of earlier experiences (à la Locke) and part of a unified conscious field (à la Kant). We need to postulate, initially at least, a locus of the initiation of action. My decisions and actions are not just events that occur, but rather *I decide* and *I act*. But now we have to proceed very carefully or else we are going to start sounding like the worst kind of German philosophers (Was ist das Ich?). So far we have postulated only a purely formal entity. It is simply an x, something capable of initiating and carrying out actions. Notice, however, that the entity that initiates actions must be the very same entity as the entity that reflects on reasons for action, and indeed the same entity that has perceptions and memories that form the basis of the reasons on which we reflect and decide on actions. Just as we had to postulate a purely formally specified entity that decides and acts, so the connection between perception, memory, and reasons for action requires us to postulate that the *same* entity that performs the action has all of these other features. Why? Well if the entity that decides and acts is different from the one that perceives, remembers, and reflects then we would not get the connection necessary to make sense of our actions. If I act on a reason R, then R must by *my* reason for acting. For example, if I jump out of the way because I see a truck bearing down on me, then the entity that initiates the jumping has to be the same one that does the seeing, otherwise the seeing gives no reason for the jumping. Furthermore once the action has been performed, the same entity that did the performing is the one who has responsibility for the performance and thus gets the credit or the blame. We can pull all these threads together by saying:

The universal urge to postulate a homunculus is based on very profound features of our ordinary conscious experiences. In order to make sense of those experiences we have to suppose,

There is some x such that

x is conscious;

x persists through time;

x has perceptions and memories;

x operates with reasons in the gap;

x, in the gap, is capable of deciding and acting;

x is responsible for at least some of its behavior.

The x in question is the self in at least one sense of the word. Notice that the postulation of the self is not the postulation of a separate entity distinct from the conscious field but rather it is a formal feature of the conscious field. The point I am making is that if we reflect on the features of the conscious field we see that we cannot accurately describe it if we think of it as a field constituted only by its contents and their arrangement. Rather, the contents require a principle of unity, but the principle is not a separate entity. To suppose we had both a conscious field *and* a self would be a category mistake, like supposing that the country most of which is between Mexico and Canada consists of fifty *states plus* the United States of America. Rather, the postulation of a self is like the postulation of the point of view in visual perception. We cannot make sense of our perceptions unless we suppose that they occur from a point of view even though the point of view is not itself perceived. Similarly we cannot make sense of our conscious experiences unless we suppose that they occur to a self even though the self is not consciously experienced. The self is not a separate thing or entity any more than the point of view is.

Let us now pull these various threads about the self together. Let us remind ourselves first that we are talking about a problem in animal biology. There is no dualism or spiritualism hiding in our account. The irreducibly mental unified conscious field is a biological, and therefore "physical" or "natural," feature of the brain. There is nothing spooky or unnatural about it. We have discovered under analysis that our bodies with their brains are capable of causing and sustaining a unified conscious field, and this unified field is qualitative and subjective, unlike other aspects of our biological life. I have claimed that the sense of permanence and coherence that we each get in our conscious field also requires memory.

But interestingly, the unified conscious field, even given a sense of continuing identity via memory, is not enough to account for the facts of our ordinary non-pathological experience. To account for those facts we need to postulate a (purely formal) self, x. What are these facts and why do they force us to postulate a self? The first fact is that, because of the gap, decisions and actions do not just happen. There has to be something that makes the decision and performs the action. In my case, decisions and actions are not somethings that just happen to me, rather *I* make the decisions and carry out the actions. And the second fact is that the existence of an agent, something that can decide and act, is not by itself enough. The very same entity that decides and acts has to be the entity that perceives, remembers, imagines, reflects, etc. I not only act but the same I that acts also reflects, perceives, remembers, etc. So, at least for non-pathological cases, we are forced to postulate a single entity x that constitutes the self and has all of the psychological properties that constitute the unified conscious field. The self in question, the x, is conscious and is capable of deciding and acting in the gap. But the same x that decides and acts must be capable of thought, because the decisions and actions are based on reasons. And those reasons themselves are based on perception, memory, and other cognitive capacities, hence the x that does the deciding, acting, and thinking must be the x that exercises all these other cognitive capacities.

Several philosophers, famously Kant, have said that all consciousness is self-consciousness. If that means that every first-order conscious state requires a second-order state about the first state, it is wrong. I can for example just enjoy the beer. I do not have to also enjoy my enjoying of the beer. But there is a sense in which it is right. All (non-pathological) consciousness, first or second order, has to be possessed by a self. The self is not the object of consciousness. If I drink the beer, the object of my consciousness is the beer I am drinking, not the self that does the drinking. Nor is the self the content of the consciousness. If I drink the beer the content of my consciousness is the experience of beer drinking, not the experience of the self. There is no experience of the self. But in order that there be a conscious experience of beer drinking that has object and content, there has to be a self that experiences the content and is aware of the object.

We will understand this point better if we pursue the analogy with vision. In order to make sense of my visual perceptions I have to postulate a visual apparatus that is necessary for visual perception but is not itself part of the object nor the content of visual perception. This apparatus will include a point of view as well as a spatially located mechanism that does the seeing. But neither the point of view nor the mechanism are seen, nor are they part of the experience of seeing. Exactly analogously in order to make sense of the conscious field we have to postulate a self that is not part of the conscious field, nor is it one of the objects of the conscious field. Finally, what has all this got to do with neurobiology? How does the brain, indeed, how could the brain produce all the features I have been describing? A neurobiological account of consciousness cannot stop with the NCC, even with an NCC that is known to function causally in producing consciousness. In order to have a scientific account of consciousness we will need more than an account of how the brain produces subjective states of sentience and awareness. We will need to know how the brain produces the peculiar organization of experiences that expresses the existence of the self.

How would one go about conducting any such research? I am too ignorant of brain functioning to have an intelligent opinion, but here is one suggestion. In other areas of brain science we have learned a lot from studying the pathological cases. Just as in vision we have learned much from blind sight, and in memory we have learned much from bilateral removal of the hippocampus, so in the study of the self we might start with some of the pathologies discussed elsewhere in this book.

REFERENCES

Edwards, P. (ed.) (1967), *The Encyclopedia of Philosophy* (New York: MacMillan & the Free Press), vol. 7.

Gazzaniga, Michael (1985), *The Social Brain: Discovering the Networks of the Mind* (New York: Perseus Group Books).

Hume, David (1951), *A Treatise of Human Nature* (Oxford: Oxford University Press), Book I, Part III, Section VI: Of Personal Identity.

Kant, Immanuel (1997), *Critique of Pure Reason*, trans. Paul Guyer and Allen W. Wood (Cambridge: Cambridge University Press, 1997).

Kinwasher, Nancy (2001), Neural events and perceptual awareness, *Cognition* 79: 89–113.

Llinás, Rodolfo (2001), *I of the Vortex: From Neurons to Self* (Cambridge, Mass.: MIT Press).

Locke, John (1924), *An Essay Concerning Human Understanding*, ed. A. S. Pringle-Pattison (Oxford: Oxford University Press).

Searle, John R. (1984), *Minds, Brains and Science* (Cambridge, Mass.: Harvard University Press).

(1992), *Rediscovery of the Mind* (Cambridge, Mass.: MIT Press).

(1997), *The Mystery of Consciousness* (New York: New York Review of Books).

(2000), "Consciousness," *Annual Review of Neuroscience* 23: 557–578.

(2004), *Mind: A Brief Introduction* (Oxford: Oxford University Press).

CHAPTER 8

Why I am not a property dualist

I have argued in a number of writings[1] that the philosophical part (though not the neurobiological part) of the traditional mind-body problem has a fairly simple and obvious solution: all of our mental phenomena are caused by lower-level neuronal processes in the brain and are themselves realized in the brain as higher-level, or system, features. The form of causation is "bottom up," whereby the behaviour of lower-level elements, presumably neurons and synapses, causes the higher-level or system features of consciousness and intentionality. (This form of causation, by the way, is common in nature; for example, the higher-level feature of solidity is causally explained by the behaviour of the lower-level elements, the molecules.) Because this view emphasizes the biological character of the mental, and because it treats mental phenomena as ordinary parts of nature, I have labelled it "biological naturalism."

To many people biological naturalism looks a lot like property dualism. Because I believe property dualism is mistaken, I would like to try to clarify the differences between the two accounts and try to expose the weaknesses in property dualism. This short paper then has the two subjects expressed by the double meanings in its title: why my views are not the same as property dualism, and why I find property dualism unacceptable.

There are, of course, several different "mind-body" problems. The one that most concerns me in this article is the relationship between consciousness and brain processes. I think that the conclusions of the discussion will extend to other features of the mind-body problem, such as, for example, the relationship between intentionality and brain processes, but for the sake of simplicity I will concentrate on consciousness. For the purposes of this discussion, the "mind-body problem" is a problem about how consciousness relates to the brain.

[1] Initially in Searle (1983); subsequently in Searle (1984, 1992), and other writings.

The mind-body problem, so construed, persists in philosophy because of two intellectual limitations on our part. First, we really do not understand how brain processes cause consciousness. Second, we continue to accept a traditional vocabulary that contrasts the mental and the physical, the mind and the body, the soul and the flesh, in a way that I think is confused and obsolete. I cannot overcome our neurobiological ignorance, but I can at least try to overcome our conceptual confusion, and that is one of the things that I will attempt to do in this article.

I think it is because of these two limitations, our ignorance of how the brain works and our acceptance of the traditional vocabulary, that many people find property dualism appealing. Before criticizing it, I want to try to account for its appeal by stating the thesis with as much plausibility as I can. Of course, there are different versions of property dualism, but what I hope to state is the version that is closest to my own views and consequently the one I find most challenging. I will say nothing about "neutral monism," panpsychism, or the various forms of "dual aspect" theories. Notice that in presenting arguments for property dualism I have to use the traditional terminology that later on I will reject.

Here is how the world looks to the property dualist:

There is clearly a difference between consciousness and the material or physical world. We know this from our own experience, but it is also obvious from science. The material world is publicly accessible and is pretty much as described by physics, chemistry, and the other hard sciences; but the conscious, experiential, phenomenological world is not publicly accessible. It has a distinct private existence. We know it with certainty from our inner, private, subjective experiences. We all know that the private world of consciousness exists, we know that it is part of the real world, and our question is to find out how it fits into the public material world, specifically, we need to know how it fits into the brain.

Because neither consciousness nor matter is reducible to the other, they are distinct and different phenomena in the world. Those who believe that consciousness is reducible to matter are called materialists; those who believe that matter is reducible to consciousness are called idealists. Both are mistaken for the same reason. Both try to eliminate something that really exists in its own right and cannot be reduced to something else. Now, because both materialism and idealism are false, the only reasonable alternative is dualism. But substance dualism seems out of the question for a number of reasons. For example, it cannot explain how these spiritual substances came into existence in the first place and it cannot explain how they relate to the physical world. So property dualism seems the only reasonable view of the mind-body problem. Consciousness really exists, but it is not a separate substance on its own; rather, it is a property of the brain.

We can summarize property dualism in the following four propositions. The first three are statements endorsed by the property dualist, the fourth is an apparent consequence or difficulty implied by the first three:

(1) There are two mutually exclusive metaphysical categories that constitute all of empirical reality: they are physical phenomena and mental phenomena. Physical phenomena are essentially objective, in the sense that they exist apart from any subjective experiences of humans or animals. Mental phenomena are subjective, in the sense that they exist only as experienced by human or animal agents.

(2) Because mental states are not reducible to neurobiological states, they are something *distinct from* and *over and above* neurobiological states. The irreducibility of the mental to the physical, of consciousness to neurobiology, is by itself sufficient proof of the distinctness of the mental, and proof that the mental is something over and above the neurobiological.

(3) Mental phenomena do not constitute separate objects or substances, but rather are features or properties of the composite entity, which is a human being or an animal. So any conscious animal, such as a human being, will have two sorts of properties, mental properties and physical properties.

(4) The chief problem for the property dualists, given these assumptions, is how can consciousness ever function causally? There are two possibilities, neither of which seems attractive. First, let us assume, as seems reasonable, that the physical universe is causally closed. It is closed in the sense that nothing outside it, nothing non-physical, could ever have causal effects inside the physical universe. If that is so, and consciousness is not a part of the physical universe, then it seems that it must be epiphenomenal. All of our conscious life plays no role whatever in any of our behaviour.

On the other hand, we may assume that the physical universe is not causally closed, that consciousness can function causally in the production of physical behaviour. But this seems to lead us out of the frying pan and into the fire, because we know, for example, that when I raise my arm, there is a story to be told at the level of neuron firings, neurotransmitters, and muscle contractions that is entirely sufficient to account for the movement of my arm. So if we are to suppose that consciousness also functions in the movement of my arm, then it looks like we have two distinct causal stories, neither reducible to the other; and to put the matter very briefly, my bodily movements have too many causes. We have causal overdetermination.

The property dualist has a conception of consciousness and its relation to the rest of reality that I believe is profoundly mistaken. I can best make my differences with property dualism explicit by stating how I would deal with these same issues.

(1) There are not two (or five or seven) fundamental ontological categories, rather the act of categorization itself is always interest relative. For that reason the attempt to answer such questions as, "How many fundamental metaphysical categories are there?", as it stands, is meaningless. We live in exactly one world and there are as many different ways of dividing it as you like. In addition to electromagnetism, consciousness, and gravitational attraction, there are declines in interest rates, points scored in football games, reasons for being suspicious of quantified modal logic, and election results in Florida. Now, quick, were the election results mental or physical? And how about the points scored in a football game? Do they exist only in the mind of the scorekeeper or are they rather ultimately electronic phenomena on the scoreboard? I think these are not interesting, or even meaningful, questions. We live in one world, and it has many different types of features. My view is not "pluralism" if that term suggests that there is a non-arbitrary, non-interest-relative principle of distinguishing the elements of the plurality. A useful distinction, for certain purposes, is to be made between the biological and the non-biological. At the most fundamental level, consciousness is a biological phenomenon in the sense that it is caused by biological processes, is itself a biological process, and interacts with other biological processes. Consciousness is a biological process like digestion, photosynthesis, or the secretion of bile. Of course, our conscious lives are shaped by our culture, but culture is itself an expression of our underlying biological capacities.

(2) Then what about irreducibility? This is the crucial distinction between my view and property dualism. Consciousness is causally reducible to brain processes, because all the features of consciousness are accounted for causally by neurobiological processes going on in the brain, and consciousness has no causal powers of its own in addition to the causal powers of the underlying neurobiology. But in the case of consciousness, causal reducibility does not lead to ontological reducibility. From the fact that consciousness is entirely accounted for causally by neuron firings, for example, it does not follow that consciousness is nothing but neuron firings. Why not? What is the difference between consciousness and other phenomena that undergo an ontological reduction on the basis of a causal reduction, phenomena such as colour and solidity? The difference is that consciousness has a first-person ontology; that is, it only exists *as experienced* by

some human or animal, and therefore, it cannot be reduced to something that has a third-person ontology, something that exists independently of experiences. It is as simple as that.

The property dualist and I are in agreement that consciousness is onto-logically irreducible. The key points of disagreement are that I insist that from everything we know about the brain, consciousness is causally reducible to brain processes; and for that reason I deny that the ontological irreducibility of consciousness implies that consciousness is something "over and above," something distinct from, its neurobiological base. No, causally speaking, there is nothing there, except the neurobiology, which has a higher-level feature of consciousness. In a similar way there is nothing in the car engine except molecules, which have such higher-level features as the solidity of the cylinder block, the shape of the piston, the firing of the spark plug, etc. "Consciousness" does not name a distinct, separate phenomenon, something over and above its neurobiological base, rather it names a state that the neurobiological system can be in. Just as the shape of the piston and the solidity of the cylinder block are not something over and above the molecular phenomena, but are rather states of the system of molecules, so the consciousness of the brain is not something over and above the neuronal phenomena, but rather a state that the neuronal system is in.

So there is a sense in which consciousness is reducible: the mark of empirical reality is the possession of cause and effect relations, and con-sciousness (like other system features) has no cause and effect relations beyond those of its microstructural base. There is nothing in your brain except neurons (together with glial cells, blood flow and all the rest of it) and sometimes a big chunk of the thalamocortical system is conscious. The sense in which, though causally reducible, it is ontologically irreducible, is that a complete description of the third-person objective features of the brain would not be a description of its first-person subjective features.

(3) I say consciousness is a feature of the brain. The property dualist says consciousness is a feature of the brain. This creates the illusion that we are saying the same thing. But we are not, as I hope my response to points 1 and 2 makes clear. The property dualist means that *in addition to* all the neurobiological features of the brain, there is an extra, distinct, non-physical feature of the brain; whereas I mean that consciousness is a state the brain can be in, in the way that liquidity and solidity are states that water can be in.

Here is where the inadequacy of the traditional terminology comes out most obviously. The property dualist wants to say that consciousness is a mental and therefore not physical feature of the brain. I want to say consciousness is a mental and therefore biological and therefore physical feature of the brain. But because the traditional vocabulary was designed to contrast the mental and the physical, I cannot say what I want to say in the traditional vocabulary without sounding like I am saying something inconsistent. Similarly when the identity theorists said that consciousness is nothing but a neurobiological process, they meant that consciousness as qualitative, subjective, irreducibly phenomenological (airy fairy, touchy feely, etc.) does not even exist, that only third-person neurobiological processes exist. I want also to say that consciousness is nothing but a neurobiological process, and by that I mean that precisely because consciousness is qualitative, subjective, irreducibly phenomenological (airy fairy, touchy feely, etc.) it has to be a neurobiological process; because, so far, we have not found any system that can cause and realize conscious states except brain systems. Maybe someday we will be able to create conscious artifacts, in which case subjective states of consciousness will be "physical" features of those artifacts.

(4) Because irreducible consciousness is not something over and above its neural base, the problems about epiphenomenalism and the causal closure of the physical simply do not arise for me. Of course, the universe is causally closed, and we can call it "physical" if we like; but that cannot mean "physical" as opposed to "mental"; because, equally obviously, the mental is part of the causal structure of the universe in the same way that the solidity of pistons is part of the causal structure of the universe; even though the solidity is entirely accounted for by molecular behaviour, and consciousness is entirely accounted for by neuronal behaviour. The problems about epiphenomenalism and the causal closure of the physical can only arise if one uses the traditional terminology and takes its implications seriously. I am trying to get us to abandon that terminology.

But if consciousness has no causal powers in addition to its neurobiological base, then does that not imply epiphenomenalism? No. Compare: the solidity of the piston has no causal powers in addition to its molecular base, but this does not show that solidity is epiphenomenal (try making a piston out of butter or water). The question rather is: Why would anyone suppose that causal reducibility implies epiphenomenalism, since the real world is full of causally efficacious higher-level features entirely caused by lower-level micro phenomena? In this case the answer is: Because they think that consciousness is something distinct from, something "over and above," its neuronal base. The typical property dualist thinks that the brain "gives rise to" consciousness, and this gives us a picture of consciousness as given off from the brain as a pot of boiling water gives off steam. In the epiphenomenalist version of property dualism, the consciousness given off has no causal powers of its own, though it is caused by the brain. In the full-blooded version consciousness has a kind of life of its own, capable of interfering with the material world.

I think this whole way of thinking of the matter is profoundly mistaken and I want to explain this point in a little more detail. The fact that the dilemma of either epiphenomenalism or causal overdetermination can even seem to be a problem for property dualism is a symptom that something is radically wrong with the theory. Nobody thinks that we are forced to postulate that solidity is epiphenomenal on the grounds that it has no causal powers in addition to the causal powers of the molecular structures, nor do they think that if we recognize the causal powers of solidity we are forced to postulate causal overdetermination, because now the same effect can be explained either in terms of the behaviour of the molecules or the solidity of the whole structure. And what goes for solidity goes for photosynthesis, digestion, electricity, earthquakes, hurricanes in Kansas, and pretty much everything else that we normally cite in causal explanations. In every case the higher-level phenomenon is causally reducible to its microstructural basis, in exactly the same way that consciousness is causally reducible to its microstructural basis. Why are we inclined to make this mistake for consciousness when we would not think of making it for other causal phenomena? I think the answer is obvious. Because the traditional vocabulary tells us that the mental and the physical are two distinct ontological categories and because consciousness is not ontologically reducible to its neuronal base, we suppose that is not a part of the physical world, in the way that these other phenomena are. That is the deeper mistake of property dualism. And that is precisely where I part company with the property dualist. The problem is not only that we have an obsolete seventeenth-century vocabulary that contrasts the mental and the physical, but that we also have a misconception of the nature of reduction. Causal reduction does not necessarily imply ontological reduction, though typically where we have a causal reduction as in the case of the liquidity, solidity, and colour we have tended to make an ontological reduction. But the impossibility of an ontological reduction in the case of consciousness does not give it any mysterious metaphysical status. Consciousness does not exist in a separate realm and it does not have any causal powers in addition to those of its neuronal base any more than solidity has any extra causal powers in addition to its molecular base.

Both materialism and dualism are trying to say something true, but they both wind up saying something false. The materialist is trying to say, truly, that the universe consists entirely of material phenomena such as physical particles in fields of force. But he ends up saying, falsely, that irreducible states of consciousness do not exist. The dualist is trying to say, truly, that ontologically irreducible states of consciousness do exist, but he ends up saying, falsely, that these are not ordinary parts of the physical world. The trick is to state the truth in each view without saying the falsehood. To do that we have to challenge the assumptions behind the traditional vocabulary. The traditional vocabulary is based on the assumption that if something is a state of consciousness in the strict sense – it is inner, qualitative, subjective, etc. – then it cannot in those very respects be physical or material. And conversely if something is physical or material then it cannot in its physical or material respects be a state of consciousness. Once you abandon the assumptions behind the traditional vocabulary it is not hard to state the truth. The universe does consist entirely in physical particles in fields of force (or whatever the ultimately true physics discovers), these are typically organized into systems, some of the systems are biological, and some of the biological systems are conscious. Consciousness is thus an ordinary feature of certain biological systems, in the same way that photosynthesis, digestion, and lactation are ordinary features of biological systems.

ADDENDUM

There is an important issue that I have not pursued in this article, but I want at least to raise as a further problem for property dualism. It is not at all easy to see how the property dualist can maintain simultaneously that consciousness is a property or feature of the brain and that there is a metaphysical dualism of the mental and the physical. How, in short, can the property dualist avoid lapsing into substance dualism? The difficulty comes out in the metaphors that the property dualist uses to express the thesis. Typical metaphors are that consciousness is something "over and above" brain processes, that brains "give rise to" consciousness and, of course, that consciousness is an "emergent" property of the brain. But all of these metaphors suggest that the picture the dualist has is that consciousness is something separate from the brain. I said the property dualist thinks of consciousness as like steam rising from a pot of boiling water, but here is another picture suggested by these metaphors: we are to think of consciousness as like the frosting on the cake of the brain (and in its panpsychist version, the frosting on the whole universe). The frosting is something distinct from the cake and is on top of it (over and above it). I have argued that these are the wrong pictures. The right picture, if we are going to persist in the metaphor of the cake, is that consciousness is the state that the cake (brain) is in. Officially, the property dualist says that consciousness is a property of the brain; but if you consider uncontroversial properties of the brain, like weight, shape, color, solidity, etc., nobody says that these "arise from" or are "over and above" the brain; and only in a special sense can some of them be described as "emergent" (cf. Searle, 1992: 111–112), and certainly not as "emergent from" the brain. The official claim is that consciousness is a property, not a thing, object or substance. But that claim is inconsistent with the conception of consciousness as something that is "over and above," that the brain "gives rise to," etc.; this conception requires that consciousness be a separate thing, object, or non-property type of entity. The dualism in property dualism forces them to postulate a separate entity. Ironically, the very dualism of the property dualist picture makes it impossible to state the theory without implying a version of substance dualism.

REFERENCES

Searle, J. R. (1983), *Intentionality: An Essay in the Philosophy of Mind* (Cambridge: Cambridge University Press).

(1984), *Minds, Brains and Science* (Cambridge, Mass.: Harvard University Press).

(1992), *The Rediscovery of the Mind* (Cambridge, Mass.: MIT Press).

CHAPTER 9

Fact and value, "is" and "ought," and reasons for action

This article deals with an issue that much concerned Hans Kelsen, the "is"– "ought" distinction. It is a fragment of a much larger work I am preparing on the subject of rationality.

A number of binary distinctions are central to our philosophical tradition. One thinks of the distinctions between truth and falsity, good and evil, reality and illusion, freedom and determinism, mind and body, and fact and value. Sometimes the belief in these distinctions creates problems because it seems that the acceptance of a certain standard conception of one of the terms of the distinction rules out the possibility of anything satisfying the other term. I will illustrate this apparent difficulty with three examples: mind and body, freedom and determinism, and fact and value. The corresponding problems can be stated as follows: How can there be irreducible mental phenomena in a universe that consists entirely of non-mental material phenomena? How can there be events that are free human actions, and thus are events not caused by antecedent events, in a universe in which every event is caused by antecedent events? How can there be objective values binding on all rational agents in a world in which all objectivity is factual objectivity and in which values are not factual?

As formulated, none of these questions is answerable. That is, in each case the answer has to be: there can't be anything satisfying the conditions set by the phrasing of the question, because the phrasing of the question would make the hypothesis of the existence of any such phenomenon self-contradictory. For example, if everything that exists is material and the mind is not material, then the mind cannot exist. The way to overcome the contradiction in each case is to go behind the crude formulation of the question and see what the formulation presupposes. In the case of the mind-body problem, the assumption is that the categories of mental and material, naively construed, are mutually exclusive. I have elsewhere[1] claimed that the

---

[1] J. R. Searle, *The Rediscovery of the Mind* (Cambridge Mass.: MIT Press, 1992).

way to overcome this contradiction is to abandon the traditional categories, and shift the terminology around so it can accurately describe the facts. When we do so, we see that mental phenomena are biological phenomena like any other. Literally speaking they are both mental and material, which shows that the traditional conception of the distinction is inadequate. I won't repeat the argument here, but I mention it as a way of leading into the present discussion. In this discussion I am going to try to perform a similar operation on the traditional fact–value distinction.

I. TRANSFORMING THE QUESTION: FROM METAPHYSICS TO LANGUAGE TO RATIONALITY

I begin by presenting the traditional conception of the distinction:

1. The metaphysical distinction between fact and value

Whatever else we can say about facts and values we must say that they are distinct from each other. What are facts? Well, they are objective features of the world such as the fact that the cat is on the mat or that there is salt water in the Atlantic ocean. What are values? Well we are not so sure about them, but one thing we are sure about is that they are subjective. Facts are objective and values are subjective. Some good examples of values are that it is good to tell the truth and bad to lie. But these values like all values are subjective. So the unbridgeable gulf between fact and value is revealed by the objectivity of facts and the subjectivity of values.

The foregoing paragraph is hardly a model of philosophical clarity, but in the twentieth century the fact–value distinction was much improved by being reformulated as a linguistic doctrine:

2. The linguistic distinction between fact and value: two different kinds of utterances

There are at least two quite distinct types of uses of languages: The descriptive or fact stating use on the one hand and the evaluative or emotive use on the other. An example of a descriptive utterance would be, "There is salt water in the Atlantic Ocean." An example of an evaluative utterance would be, "It is wrong to lie." Descriptive utterances purport to describe actually existing states of affairs in the world, evaluative utterances express feelings and attitudes of the speaker and are used by speakers to guide the actions of hearers. It is a consequence of the distinction that no set of descriptive statements by themselves can entail an evaluative statement. Statements of fact can never entail statements of value. For example, from the factual statement "John lied" we cannot derive the value statement "John did something wrong." To get to that conclusion we would have to add the non-factual, non-descriptive evaluative claim, "It is wrong to lie."

Stated as a linguistic point the thesis seemed clearer. The old metaphysical distinction was replaced by an apparently much clearer distinction between different kinds of use of language, the descriptive or fact-stating use, on the one hand, and the evaluative, on the other. Furthermore this distinction in language had a noble history. It was supposed to be a modern and sophisticated version of Hume's famous distinction between "is" and "ought." In a doctrine that came to be called Hume's guillotine, Hume had claimed that you cannot derive a statement about what ought to be the case from any set of statements about what is in fact the case. Hume's example of "is" and "ought" could now be seen to be just a special case of the more general distinction between descriptive and evaluative statements. Furthermore, it seemed that it was an updated version of Moore's thesis of the naturalistic fallacy. Moore had thought that you could not define what he called "non-naturalistic" predicates like "good" in terms of naturalistic predicates like "conducive to happiness"; and now with our more sophisticated apparatus we could see that he was really trying to describe the distinction between descriptive and evaluative statements.

A very powerful intuition supports the doctrine: It seems that no set of facts in the world can by themselves determine what I ought to do. Consequently no set of merely descriptive statements about what is in fact the case can by themselves entail an evaluative statement about what I ought to do to make something be the case. In order to determine what I ought to do I have to add to the descriptive statements some statement of an attitude, moral commitment, or desire on my part. This doctrine of the naturalistic fallacy, a generalization of Hume's guillotine, a linguistic formulation of the traditional distinction between fact and value, became one of the foundation stones of twentieth-century ethics.

Until recently, this view was so widespread in contemporary philosophy as to constitute almost an orthodoxy. And certainly it can be made to seem very plausible. What is wrong with it? Well, many people think there is nothing wrong with it, they think that it is perfectly acceptable as it stands. One difficulty with it, however, is that no one can accept it in real life. Whenever you have been raped, robbed, assaulted, lied to, burglarized, or otherwise had your rights violated, you do not feel inclined to say, "Well everybody has their own values and I have selected one set but it is up to anybody else to select any other set that they like, and their values are just as valid as mine." To nail this down to a specific sort of example, if someone that you are counting on in an important matter lies to you, you do not feel inclined to say, "Well it is just a fact that he told a lie, but there is no logical connection between fact and value, so I cannot logically derive from the fact that he told a lie that he did anything wrong whatever. In order to get to that conclusion I have to add some extra premise from outside; I have to add an extra evaluative statement, such as the expression of an attitude or some other subjective feeling I might have about lying and truth telling; and it is only given this extra evaluative premise, a premise that is outside the scope of rationality altogether, that I can criticize or otherwise assess his behavior."

I believe this is the wrong way of thinking about these matters altogether. Years ago I thought that the right way to expose the falsity of the classical model was simply to present a counter-example, and I did so in an article called "How to derive 'ought' from 'is.'"[2] This was widely discussed, but unfortunately most of the commentators missed the point of the article. Because I used the example of promising, many commentators thought that the derivation somehow depended on people accepting the institution of promising. It seems that if you approach the counter-examples in the grip of the classical model, you will literally be unable to appreciate their force or their structure. So what I want to do now is to try to shift the whole axis of the investigation around so that we can get a more accurate picture of the conceptual relations in the domain we are discussing.

So far we have reinterpreted the original question about the nature of the fact–value distinction as a distinction between different kinds of utterances. I am not sure that such a reinterpretation is fair to those philosophers who believed in the metaphysical distinction, but I am quite sure that this is in fact what happened in mid-twentieth century philosophy: the issue was perceived as one about logical relations in language. As someone stepping into that debate I will accept the reinterpretation of the issue as one about uses of language.

3. Different kinds of reasons for action

There is one more transformation I need to make. Just as we transformed the fact–value question into the is–ought question, so I want to transform

[2] John R. Searle, "How to derive 'ought' from 'is,'" *Philosophical Review*, 73 (January 1964): 43–58.

the is–ought question into the question about objective reasons for actions. I want to treat the question "Can 'ought' statements be derived from 'is' statements?" as equivalent to the question, "Can there be reasons for action which are binding on a rational agent just in virtue of the nature of the fact reported in the reason statement, and independently of the agent's desires, values, attitudes, and evaluations?" It is not obvious that such a transformation is justified and I want to justify it now.

The word "ought" is notoriously ambiguous between a practical sense and a theoretical sense. This ambiguity is revealed by sentences like the following: "They ought to be leaving the country by now." Among its many meanings are at least the following: "We have good reason to suppose that they are leaving the country by now" (the theoretical sense), or "They have good reason for leaving the country by now" (the practical sense). Notice that in both cases, the practical as well as the theoretical, the "ought" expresses reasons. I believe the practical sense is primary, and the theoretical sense is derivative from the practical sense. However, nothing in the present argument depends on this linguistic point. The important thing to get across is the thesis that "ought" is essentially connected to certain sorts of reasons, either reasons for doing or reasons for believing. To say someone ought to do something is to imply that there are certain sorts of reasons for his doing it. This is why, when anyone makes a claim of the form "You ought to do so-and-so," it always makes sense to ask, "Why ought I do so-and-so?" It is sometimes said that "ought" statements just express imperatives, but that is not true because imperatives do not rationally require reasons in the way that "ought" statements do. If I tell someone, "Leave the room," and he says, "Why ought I to leave the room?" the only reason might be that I ordered him to leave the room. An order might create a reason, but an ought statement presupposes a reason. There is an answer to the question, "Why ought I leave the room?" which goes, "Because you have been ordered to leave the room," but there is no answer to the question, "Why ought I leave the room?" which goes, without further additions: "Because it has been said that you ought to leave the room."

So far I have just made the connection between reasons and ought statements. Some authors claim that all evaluative statements are action guiding. I doubt that that is true, but there is clearly a general connection between what one thinks of as good and bad, right and wrong and what one thinks one has a reason to do or to avoid. I am not going to explore here the general connection between reasons for actions and evaluations, but shall just focus on this question: Can there be objective reasons for actions which are binding on a rational agent just in virtue of his rationality and are independent of his desires, feelings, attitudes, or evaluations?[3]

II. FIVE PRELIMINARY POINTS

As I said earlier, I will not begin by making a direct frontal assault on the is–ought distinction, but shall approach the whole set of issues by another route. In order to do that, I need to prepare the ground by making a number of points that at first sight might not seem relevant, but in the end will enable us to do what I believe is essential to do: shift the whole axis of the investigation around. I believe that if we get certain claims and distinctions right at this stage, then the final refutation of the is–ought distinction should seem obvious and even trivial. I will make five such points.

1. The irrelevance of ethics

In what follows I will have nothing to say about ethics or morality. I am discussing the topic of rationality in action and rational reasons for action. I mention this exclusion of ethics because frequently – indeed almost invariably – in these discussions people lapse into a lot of confused talk about ethics and morality. For example, many suppose that the obligation to keep a promise is always a moral obligation or an ethical obligation. I think this claim is false. But at this stage in the argument I am just sidestepping any issues about ethics. The best way to avoid any confusion is simply to stipulate at the beginning that I am not trying to solve any problems in ethics. Sometimes a reason for acting will be ethical sometimes not, but in this article I am not concerned with the distinction. The issues I am discussing are relevant to metaethics, and perhaps they have some relevance to problems in ethics as well, but it is certainly not my aim to discuss those problems.

2. Observer relative and observer independent

There is a fundamental distinction, in our basic conception of reality, between those features of the world that are observer independent such as

---

[3] I take it that this is what Bernard Williams is denying when he claims that there are no external reasons for action, that any reason to be a reason for an agent to act must appeal to the preexisting internal "motivational set" of the agent. B. A. O. Williams, "Internal and External Reasons," in *Moral Luck* (Cambridge: Cambridge University Press, 1981), pp. 101–113.

force, mass, and gravitational attraction, and those features that are observer relative, such as money, property, marriage, and government. Observer-relative features require conscious agents for their very existence. Observer-independent features do not. It is important to keep this distinction in mind in what follows because we will discover that there are many observer-relative features of the world that nonetheless can be objective matters of fact.

3. Objectivity and subjectivity

In order to understand the foregoing we will need to clarify a further distinction between different senses of the objective–subjective distinction. The distinction between objectivity and subjectivity has been very important in our culture, but it is extremely confused. In its most common sense, it involves a distinction in epistemic status. So, for example, the claim that Rembrandt is a better painter than Rubens is not, in the epistemic sense, an objective claim. It is epistemically subjective because its truth and falsity depends on the reactions and attitudes of observers. The claim that Rembrandt was born in 1606 is epistemically objective because its truth or falsity is in no way dependent on people's feelings and attitudes. But this distinction between epistemic objectivity and subjectivity should not be confused with the ontological distinction between objectivity and subjectivity. My pains have a subjective mode of existence in that they only exist as experienced by me, the subject. But mountains and molecules have an objective mode of existence because they exist whether or not they are experienced by any subject. It can be an epistemically objective matter of fact that I have a pain even though the mode of existence of the pain is ontologically subjective. I cannot exaggerate the amount of confusion that has come from failing to appreciate the distinction between the epistemic sense of the objective–subjective distinction and the ontological sense, and I hope to keep it clear in what follows.

4. The structure of intentionality

Humans and many animals have intentional states such as beliefs, desires, hopes, and fears. The general structure of intentional states is S(p), where the "S" marks the type of state it is and the "p" marks its prepositional content. Thus, if I believe that it is raining, that mental state has the structure

$$\text{Bel(it is raining)}$$

and if I desire that it be raining, the logical structure of the desire is

$$\text{Des(it is raining)}$$

The content of a belief or desire determines under which conditions it is true or false in the case of belief, or satisfied or unsatisfied in the case of desire. In both cases, I say that the intentional state determines its conditions of satisfaction. Thus, it is internal to the state's being the state that it is that it will be satisfied under certain conditions and not satisfied under other conditions. It is clear that this phenomenon is characteristic of a large number of other types of intentional states. An intention, like a belief or a desire, also has a propositional content, and the content will determine the conditions under which the state is satisfied. The intention will be satisfied if it is carried out, and not satisfied if it is not carried out.

Notice that it follows from this brief account of some of the structural features of intentionality that any intentional state already contains normative criteria of assessment. Thus, a belief will succeed as a belief if it is true and fail if it is false. An intention will succeed as an intention if it is carried out and fail if it is not carried out, and so on with all intentional states the propositional content of which determines conditions of satisfaction. Furthermore the structure of intentionality also constrains relations between different intentional states. If I both believe that p and believe that not p, my beliefs are contradictory and rationality requires that I give up at least one belief.[4]

5. Meaning and speech acts

I need also to say a few words about speech acts. Speech acts are intentional actions, typically performed by speakers in order to communicate something to hearers. The speech act has a structure much like that of the intentional state. Thus, just as the intentional state has the structure S(p), so the speech act has the structure F(p), where the "F" stands for the type of speech act that the utterance is (what Austin called its illocutionary force), and the "p" stands for the propositional content. Furthermore, just as the intentional state determines its conditions of satisfaction, so the speech act must determine its conditions of satisfaction. An assertion will be satisfied if it is true, unsatisfied if it is false. An order will be satisfied if

---

[4] The structure of intentionality is explored in more detail in John R. Searle, *Intentionality: An Essay in the Philosophy of Mind* (Cambridge: Cambridge University Press, 1983).

it is obeyed, unsatisfied if it is disobeyed. A promise will be satisfied if it is kept, unsatisfied if it is broken, etc.

However, in some important respects, speech acts are unlike intentional states. Unlike beliefs and desires, orders and assertions are meaningful acts performed intentionally by human agents, and such acts are typically designed to communicate something to hearers. A speech act is typically performed by uttering a sentence. What must be added to the utterance of the sentence in order to make the utterance into a speech act of the illocutionary type? We need to identify two separate aspects of the total speech act, which are added to the utterance by the speaker. These we may describe respectively as the meaning intention and the communication intention. When the speaker utters the sentence he means something by it, and characteristically he will intend to communicate that meaning to the hearer. Let us consider these in order. First, meaning: in the cases we will be considering, meaning consists in the imposition of conditions of satisfaction on conditions of satisfaction. Thus, if a speaker utters the sentence, "It is raining," and actually means that it is raining, in the sense that, for example, he is not just practicing English pronunciation, he will have first the conditions of satisfaction of the intention in making the utterance to produce the sound sequence "It is raining," but second he will intend that that utterance should have conditions of satisfaction in the form of truth conditions. He will intend that the utterance will have the conditions of satisfaction that it is raining. Thus saying something and meaning it involves two conditions of satisfaction. First, the condition of satisfaction that the utterance will be produced, and second, that the utterance itself should have conditions of satisfaction. It is in this sense that I say meaning is a matter of imposing conditions of satisfaction on conditions of satisfaction.

Second, typically the speaker is not just talking to himself, but trying to communicate to a hearer, and the intention to communicate is the intention that the hearer should recognize both the utterance that the speaker has made and the conditions of satisfaction that the speaker has imposed on it. Thus, the communication intention needs to be distinguished from the meaning intention. The communication intention is a matter of producing a certain knowledge in the hearer, namely the knowledge that the speaker has made an utterance and that it has certain conditions of satisfaction, by getting the hearer to recognize the speaker's intention to produce in him that knowledge.

Notice that it is a consequence of this analysis of the speech act that the speech act typically involves commitment. Once you have made an assertion, you are committed to its truth conditions. This is because, in performing the speech act, you intentionally impose conditions of satisfaction on conditions of satisfaction, and furthermore you make this commitment to the hearer because you communicate to him the fact that you were imposing conditions of satisfaction on conditions of satisfaction.

It is only because the commitment is built into the speech act that we have the possibility of lying. Lying can only occur where there is a genuine commitment to the truth conditions on the part of the agent. If the speaker is just uttering the sentence, "It is raining," as a way of practicing English pronunciation, then there is no way that he can be lying because he is not actually asserting anything. The important thing to see for the present discussion is that there is no gulf at all between making a statement and committing oneself to its truth because the very internal or constitutive structure of making a statement is already a commitment to its truth.

III. DESIRE-INDEPENDENT REASONS

The careful reader will have noted that in the discussion of intentionality and speech acts we already seem to be bridging the gap between the descriptive and the normative. Our description of intentional states has the consequence that there are certain norms of assessment built into the intentional state, and this is even more obvious in the case of speech acts. Speech acts and intentional states are already constrained by normative conditions, both conditions of their internal success and general conditions of rationality which involve their relations to each other. Thus, a speaker who makes an assertion has already created a reason for making a true assertion, and a speaker who has a belief has a reason for wanting his belief to be a true belief, because in each case it is built into the conditions of success of the phenomenon in question whether a speech act or an intentional state, that the prepositional content should be true. But this has the consequence that there is something literally wrong about a false belief or a false statement. Furthermore, there is something even more wrong about a deliberately false statement, because in this case a speaker is violating the public commitment he has made to a hearer. Another way to put this point is to say that the fact that a statement is false or that a belief is false, though it can be a completely objective fact like any other, nonetheless is already normative because a false statement is, to that extent, a defective statement. There is something wrong with it. A false belief, similarly, is defective. It also has something wrong with it.

The real paradox of the traditional discussion is that it tries to pose Hume's guillotine, the rigid fact–value distinction, in a vocabulary the use of which already presupposes the falsity of the distinction. That is, the vocabulary is one of "description," "entailment," "truth," "falsity," etc., but this whole vocabulary has literal uses that are both epistemically objective and normative. The use of the vocabulary already bridges the is–ought gap.

However, all of this is preliminary. Let us now zero in on the question and ask ourselves, under what conditions does an agent have a desire-independent reason for doing something? Notice that it is a condition of adequacy on our analysis that it must be completely naturalistic. We are simply talking about a bunch of biological beasts more or less like ourselves wandering around on the surface of the earth, who happen to have brains capable of consciousness, intentionality and intentional action, and later on we will talk about beasts exactly like ourselves who are capable of developing and using a language, but there is nothing fancy or metaphysical about our analysis. We will appeal to no noumenal world, no categorical imperative, no supernatural features. We are just talking about a bunch of sweaty biological beasts.

So we have now transformed the question about "ought" and "is" into this question: How can there be desire-independent reasons for doing something? Let us first ask, how can there be desire-independent reasons for anything?

Let us start with some simple questions about unproblematic cases. First, does an animal that sees that there is a tree in front of it have a good reason to believe that there is a tree in front of it? It seems to me that the answer to this question is obviously yes. And notice that even in this case we have already derived a normative statement, "The animal has a good reason," from the factual statement, "The animal saw that there was a tree in front of it." We can even derive an "ought" from an "is" if anyone thought it was worth the trouble. Ask yourself, ought the animal to believe that there is a tree in front of it, if it sees that there is a tree in front of it, and the answer, I believe, is, other things being equal, yes. From the factual "is" statement,

(1) The animal sees that there is a tree in front of it.

We have derived the "ought" statement,

(2) Other things being equal, the animal ought to believe that there is a tree in front of it.

Well, it might seem that this statement is question begging, because to say that the animal sees that there is a tree already implies the truth of the claim that there is a tree, since "X sees that p" implies that "It is the case that p." However, we can easily eliminate this objection if anyone thinks it is worrisome. From the fact that an animal has a visual experience of this sort, precisely the sort of experience I am having now as I look at a tree, the animal has a good reason to believe that there is a tree there. Of course, hallucinations are always possible, but, other things being equal, given the experiences I am having right now or that any other similarly endowed animal would have in a similar situation, I ought to believe that there is a tree there. Indeed, rationality requires that, other things being equal, I believe that there is a tree there. In such cases, seeing is a good reason for believing.

Let us go the next step. Given that an animal holds two inconsistent beliefs, beliefs of the form p and not p, does the animal have reason to abandon at least one of them? And again, the answer seems to me obviously yes. Because it is part of the conditions of satisfaction of a belief that it cannot be true if its negation is true. So, as in the earlier, and trivial case, an animal that believes that p and not p has a good reason for abandoning at least one of its beliefs, and, indeed, *ought* to abandon at least one of its beliefs.

Perhaps such cases seem too trivial. So, let us turn now to language. Language is possessed only by human beings, as far as we know, so from now on we are talking not about animals in general, but about a particular species, *homo sapiens*. Imagine that a man makes a statement that p, and later on he makes a statement that not p. Suppose it is pointed out to him that he is committed to a contradiction, and suppose he agrees. That is, it is a fact that he made the assertion that p and the assertion that not p, and he agrees that these statements are self-contradictory. Does he have a reason for abandoning one? Once again, it seems to me quite obvious, indeed trivial, that rationality requires that, other things being equal, he ought to abandon at least one. Of course, one can imagine all sorts of circumstances in which other things are not equal, but that is a matter of countervailing reasons. On the face of it, he has a reason for giving up at least one belief.

Why is that? Because, just as the conditions of satisfaction of a belief are that it be true, so, in making a statement, the speaker undertakes to speak the truth. Just as a belief is defective if it is false, so a statement is defective if it is false. However, there is a further constraint on statements, and that is that typically they are made from one human being to another, from the speaker to the hearer. When a speaker makes a statement, the speaker is undertaking a commitment to the hearer to speak the truth. That is, the speaker who makes a statement creates, in so doing, a reason for trying to state the truth because his statement is precisely an undertaking to speak the truth.

One way to see this is to ask yourself, how is lying possible at all? After all, for every true proposition, there is the false proposition. Why should the speaker care, and why should the hearer care which he asserts? Because it is part of the definition of an assertion that it is a commitment by the speaker to the truth of the proposition expressed. A lie is only possible where the speaker has made a commitment to the truth of his utterance. That is why fictional statements or sentences uttered while reciting a poem, for example, are not lies. There is no commitment on the part of the speaker.

We can state these points with more precision if we use the apparatus I introduced earlier. It follows from the analysis of meaning as the imposition of conditions of satisfaction on conditions of satisfaction that an utterance meant as a statement that p commits the speaker to sincerity, to the belief that p. Why? Because the speaker has intentionally imposed the condition of the existence of the state of affairs that p as a condition of satisfaction on his utterance. He is thereby committed to the existence of that state of affairs and thus to a belief in its existence. But that creation of a commitment is already the creation of a desire-independent reason.

One way to see what I am claiming is to compare it with the views that are opposed to it. It is commonly said, for example by David Lewis,[5] that for statements there is a rule that you are only supposed to make true ones. The implication is that first there is a class of statements and that, external to that, we have a regulative rule. I, on the other hand, am trying to call the reader's attention to the fact that the rule is not regulative; it is constitutive. You cannot give a definition of a statement, you cannot explain what a statement is, without explaining the notion of the statement in terms of its commitment to truth. Similarly, Paul Grice[6] says that it is a constraint on statements that speakers are supposed to be sincere. He also makes it look as if this is something external to the statement. But there is no way to define the notion of a statement without explaining that to make a statement is to make a commitment to truth, and thus a commitment to sincerity on the part of the speaker. Just as in the case of beliefs the "oughts" follow from "is's" in all sorts of trivial ways, so they

---

[5] David Lewis, "General Semantics," in Donald Davidson and Gilbert Harman (eds.), *The Semantics of Natural Language* (Dordrecht: Reidel Publishing Co., 1972): 169–218.

[6] Paul Grice, "Logic and Conversation," in A. P. Martinich (ed.) *The Philosophy of Language* (New York and Oxford: Oxford University Press, 1996): 156–167.

follow in the case of making a statement. A speaker who makes a statement, ought, other things being equal, to make non-contradictory statements, and the speaker ought, other things being equal, to attempt to make true statements, and the speaker ought, other things being equal, to state only propositions he believes to be true. In each case the "ought" statement expresses a reason that is objectively binding on a rational agent because in each case the reason has to do with the nature of statement-making as such.

To summarize the general thrust of the argument so far, typically when we find an intentional phenomenon, we find normative criteria of assessment that are internal to, or constitutive of, the phenomenon in question. Certainly that is the case with beliefs, as we have seen. Because statements are themselves intentional phenomena, they involve normative criteria of assessment, and in statements we find something additional which we did not find in beliefs. Namely, we find public commitments on the part of the speaker. In making the statement, the speaker publicly commits himself to the truth of the statement. Thus, the claim that in statement making one ought not to lie, or one ought to speak sincerely, is not a substantive claim. It follows from the nature of statement making as such that every statement is a commitment to truth. Nothing further is added by the apparently external "ought" statement that, when making statements, one ought to try to speak the truth. It is as trivial as saying that in American football a touchdown counts six points. The statement is already a commitment to truth. Consequently, the derivation of the "ought" from the "is" is utterly trivial.

IV. PROMISING AS A SPECIAL CASE

Now let us go the next step. A man who makes a statement commits himself to its truth and commits himself, therefore, to speaking sincerely or, as we would say, "truthfully." This goes for statements no matter what the subject-matter is. Consider statements about the man's own future behavior. The man might tell the hearer that he will be at a certain place tomorrow. In such case, as in any other statement, the man has committed himself to its truth, and has, therefore, committed himself to speaking sincerely when he uttered it. However, utterances about one's future voluntary actions form a very special class. In such cases, the speaker has a peculiar relation to the utterance, because he is in a position voluntarily to make the statement true. In a normal case of a statement about the weather, for example, the truth or falsity of the statement is not up to the speaker. He just reports, correctly or incorrectly, conditions that exist in the world independently of him. But in a special class of utterances, where he is making a statement about himself in the future, he is, in general, in a position to control whether or not the utterance matches reality. Now in such cases, it is not a mystery to suppose that human beings might evolve a practice whereby, in the making of an utterance about his future, the man undertakes, not only that the utterance will be true, *but that he will see to it that the utterance comes true.* He will see to it that he performs the act described in the prepositional content of the utterance.

Once again we can state this point more precisely if we use the apparatus I introduced in Section II. In the case of such utterances about his future, the condition of satisfaction imposed on the utterance is not merely that such and such events will occur, but rather that the speaker will make it the case that they occur, precisely because he has imposed these conditions of satisfaction on his utterance.

Furthermore, it is not at all unreasonable of us to suppose that human beings might evolve a general practice whereby the reason for the man behaving in the future in the way expressed in the proposition is that he said he would so behave. That is, we are imagining that human beings evolved a type of speech act which involves a further commitment that goes beyond the commitment of statements. We imagine speech acts where human beings evolve a practice of making utterances where the prepositional content is such that, in making the utterance, the speaker commits himself, not only to the future truth of the utterance, but to acting in such a way as to make the utterance true. In short, we imagine a case where the speaker commits himself to doing something simply because he said he would do it.

The social value, of course, of any such practice would be that more stable expectations would be produced in hearers if such utterances were regularly made and could be counted on by hearers. Notice that in this new class of utterance we have a different direction of fit from that of the statement. A statement matches an independently existing reality. But in this case, reality in the form of the speaker's subsequent behavior is supposed to change to match the content of the speech act. In making the utterance, the speaker commits himself to acting in such a way so that his future behavior will come to match the prepositional content of the utterance.

This type of speech act, like statements, involves a commitment. However, it is a different sort of commitment from the commitment we found in statements. In a statement, the speaker is committed to something's being the case, but he is not committed to doing anything about it. He is not committed to making something be the case. He is only committed to truth and, thereby, also committed to sincerity. But in this new type of speech act he is actually committed to doing something in the future. Now notice in this case, if we ask the question, "Does he have a reason for doing the thing that he has committed himself to doing?" the answer is as trivial as the answers we gave to similar questions about intentional states and speech acts. A speaker who makes a commitment to a hearer to do something in the future has thereby created a reason for himself to do it. That is, he has created a desire-independent reason, or an objective reason, to do something in the future. And again, as in our other cases, since the phenomena we are talking about are ontologically subjective, let us state the situation from the first-person point of view. I can attempt to create desire-independent reasons for myself to do something in the future. The way that I do this is by saying that I will do something, and the reason that I will do it is that I said I would do it. When I make any such attempt, I succeed if I create a desire-independent reason for doing something. It is no more mysterious that I can create desire-independent reasons for doing some future act, than that I can create desire-independent reasons for speaking the truth, whenever I make an assertion. Just as the point of making an assertion is to commit myself to the truth of a proposition, so the point of this sort of speech act is to commit myself to a future course of action. The one is no more mysterious than the other.

The reader, as a speaker of English, will recognize that this last type of speech act also has a name in our language. Such speech acts are called *promises*, and we should think of the institution of promising as having evolved as innocently as the institutions of making statements or asking questions or giving orders.

Once the practice becomes generally accepted, then there will evolve certain general procedures for making and recognizing promises. There will evolve constitutive rules, whereby such and such a sort of utterance counts as the making of a promise, and there may indeed be complex legal systems, such as the law of contract, which exist to provide public enforcement of promises, that is, enforcement of promises by agents other than the speaker and the hearer in the speech act in question. But this complex structure of the institution of promising in advanced civilizations, with elaborate legal systems like our own, should not blind us to the fact that the actual guts of the practice, the basic features of the practice, are perfectly natural extensions of simpler forms of speech acts, just as speech

acts themselves are a public form of prelinguistic intentionality. All of
these phenomena, intentionality, speech acts in general, statement making
and promise keeping, involve normative standards that are internal to the
intentional facts in question. In each and every case we can easily and
trivially derive an "ought" from an "is." There is nothing whatever here
that is problematic. Notice that in every case we have an epistemically
objective class of facts that are observer relative and hence ontologically
subjective. The fact that someone made a promise, the fact that someone
made a statement, the fact that someone undertook an obligation, are,
in each case, completely objective epistemically, but they are all observer
relative in that they only exist as so created and recognized by human
agents.

And this leads to a general point that I have not yet substantiated, but
want now to assert: *all values, other than those internal to intentional states
themselves, are observer relative.* All reasons for action, obligations, commitments, undertakings, etc. exist only relative to human and animal agents,
and they are either in the form of internal features of the intentionality
of such agents, or they are created by the intentionality of such agents. It
is important to point this out, because many philosophers suppose that
the possibility of any epistemically objective values would require that
somehow we find such values lying about in the world like stones and
mountains and molecules. Of course, that dream is self-defeating. Stones
and mountains and molecules could never have any binding force on rationality by themselves. Only where there are conscious agents possessed of
intentionality, and prepared to intentionally create phenomena subject to
assessments of rationality, do we have the possibility of reasons for action
and values in general.

The upshot of the discussion so far is that there is a very large number
of valid forms of derivations of "ought" from "is." Most of the examples I
have presented are obvious and, indeed, trivial. The reason that people have
failed to see this, I believe, is because they have failed to understand the
nature of intentionality, the nature of speech acts, the nature of reasons in
general, and reasons for action in particular. The question whether "ought"
can be derived from "is" is the same as the question whether there can be
objective or desire-independent reasons for actions. The answer is that the
whole notion of intentionality in general, and of speech acts as a form of
intentionality, already involve the notion of normative criteria of rationality
and hence criteria of rational constraints that are partly constitutive of the
phenomena in question. The most obvious case and the most salient case
as far as action theory is concerned is the case of promising. In the case of

promising the whole point of the action is to create a desire-independent reason for action, so it should not seem mysterious to us that the person who successfully promises precisely creates such a reason.

SOME MISTAKES ABOUT PROMISING

I will conclude this entire discussion by removing a number of pervasive mistakes that one finds in the philosophical literature about the obligation to keep a promise and correspondingly about the derivation of "ought" from "is."

(1) It is frequently said that the obligation to keep a promise must derive from the institution of promising. Consequently, so the story goes, for someone who does not endorse the institution of promising, there is no such obligation.

The reply to this objection is that it is a hopeless muddle. The obligation to keep a promise does not derive from the institution of promising, the institution is simply a vehicle, it is a device, or a tool, whereby an agent can, through his voluntary intentional action, create a reason for himself to do something. This point cannot be overemphasized. In the act of promising, the agent voluntarily undertakes to create a reason for himself, and the existence of the reason derives from his creation of it, not from the institution. The institution is just a device that he uses for this purpose.

(2) It is sometimes said that the obligation to keep a promise is merely a *prima facie* obligation, and not a real or honest-to-john obligation. This view is also hopelessly confused, and I have exposed it in detail, in an article entitled, "Prima facie obligations"[7] which I won't repeat here. But I shall just state a main point. The doctrine of *prima facie* obligations was developed by Sir David Ross, to account for the fact that sometimes quite genuine obligations can conflict with each other. One can have an obligation to do one thing, and a conflicting obligation to do something else, where both are genuine obligations. It bothered Ross that you could have two genuine obligations in conflict, so he tried to devalue one of them by saying that it was merely *prima facie*. This is confused. "*Prima facie*" is an epistemic sentence modifier derived from the Law, and it means "the preliminary evidence suggests that." But the obligation to keep a promise is not in this sense *prima facie*, because its status has nothing to do with

---

[7] John R. Searle, "Prima facie obligations," in Joseph Raz (ed.), *Practical Reasoning* (Oxford: Oxford University Press, 1978): 81–90.

the degree of our knowledge or with epistemology. Whatever the status of our knowledge in a given case, the obligation to keep a promise is a genuine, honest-to-john obligation. The point is that, like any obligation, the obligation to keep a promise can be overridden by other obligations or other sorts of reasons. I can have an obligation to come and visit you because I promised, and on the way I discover a man crushed beneath a car, and consequently I have a good reason to stop and help the man, even though in so doing I break my promise to you. What is the problem? I have two inconsistent but valid reasons for action, and I have to choose which is the more pressing. In this case the choice is obvious, but it does not imply that there was no obligation to keep the promise in the first place. It just shows that that obligation, like any obligation, can be overridden by other considerations.

(3) It is sometimes said that if one makes a promise to do something evil, one has no obligation at all. This, again, is confused. Pick the most evil promise you can imagine. An evil dictator promises his followers that he will destroy the whole world. Now, does he have an obligation to do that? In this case, there must be a distinction between the case where he actually made the promise, and the case where he failed to make any promise at all. The problem with the standard view is that it makes it as if he had never made a promise in the first place. But of course he did. The point behind the example is that in the case of a promise to do something evil, the obligation to keep the promise is vastly overridden and overpowered by the evil of the thing promised. So, of course, on balance, the agent ought not to do something evil, even though he promised to do it. But to say that his obligation to keep the promise is overridden by other considerations precisely presupposes that there was an obligation there in the first place, otherwise it could not have been overridden.

(4) I have often heard the following strange objection. "All the same, even if everything you say is true, the agent still might not do it. He might not keep his promise. Nothing in the account guarantees that he will actually do what he promised to do." The answer to this is, "Of course! But it is not an objection." No theory of mind, language, and rationality will guarantee that people act in accord with their self-created desire-independent reasons. The question we are discussing is not which reasons will actually prevail in every case, but rather how it is possible that there are desire-independent reasons for action.

In conclusion, I believe, that all the points I have made here, though contrary to orthodoxy, are fairly obvious, and I hope that most of them are indeed trivial. The fact that we have had so much trouble seeing these points, I think derives from the fact that we are unwilling to look at the details of the actual logical structures. It seems much more exciting to talk grandly of something called "ethics" or "morality," and not pay attention to the actual structures of more humble phenomena like beliefs, desires, actions, meaning, and reasons. If you examine those phenomena you shift the whole axis of the investigation around so that you can see matters correctly. As Wittgenstein says, "Nothing is hidden."

The unity of the proposition

I

This article is about an old problem, but one that is seldom discussed in contemporary philosophy. Here is the problem: because a proposition, such as for example the proposition that Socrates is bald, consists of more than one element, how is it that the different elements of the proposition are connected together to form a unified whole? The problem has both a semantic and a syntactical version. In the semantic version it comes out as: How are the meaningful elements of the proposition connected to produce a single unified proposition? And in the syntactical version it comes out as: How are the words in the sentence organized to produce a meaningful sentence, as opposed, for example, to a meaningless jumble of words, or simply a list? I think contemporary discussions in both semantics and syntax just miss the problem and do not see how it presents a difficulty for their analyses. Thus, for example, on some versions of the direct reference theory and the corresponding doctrine of singular propositions, we are to think of the proposition that Socrates is bald as an ordered pair consisting of the man "Socrates" and the property "baldness." But that cannot be right, because then the proposition would consist of two ordered elements. There is this man and this property, what do they have to do with each other? How does any unity emerge from that? The situation in syntax is just as bad, maybe worse. Thus, for example, according to many versions of the syntax of English, it is just a rule of syntax that sentences consist of noun phrases plus verb phrases, and the rule is

$$S \rightarrow NP + VP$$

but now, that looks just arbitrary. It looks, on this account, as if there could perfectly well be a language where the rule was

$$S \rightarrow NP + NP + NP$$

or

$$S \rightarrow Det + Det + Det.$$

That is, unless you give some functional analysis that shows how the sentence is unified, it seems utterly arbitrary that the rules of grammar should allow for certain forms and not others. When I did research at MIT in 1963 I pointed out these difficulties to the linguists there, and suggested that the right way to understand the issue was to see that the noun phrase and the verb phrase do certain jobs in the sentence. They have certain functions, and the sentence also has a function, and by analyzing these according to their functions, we could give some explanation, some motivation, for what looked like absolutely arbitrary rules of syntax. MIT linguists typically objected to my proposals by saying that they violated the principle of the autonomy of syntax. It was taken for granted that the syntactical rules should be entirely self-enclosed and should not make any reference to any semantic or pragmatic considerations. Furthermore, they also objected that just specifying the functions would not be sufficient to determine the syntactical rules, because different syntactical rules could all perform the same function. I agree with that, but that still does not show that we should not make reference to function when doing syntax. One might as well say that because the function of hammers could be performed by something that is not a hammer (you could, for example, drive nails with something other than a hammer), therefore we need not make reference to the function of a hammer when we are discussing the design of a hammer. That seems to me a mistake. You will not understand hammers unless you understand it is their function, among other things, to drive nails, even though you cannot infer the design of the hammer simply from knowing that it is going to be used to drive nails. And similarly you will not understand sentences unless you understand it is their function, among others things, to be used to express propositions and perform speech acts.

Similarly, the semantic proposal of treating the proposition as consisting of ordered pairs, ordered triples, and ordered n-tuples generally seems to me to make it impossible to give an intelligible account of propositions. An ordered pair is specified by giving a list of two elements with a condition on the identity of the pair that the order of the pair is essential to the identity of the pair. Thus <A B> is a different ordered pair from <B A> even though they both contain the same elements. But we still do not have any explanation of the unity of the proposition by giving any list that determines an ordered pair or ordered n-tuple generally.

This difficulty is not merely a problem for externalist theories of the proposition, theories that say that the content of the proposition cannot be in the head of the speaker, but they arise even for an internalist. Suppose I am a complete internalist and I think that the concept *Socrates* or the description associated with the name "Socrates" is entirely in my head, then still I do not get the unity of the proposition simply by saying "the proposition consists of the concept of 'Socrates' and the concept of baldness." How are they supposed to be linked together?

It is interesting to see how philosophers have evaded this question. Strawson describes the relation between the object referred to by the subject expression and the property expressed by the predicate expression as "non-relational tie."[1] But how could there be such a thing as a non-relational tie? If we try to take that literally, it defies explanation.

II

So much by way of a statement of the problem. The solution that I am going to propose to this problem is rather simple, but like a lot of simple solutions to complex problems, it takes some groundwork to prepare the way for the statement of the simple solution. Let us start with Frege. Frege revolutionized the subject of logic by the invention of the predicate calculus. This fact is well known. What is less well known is that he also revolutionized our understanding of sentences and propositions, and I want to say a few words about his revolution.

Prior to Frege it was assumed that the paradigmatic form of the sentence was the subject-predicate form, and the paradigmatic form of the proposition was the specification of an object by the subject expression in the sentence, and the ascription of a property to that object by the predicate expression in the sentence. Thus, "Socrates is bald" would be a paradigmatic sentence because it contains a subject and a predicate, and the proposition that Socrates is bald would be a paradigmatic proposition because it contains an element referring to Socrates and an element predicating baldness of Socrates. On this account the quantified forms are simply seen as special cases of the subject-predicate form. So, "Socrates is bald," "some men are bald," "all men are bald," are all regarded as of the same form. In each case the subject expression refers, and the predicate expression predicates. What could be simpler? On this account existence sentences such as "horses exist" were always an embarrassment, and indeed

[1] P. F. Strawson, *Individuals: An Essay in Descriptive Metaphysics* (London: Methuen, 1959): 169.

it was probably not until Kant's famous refutation of the ontological proof that people were satisfied that there was something special about existential sentences, and, as Kant said, "existence is not a predicate." Actually, the difficulties with the ontological proof were known even at the time of Aquinas, and Aquinas has quite an effective attack on the ontological proof, but it was not until Frege that we had an alternative account of propositions in such a way that existential propositions could be easily assimilated to it.

Frege begins his account by saying that we should not think of the proposition as something that is arrived at by assembling the elements and putting them together in a certain way, nor should we think of the sentence as something that is arrived at by putting the syntactical elements together. Rather, we should think of the proposition and the sentence as primary, and the elements as arrived at by decomposing the proposition or the sentence respectively. When I read this account as an undergraduate, I thought it was confused. It seemed to me one might as well say we shouldn't think of a car as made by assembling the parts, we should think of the parts as gotten by disassembling the car. Analogously, we can say either, the proposition is arrived at by assembling the parts of the proposition, or the parts are gotten by decomposing the proposition. There is no difference between these two claims. But I now think that at a deep level Frege was right, and I want to explain how. As on so many issues where I thought Frege was wrong and I was right, it turned out that Frege was right, and I now want to explain why. Consider the sentence, "Socrates is bald." Now knock out the word "Socrates," and what you have is:

"... is bald."

So we took the complete expression "Socrates is bald," and now we have something incomplete. Frege wanted the syntax to map neatly onto the metaphysics, so he said that the incomplete expression stood for an incomplete kind of entity, a concept (Begriff). We do not need to worry about his metaphysics, but he is surely right and intuitively correct when he said that the expression "... is bald" is incomplete, in a way that the expression "Socrates" and the sentence "Socrates is bald" are both complete. To make the words on the page look less rebarbative, we can put in a letter to fill in the gap, and write "x is bald," but the "x" does not stand for anything, it is just a way of filling up the hole syntactically, but semantically there is still a hole there. The result is still incomplete, even though it now looks more like a grammatical sentence. But now we have this syntactical thing with a hole in it, an open sentence, and the corresponding proposition is not even a proposition, but is a proposition with a hole in it.

Notice that we have already made an important shift from the conception of the sentence as consisting of a subject and a predicate, and a conception of the proposition as consisting of the object and a property. The sentence now consists of a subject expression or noun phrase, and an open sentence. There is no predicate "is bald" any more, rather there is the whole open sentence "x is bald." And this open sentence, as we noticed, has a hole in it. How can we fill the hole?

Well, we might fill the hole with the same sort of thing that we knocked out. We might put in a proper name. So, we might say, "Socrates is bald," or "Xanthippe is bald," or "Plato is bald." On the left-hand side we have an expression standing for an object, and the open sentence, now closed, predicates a property of that object.

Now, what I have just said is not innocent, so let us stop and examine it a little more closely. In a perfectly ordinary sense, the proper name is used to name, refer to, or stand for, an object, Socrates, Plato, etc. The open sentence "x is bald" does not in that way stand for any object or, for that matter, anything. It does not stand for anything in the relation in which the name "Socrates" stands for the man Socrates. I have said something that sounds innocent; I have said that it predicates a property. I think that is right, but it is important to emphasize that it does not stand in relation to the property of baldness in the way that the expression "the property of baldness" stands to the property of baldness. The expression "the property of baldness" refers to (or names or identifies) the property, but the open sentence does not in that way just identify the property. (Frege, by the way, had some very heavy going over precisely these points, but I am for these purposes just ignoring what he said about the concepts and the reference of grammatical predicates because I think it is inadequate.)

We have already seen that the open sentence is incomplete, because we had to complete it by sticking in a proper name, but Frege noticed that you can complete the incomplete concept expression with other concept expressions. Now these other concept expressions he called "second-level concept expressions." And the concepts they express he called "second-level concepts." Most famously, these are the quantifier expressions: "There is an x such that," and "for all x, x is such that." Notice that these expressions are just as incomplete as our original open sentence "x is bald." But notice how we can complete the original incomplete "x is bald" by prefixing it with one of these other incomplete concept expressions. "For all x, x is such that x is bald," and "There is an x such that x is bald." Now Frege noticed not only that these expressions function in a way that is radically unlike the way that proper names function, but he also noticed that they have a further semantic feature. They do not stand for any object. The name "Socrates" stands for the man Socrates. But the expression "there is an x such that" or "for all x, x is such that," does not stand for any object at all.

On Frege's account the standard subject-predicate model, "Socrates is bald," even as modified by Frege himself, where the subject expression refers to an object, and the open sentence completes the subject expression to form a complete sentence, is now regarded as a special case, not the model for all cases. So if you take a sentence such as, for example, "horses exist" or "a horse exists," it is not the case that the subject expression refers to horses, and the predicate expression says they have the property of existing. On the contrary, thanks to Frege we can now state a positive account of how existential statements work. Aquinas and Kant had both seen that existence is not a property. Another way to make the same point would be to say that in existential statements the subject expression does not refer to an object, or we can say that in existential statements the predicate expression does not predicate a property of an object. But until Frege we did not have a way of saying what actually does happen in these statements. It turns out on the Fregean analysis the perspicuous way to state the proposition "a horse exists" is to say "there is some x such that, x is a horse." In this sentence we have two concepts expressed. One concept, a first-level concept, is expressed by the open sentence "x is a horse," and a second-level concept is expressed by the expression "there is some x such that." So what actually happens in an existential statement, such as, for example, the statement that horses exist, is that the subject expression expresses a concept, and the predicate expression expresses a second-level concept, a concept of a concept. If we describe the proposition from outside, we can say what is going on is this: the subject expression expresses a concept, and the second-level concept tells us whether the first-level concept has any instances. This does not mean that the original sentence is a meta-level sentence, it is not synonymous with "The concept 'horse' has instances", but rather if we are describing the operation of a sentence in a way that we can say that in "Socrates is bald" the subject expression refers to the man, and the predicate expression tells us some feature about him, in this case we can say the subject expression expresses a concept, and the predicate expression functions to tell us whether that concept has instances. And we are then told by the proposition that the first-level concept has instances, that is to say in this case that "there is at least one x such that x is a horse".

We may summarize this account of existential statements as follows: there are really three ways of saying what is special about existence and existential statements. First, existence is not a property of objects. This is a familiar point made by philosophers from Aquinas to Kant. Second, subject expressions in existential sentences such as "horses exist" do not refer to objects. If they did, the sentence would presuppose its own truth if it were in the affirmative, and it would presuppose its own falsehood if it were in the negative. In order to say that horses exist they would already have to exist, and in order to deny that horses exist they would already have to exist. But third, and this is Frege's contribution, what actually happens in an existential statement is that the subject expression expresses a concept, and the grammatical predicate "exists" tells us whether or not that concept has any instances.

Frege clearly thought that in order to produce the special unity of the proposition you had to have something in it which is incomplete and that is completed by some other element. The other element completing may be complete or not complete. So the name "Socrates" is complete, the element "x is bald" is incomplete. "There is an x such that x . . ." is incomplete, but either the complete "Socrates" or the incomplete "there is an x such that" can complete the incomplete "x is bald" to produce a complete proposition. Well, one sort of sees what he is driving at, but it does not seem to explain anything, it does not seem to have any explanatory power. Why should it be like that? Why isn't "Socrates Plato" a proposition? Or, "Socrates baldness" a proposition? To these questions which form the main topic of this article I now turn.

III

Let us begin by asking why we have propositions anyhow. I do not mean why we have the philosopher's notion of a "proposition," but rather why humans, and some animals apparently, have evolved anything that we would think of as a proposition. It is always easier when trying to answer questions like that to turn to the case of sentences, where you actually have something you can look at. And if you ask why we have sentences, well the answer to that at its simplest level is that we have sentences in order to be able to perform speech acts. And why do we want to be able to perform speech acts? Well, we need to communicate with each other, and we need to communicate with ourselves about – well, about what? About how things are in the world, or how we would like them to be, or how we commit ourselves to making them be, etc. And the proposition is the abstraction from all of these different kinds of speech acts, it is that part of the speech act which represents how things are or how we would like them to be, etc. in the world. Familiar examples will make this point clear. If I say to you, "please leave the room," "you will leave the room," or "will you leave the room?" in each case I have expressed the proposition that you will leave the room, but I have done it in these different illocutionary modes. The first is a request, the second is a prediction, the third is a question. So we might say, generalizing from this example, if we abstract the notion of a proposition from all of these different speech acts, then the job of the proposition is to form a representation. A representation of how things are, in the case of statements, or how we are trying to make them be, in the case of orders, or how we commit ourselves to making them be in the case of promises, or how we wish to know how things are, in the case of questions.

But if the proposition is just a matter of representing how things are in the world (in one or more of these illocutionary modes) we already have a way of representing how things are which is common to ourselves and to certain other biological species, and that is perception. In order to represent to myself that Socrates is bald, I do not have to actually *say* that Socrates is bald, if he is around I can just have a look at him and *see* that Socrates is bald. Notice that when I saw that Socrates is bald, I represented that to you in the form of a sentence, but the actual experience in which I see that Socrates is bald need not be sentential. My dog can see that the cat has run up a tree, but he does not require any sentences in order to see that.

We ought to be struck by the fact that when we report the *content* of our perceptions we use exactly the same locutions that we use to report the content of our beliefs, desires, and intentions, as well as our speech acts such as statements, orders and promises. When I said that in perception we represent how the world is, that will mislead if you think I am endorsing the representative theory of perception. I am not. I am not claiming that we see representations of things rather than real things. On the contrary, I am a realist, perhaps even a naive realist, where perception is concerned. What I am claiming now is that the actual experience of perceiving, the conscious visual experience, has informational content about the world in the same sense as beliefs and statements. It is only in that sense that I am saying perceptions represent things in the world for us.

But this leaves us with the idea that the perception has propositional content in the same sense as a speech act or an intentional state such as a belief. The idea that we seem to be moving toward is this: A proposition is any mental entity whatever that is sufficient to determine truth conditions or other conditions of satisfaction. It does not have to be expressed in words. I want to explore this idea more fully in the next section.

IV

The most biologically primitive, the most basic cognitive relation in which humans stand to their environment is perception[2] and in particular in our case, visual perception. For us seeing is believing. I will concentrate on vision rather than any other sense, though what I say should be perfectly general. If we were talking dogs, I could perhaps write a chapter about smells, but our sensitivity to smells is nothing like as good as that of the canines.

The biologically primitive form of intentionality is perception, and in the case of visual perception, we have to ask what is it that is seen when we literally see something? The natural answer to that is we see objects. We see chairs and tables, dogs and cats, trees and mountains, etc. There is something right about that, but there is also something wrong. In order that we can see a dog, we have to be able to see such things as "that there is a brown dog over there on my left." And even that sentence does not capture all of the features of the visual experience, but only picks out some. The point that I want to make for the present purposes is this: *you never see just objects, you always see states of affairs,* for example, you see the dog on your left chasing the cat on your right. This is further indicated by the fact that if you ask, "What must be the case in order that your visual experience should be satisfied?" (in the traditional jargon, that it should be veridical rather than illusory), the answer always has to be that there must be certain conditions which satisfy the experience, and those conditions will be what I call the "conditions of satisfaction" of the visual experience. But now, and this is the crucial point for the present discussion, the notion of a condition is already a propositional notion, because the notion of a condition is always a condition that such and such is the case. From the agent's point of view, the visual experience is indexical; for the agent, from the agent's point of view, it may be just "I see this." and then the agent concentrates his or her attention on the visual scene presented. But the important thing in this case, and the important thing in general, is if the

---

[2] Strictly speaking, it is both perception and action, which are on the same footing. In order to avoid complexity, I am confining this discussion to the case of perception. Similar points would apply to action.

intentionality of the visual experience is satisfied, then it must be the case that such and such.

Once you see that in the visual experience the unity of the propositional content derives from the unity of the condition in the world that satisfies that content, then the question is turned around. Instead of asking how is it possible that the various sentence fragments can be united to express a unified coherent proposition, we should ask how is it possible that in language we can break up the parts of the proposition into different components in a way that they are not broken up in the actual flow of our experiences. In language we can separate Socrates from his properties, but in the perception you cannot make that separation, there is no way that you can perceive Socrates without perceiving the visual properties that he exhibits to you then and there.

These reflections suggest the following hypothesis: We cannot understand the functioning of language except in terms of its relation to other more biologically fundamental forms of intentionality. For us, the most basic forms are perception and action, and I am here concentrating on perception. If we ask the question, "How is it possible that there can be a unified propositional content in the case of language?", the way to see the answer to that is to consider the case of perception, where the perceptual content comes to us as necessarily unified, because it necessarily represents entire states of affairs. We cannot break up the perception as we can break up the sentence. So on this account, the unity of the proposition derives from the unity of the state of affairs that the proposition must represent. We can see now the insight behind Frege's claim that we should not think of the proposition as composed of elements, but rather think of the proposition as itself a unity, and the elements as something derived by abstracting them from the propositional unity. I will explore this idea further in what follows.

What would it be like if language did not allow us to break up the proposition into bits, if languages were like our experiences, and gave us whole conditions of satisfaction chunk by chunk? Well, we might have such a language, but it would be severely limited in its expressive power. Some codes, in fact, are like this: the famous "one if by land, two if by sea" allows us to express the whole state of affairs in a single, simple signal. One light means they are coming by land, two lights means they are coming by sea. But even in that case we understand the lights because we have a prior way of articulating the complexity of the proposition involved. If we just had a language where you could name a state of affairs the way you name an object, then the language would be severely limited in its expressive power. We would have a finite list of possible types of affairs that you could specify.

You cannot break up the unity of the state of affairs, but you can break up the elements of the language that are used to represent the state of affairs. But now, this is the key point: The perception determines conditions of satisfaction, and those conditions are always entire states of affairs, not just objects. But that has the consequence that the intentional content of the perception must be sufficient to determine the entire state of affairs as its condition of satisfaction. But if that is the case, then the content of the visual experience is a proposition. Even though it is not in any sense articulated verbally or conceptually. Because a condition is always a condition "that such and such" is the case, or "that such and such should be the case," etc., it follows that the determination of those conditions must be in the important sense propositional, because they must be rich enough to determine an entire state of affairs. The points that I have made so far can be stated independently of any claims about language. So far, we are just talking about perception determining conditions of satisfaction, and for that reason, the perceptions must be propositional.

Now what happens when we introduce language? Well, of course, a whole lot of things happen. But from the point of view of our present investigation, two crucial things happen. First, we are no longer bound to represent only actually existing states of affairs. In the case of perception, we can only see, or purport to see, what is actually the case here and now. You may be mistaken, you might have a hallucination or otherwise be deluded visually, but your perception at least purports to give you information about how things are in the world. The visual experience is satisfied only if there is some actual state of affairs there causing you to have that very visual experience. A state of affairs such as the cat is on the mat, the rose is red, or Socrates is bald. But, as soon as we introduce linguistic devices of representation, we are no longer tied to the here and now. We can represent imaginary states of affairs, possible states of affairs, and we can even lie – we can claim that there are states of affairs even when the state of affairs does not exist.

But second, we can break up the state of affairs into different components. We can have one component that represents Socrates, and another component that represents some feature of Socrates. We can have not only "Socrates is bald," but "Socrates is fat," "Socrates smokes too much," and "Socrates works too hard at philosophy."

It is a consequence of the analysis I have given so far that the fundamental intentional relation, whether realized in language as semantics or in the mind as intentionality, is not *reference* in the sense in which the word "Socrates" refers to the man Socrates, but *satisfaction* in the sense that my thirst is satisfied if I drink, my hunger is satisfied if I eat, my belief that it is raining is satisfied if it is raining, and my perception that the dog chased the cat is satisfied if the dog chased the cat. Notice that in the cases of hunger, thirst, and perception, there is not any question about the unity of the proposition, it already comes to us as unified. There are not in that way any components to the hunger, the thirst, or the visual perception. I am not saying, by the way, that there are not discriminable features of hunger, thirst, and visual perception. Of course there are. The point, however, is that so far there is nothing analogous to subject and predicate.

Why is it, then, that we get a problem for the linguistic form which we do not have for the prelinguistic form? The answer is that language allows us to break the natural unity of the proposition by introducing an articulation which the prelinguistic forms do not have. I will say more about that in a moment.

If I am right in thinking that the fundamental relation is not reference but satisfaction, and that truth is only a special case of satisfaction, then we are left with the puzzle why objects loom so large on our cognitive horizon. The entities or phenomena which constitute the conditions of satisfaction are not objects of the kind that you can sit on or weigh or throw at somebody. But they are fact situations and states of affairs. Objects are derivative from facts. But that leaves us with a question: to repeat, why are objects such a big deal to us? And I think the answer has to do with our evolutionary needs. Our basic causal relations to the world, especially those relations that we can actively deal with, are to discrete objects. Each of us is himself or herself a discrete object, and the other people and animals that we encounter are discrete objects. The entities we eat, and the phenomena that we fear are for the most part objects.

The biologically most primitive forms of representation have a natural unity in the sense that they have no prior articulation. By introducing linguistic devices to do a comparable job of representation, we introduce enormous flexibility, because we are now no longer required to represent actual states of affairs, nor even singular concrete states of affairs. In addition to "Socrates is bald," we can have "some men are bald," "all men are bald," "no man is bald," etc. However, it is a requirement on this introduction of flexibility that any resulting representation should be capable of representing an actual or possible state of affairs. It should be capable of having conditions of satisfaction. It is this requirement that accounts for the unity of the proposition. *A proposition is anything at all that can determine a condition of satisfaction. And a condition of satisfaction, as we have already seen, is "that such and such is the case."* Its identification requires a propositional mode of representation precisely because a condition is always a condition that such and such, it is always a fact or state of affairs.

So our original question: "What accounts for the unity of the proposition?", is that the requirement that a proposition represent a state of affairs automatically places a requirement of a certain sort of unity, a unity not possessed by noun phrases or predicate expressions alone.

Now, it does not really matter what kind of grammatical device we use to indicate a unity of the proposition. In our languages it has to do with certain syntactical constraints on predicate expressions. But anything at all will do, provided only that it is understandable to the hearer and the interpreter of the expressions as marking that a given sequence represents a whole state of affairs. It can be done with conjugated verb phrases, or it can be done just with a certain ordering, or it can be done just by arbitrarily selecting certain syntactical units. So, for example, in logic "fa" is a sentence because we have a convention that "a,b,c . . ." sequences are singular noun phrases, and "f,g . . ." sequences are verb phrases. But it does not matter what device you use; the only requirement is that there must be a whole state of affairs, represented by a well-formed formula.

Let us try to summarize some of our results so far. We started out with a question how a proposition which obviously has discrete elements and a sentence which equally obviously has discrete elements combine to form a unity. In the end we turned that question on its head. In the course of our analysis we argued that the basic intentional relation between the mind and the world has to do with conditions of satisfaction. And a proposition is anything at all which can stand in an intentional relation to the world, and since those intentional relations always determine conditions of satisfaction, and a proposition is defined as anything sufficient to determine conditions of satisfaction, it turns out that all intentionality is a matter of propositions. And this does as much for intentional action or visual perception or thirst or hunger as it does for speaking a language. When we turn to language we find that language gives us enormously greater representational capacities for representing states of affairs in the world because it is not tied to the immediate perceptual impact of states of affairs on our perceptual apparatus. We can talk about things that might exist, or will exist, or are not present to us, or we might imagine exist, etc. The actual conventions of natural languages can be as arbitrary as you like, provided that they meet this one condition: they must have the result that the resulting unit is sufficient to determine a condition of satisfaction.

It may be a truth condition, or some other kind of condition, but it must be a condition, and consequently the corresponding formula must be propositional on our definition.

v

The primacy of situations and states of affairs over objects is both explanatory and puzzling. It explains a great deal, or at least so I have claimed, and there are some other areas in which I would like to invoke its explanatory powers, but for the present I want to explore further a puzzle I have already briefly mentioned. It is this: If the primary terms of the cognitive relation are intentional states and their conditions of satisfaction, and if in consequence the content of any intentional state is therefore a proposition, then what is an object? And how exactly do we relate to objects?

It is by now, I hope, a familiar point that what we count as an object is up to us. It is up to us and we can devise any arbitrary scheme we like for individuating and counting objects. So, for example, I count the cup in front of me as one object, and the desk on which the cup sits as a second object, but I could equally well have refused to count those as separate objects, but have treated the combination of cup and desk as one object. Or I could treat the bottom half of the cup and the immediately surrounding area on the surface of the desk as an object, and given a general name to objects of that type. But, though this logical point is valid, it does not override an empirical disposition that we have. We naturally, for reasons that I earlier tried to suggest, discriminate certain sorts of things as objects, and not others. We naturally pick out certain sorts of things and not others as objects. Our favorites are discrete chunks of hard matter like stones, and chairs and tables. We have a preference for functional units, and will treat the car as a single object even though a lot of its parts are detachable and again the chair is a single object even though the cushions may not be attached to it. Sometimes we take a series of discrete bits and count them as a single object. To take an example close to hand: this article that I am now working on contains lots of separate sheets of paper, but we treat them together as a single article, the text of my article on the unity of the proposition.

The analysis so far explains why the correspondence theory of truth will not go away. Every generation has a refutation of the correspondence theory, but it is kind of a default position. It is the position we always come back to. Like realism in the theory of perception, no matter how often we refute it, it always returns. And what it tries to say can hardly be wrong:

in its most general form, the correspondence theory of truth says that a statement is true if and only if there is something in virtue of which it is true or because of which it is true or which makes it true. The condition that makes a statement true, if it is true, is called a fact. And the relation between a statement and a fact can be described in a number of ways. We can say that a true statement states a fact, or that it fits the facts, or that it corresponds to the facts. The mistake in philosophy is always the same: it is to misunderstand the logic of these terms. We naturally tend to think of the noun phrase "the fact that p" as naming an object, and then we want the sentence or statement to stand in some kind of a genuine relation to the object, something in addition to stating. But that is wrong. The variety of relations in which statements stand to their truth conditions is as great as the variety of statements. There is no single matching or picturing relation, nothing of the sort. But properly construed, the correspondence theory of truth can hardly be mistaken. It simply says that if a statement is true, there must be something in virtue of which, or because of which, it is true. There is a condition in the world that satisfies it, a truth condition, and the name for those truth conditions is "facts."

VI

It must seem as if implicit in everything I have said so far is the idea that the existential proposition is somehow fundamental. For if it is true that Socrates is bald, then it can only be because there exists such-and-such a person with such-and-such characteristics who is bald. This analysis fits an old urge in philosophy. Russell's extension of the theory of descriptions to cover ordinary proper names, and Quine's attempt to eliminate singular terms by treating them as predicates, are both expressions of this fundamental metaphysical urge. Instead of thinking "Socrates is bald," we should think "there is a unique x such that x Socratizes and x is bald." If objects are somehow dependent on states of affairs, then surely any statement about an object must reduce to statements about states of affairs with no mention of the object. As an undergraduate I was very much attracted to this view. I never published it in *Speech Acts* or in any other of my writings on the philosophy of language because I did not have the nerve. But now it seems to me at a deep level mistaken. Here is why.

Paradoxically the very attempt to state the thesis seems to deny it. For in the statement of the thesis we appeal to the qualificational notation, and on the standard interpretation of the quantificational notation, we are to think of the variables of quantification as *ranging over* a previously identified domain of *objects*. But if that is right, we cannot get rid of objects by reducing them to existing states of affairs, for the articulation of the existing states of affairs is an articulation of states of affairs about objects.

But perhaps this is just an artifact of the notation. Perhaps we should think of the most fundamental metaphysical form as something like the identification of *features*, not objects. Thus, along with Strawson's notion of "feature placing,"[3] we would have the idea that the feature of Socratizing is here instantiated and it is coinstantiated with baldness.

But there is something wrong about that. What is wrong is the idea that, if we recognize the primacy of states of affairs over objects, then it would be inconsistent to recognize objects as irreducible components of states of affairs. But it is not inconsistent. We can acknowledge both that we recognize a domain of objects, and that we are just biologically predisposed to recognize the domain of objects, together with the idea that we can only represent objects to ourselves as components of states of affairs.

[3] Strawson, *Individuals*.

Name index

Andrade, R., 51
Aquinas, T., 184, 186, 187
Aristotle, 10, 28
Austin, J. L., 49

Bacon, F., 4
Batali, J., 94
Berkeley, G., 63, 64, 107
Block, N., 91, 97
Borash, D., 35
Bourdieu, P., 29
Bradly, F., 63

Chisolm, R., 111, 114
Chomsky, N., 102

Dennett, D., 73, 96
Descartes, R., 4–6, 63, 64, 138
De Soto, H., 38
Dreyfus, H., 90, 108–110, 112, 117, 121–123, 126–132
Durkheim, E., 28–29

Eccles, J., 138
Einstein, A., 11

Feyerabend, P., 7, 24, 77
Follesdal, D., 112, 115
Foucault, M., 29
Frege, G., 18, 111, 112, 117, 183–187, 190–192

Gazzaniga, M., 142
Godel, K., 80
Goel, V., 94
Grice, P., 173

Habermas, J., 29
Haugeland, J., 97
Heidegger, M., 107, 112, 117–119, 125–126
Hegel, G., 63
Hempel, C., 19, 23

Hofstadter, D., 73
Hume, D., 21, 28, 138, 147, 148
Husserl, E., 107–113, 124–125

Johnson-Laird, P., 91

Kafka, F., 139
Kant, I., 22, 142–143, 147, 148, 150, 184, 186, 187
Kasparov, G., 81
Kelsen, H., 161
Kinwasher, N., 145
Kuhn, T., 6, 23–24, 76–77, 132
Kurzweil, K., 80

Llinas, R., 145
Locke, J., 4, 139, 140, 145–147

Marr, D., 95
Merleau-Ponty, M., 107, 110, 112–113, 121, 125
Moural, J., 51

Penfield, W., 120
Penrose. R., 80, 90
Plato, 10
Polt, R., 126
Popper, K., 23, 76
Pylyshyn, Z., 92

Quine, W., 195

Rawls, J., 19–22
Rosaldo, M., 45
Ross, D., 178
Royce, J., 63
Russell, B., 117
Ryle, G., 114

Searle, D., 51
Searle, J. R., 45, 110, 117

197

Subject index

externalism, 18

fact–value distinction, 162
  and descriptive utterance, 162
  and evaluative utterance, 162
  and Hume, 162–163
  and linguistic description, 162–163
features
  observer-dependent, 78–79
  observer-independent, 27–28, 78
  observer-relative, 27–28, 166–167
freestanding-Y terms, 39
  and corporations, 41
free will, 147
function
  assignment of, 32
  the problem of, 118–119
functionalism, 56–57
  black box, 56
  and cognition, 56
  and computation, 56

homunculus, 101, 102, 105
homunculus fallacy, 95–97
Husserl's method, 112–113
  and intuition of essences, 113
  and Noema, 115, 116
  and transcendental reduction, 113, 115
hypothethico-deductive method, 23

idealism
  definition of, 107
  and *de re* reference, 107
  and perspectivalism, 108
  and phenomenology, 107
institutional facts, 31–32
  types of, 43–44
institutional power, 43–44
institutional reality
  and declarations, 49–51
  and language, 35–38
institutions
  recognition of, 38
  types of, 48
intelligence
  as ambiguous concept, 57
intensionality–intentionality distinction, 111
intentionality
  structure of, 167–168
internalism, 18
is–ought distinction

language
  constitutive role of, 29
  and institutional reality, 35–38

  and recognition of institutions, 38
  and social reality, 28–29
Locke's consciousness criterion, 139, 146, 147
  and coherence of spatial-temporal continuity, 140
  and continuity of personality, 140
Logical Positivism, 74

machines
  and thought, 72
Mind-Body problem, 10, 153
  and Cartesian dualism, 11
  and neurobiology, 10, 11
modernism, 9
money, 39–40
Moore's naturalistic fallacy, 163
  and Hume's guillotine, 163, 171–173
motor intentionality, 121
multiple realizability, 15
  implications of, 92

Neuronal Correlate of Consciousness (NCC), 13, 143–144
  as building block approach, 13, 144

object
  and correspondence theory of truth, 194–195
  and facts, 195
  as observer-relative, 194
objectivity–subjectivity distinction, 167
ontological subjectivity–objectivity distinction, 29–30

personal identity, 139
perspectivalism, 108, 128–132
  and Heidegger, 128–130
phenomenological illusion, 116–124
  diagnosis of, 124
philosophy
  of language, 14, 17–19
  of mind, 14
  of science, 9–22
  of society, 21
Phineas Gage, 140
post-modernism, 6–7
  and extreme skepticism, 6
practical reason, 22
programs
  as constitutive of minds, 68
  and lack of ontology, 98
promises, 174–176
  and obligations, 178–179
  and prima facie obligation, 178
property dualism, 153–154
  and causal overdeterminism, 153–154